BUILDING A
DIGITAL HUMAN

BUILDING A DIGITAL HUMAN

KEN BRILLIANT

CHARLES RIVER MEDIA, INC.

Hingham, Massachusetts

Publisher: Jenifer Niles
Production: Publishers' Design and Production Services, Inc.
Cover Design: The Printed Image
Cover Image: Ken Brilliant

CHARLES RIVER MEDIA, INC.
10 Downer Avenue
Hingham, Massachusetts 02043
781-740-0400
781-740-8816 (FAX)
info@charlesriver.com
www.charlesriver.com

This book is printed on acid-free paper.

Ken Brilliant, *Building a Digital Human*
ISBN: 1-58450-216-9

Library of Congress Cataloging-in-Publication Data

Brilliant, Ken.
    Building a digital human / Ken Brilliant.
        p. cm.
    ISBN 1-58450-285-1 (Paperback w/ CD-ROM : alk. paper)
    1. Androids.   2. Robotics.   3. Artificial intelligence.   I. Title.
    TJ211.B686 2003
        006.6'9—dc21

                            2003004017

Printed in the United States of America
03 7 6 5 4 3 2 First Edition

CHARLES RIVER MEDIA titles are available for site license or bulk purchase by institutions, user groups, corporations, etc. For additional information, please contact the Special Sales Department at 781-740-0400.

For my father

CONTENTS

PREFACE

In the universe of 3D animation and graphics, the final frontier isn't the vast unknown depths of outer space but rather the intimately familiar human form. Replicating this body is by far the most challenging journey to undertake as a digital artist. Why? Because all of us know what a human looks like. Even if we don't know how to draw or sculpt one, we do know instinctively when there is something off or wrong with a recreation.

Digital humans are in our midst already. They are stuntmen and background extras in movies such as *Titanic*. They are your favorite hero or heroine in video games like *Tomb Raider*. They are the main characters in Saturday morning children's shows such as *Max Steel*. Finally, they have stepped out of the shadows and from behind the scenes to hold their own at center stage as full-fledged photo-realistic actors in such feature films as *Final Fantasy*. It is clear that they are here to stay.

Acceptance of digital humans in the various media depends much on the characters' appearance. That is, do they look natural, or well designed? Even in stylized forums such as video games, where a certain lack of realism in appearance due to artistic choices or the technology's limitations is naturally accepted, a poorly realized digital human will still be noticed.

The artists who create memorable digital characters understand the human form well. They know how to exaggerate it to suit their needs. They understand the subtleties and forms in life and can replicate them in the digital medium. It all starts with the human form.

WHERE THIS BOOK COMES IN

This book is for those of you who desire to be able to reproduce a 3D digital human, from the hair down to the toenails. It will also serve as a book of modeling and texturing instruction that can be applied to any 3D project.

During the main part of this book—Chapters 1 to 9—you will construct a realistic male model. In the process, you will gain both a technical and artistic understanding of what goes into replicating the forms on the body. Once we complete the male model, we will then transform it into a fantasy character and a female. Reworking the character in this way will illustrate the type of mileage you can get by having a good human model in your library.

In this book, we are going to build the model over a live model as a reference. The live model images are supplied on the accompanying CD-ROM (in the reference images folder), but you can use your own live model if you choose. Chapter 1 will show you how to take the best photographs for reference when building from a live model.

ON THE CD

Lastly, this book is non-software specific. Although the model was built using NewTek's LightWave 3D, the techniques taught here can be applied to just about any 3D package on the market, from the free to the multi-thousand-dollar variety. Therefore, it is important that you know and understand your software's interface and commands. For more information on the system requirements, please see the System Requirements page.

Although programs vary in features, many do share similar features, although they may be named differently. The model constructed in this book utilizes a relatively small toolset. Table P. 1 shows the terms used in this book and their corresponding tool names in three popular programs. See Chapter 2 for more detailed descriptions of the tool types. Be sure to

TABLE P.1   Comparative Terms and Tool Names

TERM USED HERE	3DS MAX NAME	MAYA NAME	LIGHTWAVE NAME
Split	Cut, slice	Split polygon tool	Knife, Bandsaw, Add edge (plug-in)
Weld	Weld	Collapse, Merge vertices	Weld, Merge
Subdivide	Mesh smooth, Subdivision surfaces	Smooth, Subdivide, Sub Patch Subdivide polygons subdivision surfaces	
Smooth	Relax	Average vertices	Smooth
Spin faces	Turn edge	Flip triangle edge	Spin quad
Extrude	Extrude, Bevel	Extrude face	Bevel, Smooth shift
Magnet	Soft selection, freeform deformers	Sculpt polygon tool, lattice deformers	Magnet, Dragnet
Mirror	Symmetry	Mirror geometry	Mirror
Symmetry mode	No	No	Yes

become familiar with the features in your software so that you can take full advantage of the tools.

If you do not have a software package yet, be sure and read on for suggestions.

3D Software

You might already have your favorite modeling software on your computer. Or perhaps you have a clean hard drive and are looking to fill it but do not know where to begin. Here is a quick breakdown of some popular choices available. They vary in price and features, but fortunately, most have the common polygonal subdivision and other features used in this book.

- **Amapi 3D™ ($400).** This is mainly a modeler, with minimal animation capabilities. It has an unconventional interface compared to most, but it has plenty of powerful modeling features. A fully functional free version is available, but it is not the most current version of the software. *www.eovia.com*
- **trueSpace ($600).** This is a low-cost modeling, surfacing, rendering, and animation software package. *www.caligari.com*
- **LightWave 3D® ($1,595).**This is a popular modeling and animation program. It features an excellent rendering engine and good character-animation tools. The models in this book were created with Light-Wave. *www.newtek.com*
- **Maya® ($1,999 and $6,999 price structure).**This is a high-end, full-featured modeling and animation software package that is used on most major films these days. *www.aliaswavefront.com*
- **3ds max™ ($3,500).** This software is predominantly used in the gaming community but it is totally capable of creating photo-realistic high-resolution work. Max has a large user base as well as numerous modeling and animation features that make it good for character work. *www.discreet.com*
- **Softimage XSI ($6,750 to $13,995 price structure).** This is the newest version of the long-used Softimage software; it is a full-featured, high-end package. *www.softimage.com*

Alternative 3D Software

Some 3D software is more off the beaten path than most, but it still has uses in the workflow described in this book. The two programs mentioned below offer natural 3D sculpture tools. These tools allow you to take a "brush" and drag it over the model to invoke modeling changes.

This feels similar to 2D painting, but in this case you are changing geometry instead of applying color to a canvas. Chapter 11 illustrates this in use.

- **Amorphium ($139).** This has 3D modeling brush tools similar to those in ZBrush, as well as modeling, painting, and rendering capabilities. *www.amorphium.com*
- **ZBrush ($399).** A unique hybrid of 2D and 3D, this software has natural 3D modeling tools, as well as texturing, painting, and rendering capabilities. *www.pixologic.com*

Most software companies have demo versions of their programs available for you to try out. Some companies also offer student discounts should you qualify. If the lowest-priced software on this list is too much for your wallet, keep reading.

3D for Free

Nowadays, you can set yourself up with some nicely featured 3D software for no money at all. Certain generous individuals out there have produced 3D software and made it available for free. Here are a couple of recommendations:

- **Wings 3D.** This is just a modeler, but it has many powerful features. It's very easy to start with. The Web site has an active forum and links to free 3D rendering software. *www.wings3D.com*
- **Metasequoia.** This Japanese-made modeler is easy to use although there is no English documentation. With a little experimenting, you will understand the features in no time. It contains a good feature set for modeling. *www.sphere.ne.jp/mizno/main_e.html*
- **UVMapper.** This is a free UV mapping utility. There is also a low-cost ($50), larger version available from the same site. *www.uvmapper.com*
- **Satori Paint.** The freeware version of this, which is used for painting, has layer capabilities as well as decent brush options. *www.satoripaint.com*

If you are working with several different programs and are concerned about converting model files to the various formats needed, check out Ed: Slang Crossroads, a free file conversion program. *http://home.europa.com/~keithr/Crossroads/index.html*

So, you see, there is no excuse for not getting into 3D modeling if you are truly interested. Don't be deterred if you don't have the hottest name-brand software. Many of the basic skills you will learn from this book will benefit you when you move to another modeling package.

Paint Programs

At some point, you will get down to painting your texture maps. What is the best program for this? Numerous paint programs are out there, and you might already have your favorite. But one feature that's pretty essential, no matter which program you use, is being able to work in layers. As the name implies, layers allow you to place virtual clear acetate over an image. You can build any number of layers, and you can set the transparency for each layer. The most basic way to use layers, as far as we're concerned, is taking a template background of the model mesh and using that as a guide to paint the textures in a layer above it in the paint program. There, you will be able to see key landmarks in the model's mesh, and you will be able to line up your detail accordingly.

Using layers isn't limited only to that, however. You can use them to experiment with specifics of your texture design. For example, you could try out variations of spotted patterns on your dinosaur's back. You could also turn layers on and off, and you could jump back and forth between variations, all without disturbing the work underneath. To get different effects, you can set opacity and blending modes for each layer.

Another way to create texture is to use 3D paint programs. Bear in mind that you are still producing 2D texture maps through these programs. The advantage of using them is that you can see how the texture looks on a 3D model as you paint. Before you enter a 3D paint package, you still need to properly set the texture coordinates. However, some 3D paint programs allow you to edit UV coordinates while in the paint program. The model, along with the maps, is then saved back out again. Before you use such programs, make sure to find out if this aspect is compatible with the object file format of your 3D software.

2D Paint Software

This type of software allows you to paint and edit two-dimensional images.

- **Paint Shop Pro® ($100).** This is an inexpensive alternative to larger paint programs, yet it contains many powerful features. *www.jasc.com*
- **Painter ($480).** This natural-media paint software features a large variety of brushes that can simulate effects such as oil paint and chalk. Paper textures and pattern brushes make this ideal for creating

texture maps. Painter 7™ improves the layer capabilities greatly over Version 6. *www.procreate.com*

- **Adobe® Photoshop® ($600).** This is by far the most popular image-editing software used. It supports excellent layer features. It's a favored choice for texture painting. *www.adobe.com*

3D Paint Software

This software allows you to paint and edit two-dimensional images, with the added bonus of seeing them applied to the 3D model.

- **BodyPaint 3D ($595).** This is another 3D paint package with natural-type brushes and UV editing capabilities. *www.maxoncomputer.com*
- **Deep Paint 3D™ ($795–$1,290).** This is a 3D painting program that has many of the best features of Photoshop and Painter. In addition, it allows you to paint directly on your 3D model and even edit the UV coordinates. *www.righthemisphere.com*

Image Map Resolution

A brief word on image map resolution: For memory and resources, it's important to keep tabs on your image map sizes and formats. As with the model resolution, image resolution is determined by the output (whether it's video, film, or print) and by how close the texture is to the camera. If you can reduce the image without a noticeable difference in the display, then do so. But if you can't paint fine enough detail, consider increasing the resolution.

All grayscale maps should be 256-tone grayscale. Even color maps can be reduced from millions of colors to 256 colors in many cases, especially if the output is video. Do a test with an image map that contains millions of colors and then another test with the same map reduced to 256 colors. Do you notice any degradation or loss of quality in the results? If not, then go with 256 colors, but keep a backup copy of the high-color image. You can save a lot of memory if you reduce the image color.

HARDWARE

This section covers a few items of hardware that are worth owning.

Drawing Tablet

The first and foremost must-own item is a drawing tablet. Once you've painted with a drawing tablet, you'll never want to touch a mouse for painting again. A tablet lets you work as if you were drawing naturally. Most are pressure sensitive, which means that the harder you press the pen down, the darker or thicker the painted line will be. Some even respond to the pen's angle. Wacom is perhaps the most popular manufacturer of drawing tablets. *www.wacom.com*

Scanner

Flatbed scanners are useful for bringing outside image sources, such as photos, into your computer. Sometimes you can even lay an actual item on it to be scanned. These imported images can be used as reference, or with some manipulation, they can be translated into texture maps. You can get a scanner for under $100 these days.

Digital Camera

In many ways, a digital camera can save you the steps of processing regular film and scanning. You can directly load digital images into your computer through a connection cable. Some digital cameras allow you to save directly to floppy disks or a CD-ROM. There are many brands on the market with numerous features. In general, most consumer-level cameras won't give you the resolution of a traditional 35mm camera, but that doesn't usually matter because the highest resolution a digital camera can reach is more than enough for our purposes.

We have a lot of work ahead of us, so when you are ready, turn the page.

ACKNOWLEDGMENTS

I wish to express a huge thank you to Mark Deamer. His generosity and expertise helped me out greatly.

Thank you also to the live model used in this book, Frank Villafranca. And always, thank you to all the artists who share their knowledge.

1

ASSEMBLING REFERENCE MATERIAL

PHOTOGRAPHING A LIVE MODEL

The tutorials in this book are based around building a 3D computer model from a live human reference model. It is usually a good idea to have a live model reference for a roadmap so that you stay on track in terms of proportions.

Another method of capturing your live model's likeness as a reference is to laser scan the person. In this process, the subject sits or stands still while lasers scan the person from all angles. This data is then turned into a 3D model that you can load up using your modeling software. You can never use this model as is, however, since a scanned model is often quite dense, polygon wise, and often needs to be cleaned up in areas such as the hair. After the model is scanned, you can rebuild it into a lighter, user-friendly version using the scanned model as a reference. Laser scanners are typically very expensive to own, but some companies offer scanning services. If you have the means or the option, having 3D scanned data of your subject is certainly helpful. The tutorials in this book, however, will operate on the assumption that you will not have a scanned model to work from. Photographs are more accessible and cheaper to acquire.

ON THE CD

The live reference images used throughout this book are provided on the CD-ROM in the reference folder, but you may want to photograph your own live model for reproduction. If you choose to do so, here are some pointers to keep in mind.

Good and Bad Camera Angles

If you want accurate reference photos, it is not sufficient to arbitrarily point the camera and shoot. The camera angle and lens type will make a huge difference in how useful the photos are as background templates to build the model over.

For example, most camera angles for background templates should be as straight on as possible. That is, avoid any low, high, or odd angles that would introduce unnecessary perspective distortion. See Figure 1.1.

Something else that's important when you are taking photos of a model from several angles (such as front, side, and back) is to use a tripod because this helps ensure even alignment with each new pose. If you don't have a tripod, try to stand in the same position when the model changes poses. Or, if you have to move for some reason, do your best to remember the position your body was in and how far away you stood. You should tape markers on the floor to help with this.

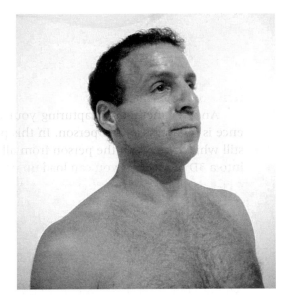

FIGURE 1.1   This is a bad angle from which to photograph your subject if you need a modeling reference.

The next feature you should be aware of is the camera lens type. Camera lenses are measured in terms of millimeters (mm), with the average being 50mm. A wide-angle lens, such as 25mm, will allow you to capture more in the frame while being closer to the subject, but the downside will be image distortion. An extreme example of this is the "fish-eye lens" look. See Figure 1.2. Therefore, the wide-angle lens is the one we want to avoid the most.

You might feel that all this is moot since your camera has only one lens. But take a look; does your camera have a zoom feature? This will interactively change the lens, so you do have multiple lenses at your disposal. Zoom capacity can vary greatly depending on your camera. Some cameras have built-in lenses, and some have detachable ones that allow you to swap different lenses to suit the photographer's needs. Most consumer-level digital cameras have built-in lenses. If you want the extra option of lens types, look into traditional 35mm cameras.

The opposite of the wide angle is the zoom lens. The most common use of a zoom lens is to get a close shot of something from far away. What this also does to the image is flatten it out—that is, it removes perspective distortion. For our uses, this is desirable. Most 3D modeling software view ports (front, top, left) are orthogonal. That means there is absolutely no perspective distortion at all. This is not realistic for rendering but works well for the technical side of modeling. Since we will be working in

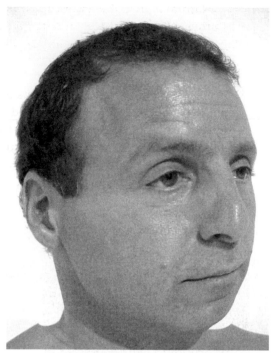

FIGURE 1.2 Wide-angle lenses can cause unwanted distortion.

these view ports with the background photos as a reference, we want those photos to match the orthogonal look as much as we can. They won't be perfect in alignment since a photo will always have real-world distortions, but the goal is to have the image as close as possible to an orthographic view.

Lighting the Live Model

Naturally, you need light to get a usable picture of your subject. The lighting you use can help or hinder how useful the image will be as a reference. You'll want the lighting to be revealing, but not so light as to wash out the subtleties of the subject. Some soft shadows are desirable to illustrate the forms of the subject. Harsh, dark shadows can also be helpful to further study the forms, but they shouldn't be your main reference images as they might hide information as well.

The type of lighting, whether artificial or natural, is important to consider as well.

Natural light is the easiest to come by. The sun is almost guaranteed to provide useful lighting. It's free and usually plentiful. Direct sunlight has a tendency to be too harsh, however. It can also cast harsh shadows. While this may be good for reference at some point, it will be distracting to model over. See Figure 1.3.

Photographing the subject in a slightly shaded area will give a softer quality to the shadows, which is good. If you are working during a sunny day, then photographing the subject on the shaded side of a building would work in this case. Just make sure there is decent bounce or ambient light. Overcast days also provide a good, even lighting situation. See Figure 1.4.

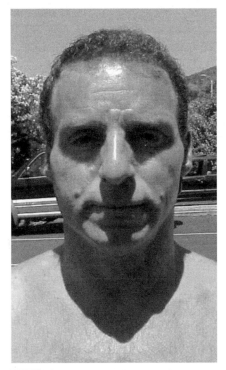

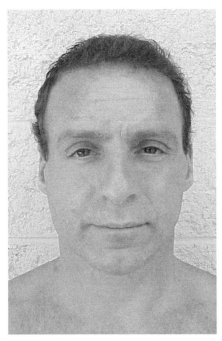

FIGURE 1.3   Direct sunlight creates hot spots and harsh shadows.

FIGURE 1.4   Photographing a subject when it's overcast or in indirect sunlight provides good, even lighting.

The trouble with natural lighting comes in its actual color. For instance, photos shot in a shadowed area or on an overcast day will have a bluish tint to them. Direct sunlight will produce a warm, yellowish tint in your photos. What is the big deal about this? The color of the subject in the photos will come into play farther down the construction line (when we create the image maps). For the purposes of color map reference and re-creation, we want to accurately reproduce the subject's skin tones. If your photo reference is tinged blue, then it will be difficult to recall the more accurate tones. If you have easy access to your live model, then it might not be as much of a problem. However, we will assume that the model won't always be sitting by your computer (unless you are the live model, which is always an option).

Artificial light will give you more control over every aspect of your photos. It will allow you to shoot indoors regardless of any weather conditions. However, as with natural light, you need to keep certain things in mind.

The simplest and most common artificial light—the flash—is found on most cameras. The flash provides a brief burst of light, bright enough to illuminate the scene for a decent exposure. Many flashes, however, are fixed on the camera so that they point directly at the subject. This arrangement will most certainly create flat, harsh, or washed-out lighting. See Figure 1.5.

Some flashes, either built-in or attachable, allow you to adjust the angle in which the flash faces. This goes a long way toward alleviating the

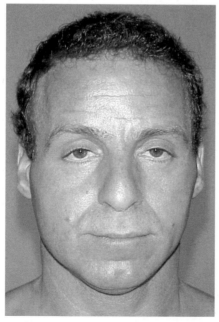

FIGURE 1.5   A direct flash can be too harsh.

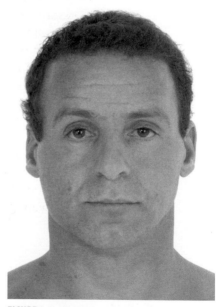

FIGURE 1.6   If you bounce flash lighting, you achieve good, even coverage.

harsh direct flash by allowing it to bounce off of ceilings or walls. See Figure 1.6.

The lights and lamps that are in our homes usually won't do a proper job for these purposes. Such light is most likely too much of a single-source point light and hard to position with any control. Fluorescent lights can provide softer, broader illumination, but their curse is that they produce light that is very green.

That leaves us with studio or photography lights. Such light can be as simple as a regular soft white bulb screwed into a half-dish reflector with a clamp. Or these lights can be higher-end professional lights with intensity adjustments and barn doors (to keep unwanted light off of portions of the scene). If you don't own these lights, you can rent them. Check your phonebook under "Photographic Supplies."

The lighting setup can follow the traditional three-point lighting arrangement. The first light is the *key light*. This is the main source of illumination and the brightest. Its best position for our purposes is slightly above the subject's head, but not so much so that it causes deep shadows in the eyes.

The *fill light* is less intense than the key light. This is positioned opposite the key light, and is used to fill in some of the shadows. However, you might not need this if there is enough bounce or reflected light in the scene. You can create bounce light by placing a large white card near the subject, and angle the card so that it reflects, or bounces, the key light's illumination back onto the subject.

The third light is the *back*, or *rim*, *light*. This isn't as important as the others for our purposes but it can help define the subject. This is positioned behind the subject and is adjusted to catch the edge of the person's forms, such as the hair or shoulders.

The last photographic detail to pay attention to is the background. Ideally, this should be a smooth, neutrally-colored surface that is void of distracting details. Plainly painted walls are the first option, but a large roll of seamless paper or fabric is the best. Of course, in our digital age, a distracting background can be painted out in the computer, but the optimal solution is to do your best to avoid that extra work by taking the time to get clean photos up front.

Poses

ON THE CD

If you are using the live model images from the reference folder of this book's CD-ROM, the poses are taken care of for you. If you are going to photograph your own live model, here is a minimum rundown of angles you should take:

Full body. Front, side, back, and top (this can be accomplished by laying the subject down on a table).

Head close-up. Front, side, and back (if the subject has a good amount of hair, this angle might be of minimum use).

Head details. These include close-up shots of the eyes, nose, mouth, teeth, and ears.

Facial expressions. Capturing your subject's facial expressions is very helpful, especially if you plan to animate them. Some base expressions are the smile, frown, sadness, surprise, and anger.

You can also photograph your model from angles that would not be useful as background reference in the modeling windows but just as visual reference. These views can include lower and higher camera angles compared to those of the straight-on shots.

The full-body shots of the live model for this book were done with his arms outstretched, palms forward. This position will allow for easy modeling of areas such as under the arms. A point was made to have the model face his palms forward by rotating his whole arm, not the forearm. Rotating at the forearm twists the two forearm bones, the radius and the ulna, thus twisting the muscles slightly. This is perfectly natural in appearance but will make modeling this area more difficult. This motion, and all other poses, can be accomplished with the 3D bones you insert into your models for animation.

The last bit of work to do with your reference shots is to make sure the different views, such as the front and side, line up accurately when laid over each other. You'll want major landmarks like the eyes, mouth, etc., to line up in the different views. This will be crucial when you import these images into your modeling software. If the different angles do not line up there, you will be modeling in circles as you attempt to make the geometry line up.

Getting the photography correct is the first step in assuring that the different angles of your model line up. As mentioned earlier, securing the camera on a tripod will keep the viewpoint consistent. You can then bring these images into a paint program to check for further alignment. Most paint software has Ruler and Guides features, in which you can draw visual guides across the images for such uses. These guides are not a permanent part of the image and will not print.

You can do this lining-up process either with two separate images, or you can copy and paste one into a new layer of the other. You should turn down the layer's opacity slightly to allow for visual alignment of the underlying layer. When you're done, return the opacity to 100 percent, and then copy and paste the layer back into a separate document.

If your images are of different sizes, you will need to resize them to fit them the best you can over each other. Figure 1.7 shows the front and side full-body images lined up using layers and guides in a paint program.

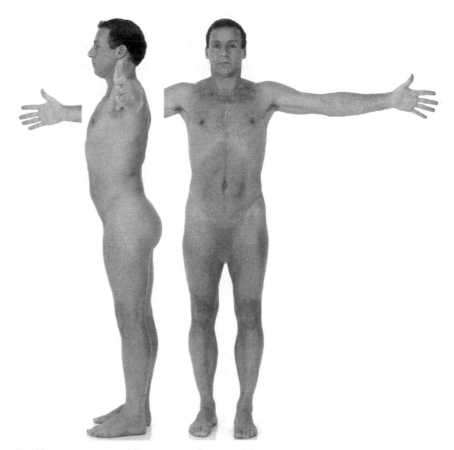

FIGURE 1.7   Line up the different views of your model in a paint program.

Incidentally, you should apply the same coverage and care to imaginary character designs, such as fantasy beings. When constructing the model for such characters, it's crucial to have a good, clear representation of their proportions from views that are easy to model over. The process of creating views that line up with each other is the same whether you are utilizing guides and layers in paint program, or grid paper if drawing with a more traditional medium. See Figure 1.8.

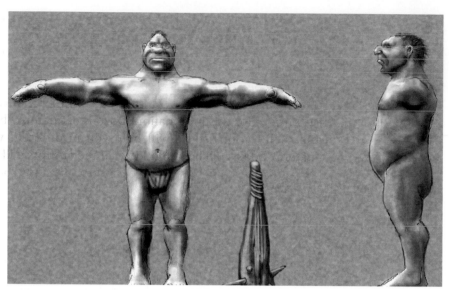

FIGURE 1.8   A character design for modeling.

ANATOMY STUDY

So, we have our model well photographed. It's time to start some 3D modeling! Well, not quite. Having a good visual reference of the live model is only part of the process of bringing a digital human to life.

The photos capture the surfaces of the model quite well. If you are an adept modeler, you may be able to reproduce those surfaces accurately. However, you do yourself a disservice if you don't attempt to understand what is going on underneath those surfaces. What causes the topological forms you see on the model?

Yes, this means a bit of anatomy study. Learning about human anatomy will help you greatly while doing 3D modeling because you will have a strong understanding of the shapes you are seeing. You will therefore be able to reproduce them more efficiently in 3D data. If you do not have the best photographic images of your live model, then your anatomy knowledge will help fill in the blanks where the photo is not that clear, if it has a covering shadow, or if an angle is missing. In short, you will only benefit by taking the time for some anatomical study.

A good place to start is the human skeleton. Do not dismiss our bones as less than important even if they appear buried deep within a bulk of muscle. All those muscles are built upon bones, and those bones determine the broad angles and forms you ultimately see in a human. Do not ignore the effects that the bones have on the surface topology. If you are planning to build an animation skeleton for your 3D model, studying the skeleton and how it moves will be of great benefit.

This book is not meant to serve as a thorough anatomy guide, but at the end of this chapter there is a list of a number of reference books you can turn to for this information. Dozens of anatomy books are out there, and their various styles will help you in different ways. The art-type anatomy books will be helpful in that the authors will help you break the body down visually in terms of easy-to-understand forms. If you're shopping in a bookstore, look at many of these books and determine which artist's style appeals to you the most. This can be a highly individual process. Then there are books that are good for understanding the body in a more clinical manner; these contain photos of real bones and such. You should have both types of books in your collection, and refer to them often.

After you study the anatomy, the next step in understanding it is to sketch from a live model. The most common place to do this is in a figure-drawing class. See Figure 1.9. Many schools offer these courses, and they are helpful on many levels. In fact, schools that primarily teach 3D and computer graphics also offer figure-drawing classes. Computer modelers

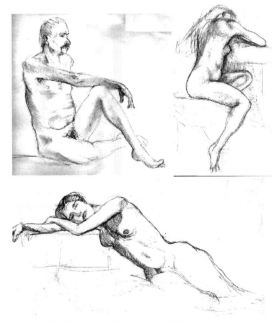

FIGURE 1.9   Sketching from live models.

and animators can benefit from learning about gesture, form, and weight, which studying a live model offers. Do not feel intimidated if you are not strong with a pencil. You will certainly benefit from this study.

SUMMARY

This concludes the preliminary work you need to do before we start constructing a digital human. Taking the time to get good photographic coverage of your live model, coupled with personal anatomical study, will lay a solid groundwork for proceeding into the 3D realm. As you can see, it all starts with strong observation of the real-world object.

REFERENCE MATERIAL

Here is a short list of some good anatomy reference books:

Atlas of Human Anatomy for the Artist by Stephen Rogers Peck. ISBN 0-19-503095-8
> This is a terrific overall anatomy book that was originally published 50 years ago and is still as useful as ever. If you have only one anatomy book, make this it.

Human Anatomy for Artists: The Elements of Form by Eliot Goldfinger. ISBN 0-19-505206-4
> This is a comprehensive, extensive study of the muscles; it covers their shapes as well as insertion and origin points on the skeleton.

Artistic Anatomy by Dr. Paul Richer. ISBN 0-8230-0297-7
> This is a complete study of the skeleton and muscles.

Bridgman's Life Drawing by George B. Bridgman. ISBN 0-486-22710-3
> Bridgman wrote a series of these artistic books on drawing the human form. All are still available, inexpensive, and unequaled in their teachings. You can also purchase the series in a single-book compilation.

This is just a small fraction of the books available to you. Build your personal library with these suggestions and with any other books you may find on bookstore shelves that appeal to you.

2

POLYGONAL MODELING TERMS AND TECHNIQUES

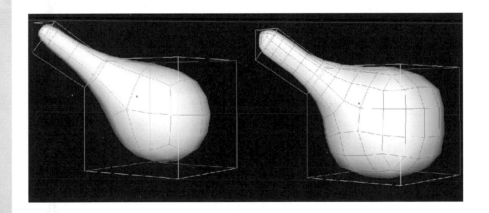

TECHNIQUES COVERED IN THIS BOOK

All geometry constructed in this book is polygonal models. No spline modeling will be covered. A spline is a curve that is defined by two or more points placed in the 3D space. It does not have any volume and therefore is not rendered. Several splines can be assembled together to form a surface that will render. A benefit of a spline surface is that it requires very few points to define a large, smooth surface. However, when you're attempting to create a complex shape, it may be more difficult to visualize with splines. With straight polygonal modeling, it is easy to define the whole, rough volume of the model, and then divide it as you go to add the detail. When you couple polyonal modeling with subdivision techniques for smoothing (discussed later in this chapter), you can obtain the best of both worlds in terms of the ease of polygonal modeling and the smoothness of splines.

POLYGONAL MODELING TECHNIQUES

All examples in this book and the resulting models will take advantage of the software's subdividing capabilities (see Table P.1 in the Preface for terminology differences). The smoothing algorithms can differ slightly from program to program, but the basic principles are the same; a low-resolution model is built and then smoothed; that is, its polygonal resolution is increased to get rid of the blocky and jagged-edge look of the low-resolution model. It's much easier to build and edit a low-polygon model than to work directly with a higher-count mesh. Typically, the low-resolution version (controller) is used to drive the higher resolution (controllee) during animation. The controller isn't rendered; instead, the controllee is at a user-defined resolution. The controller is usually the model that is rigged with bones, and the one the animators see on their screen. Because the controller's polygon count is low, you can usually display it in real time while you are working. The low-polygon version is sometimes called the *cage*.

Understanding how the polygons subdivide is crucial when you are constructing your model. A blessing and curse about most subdivision algorithms is that they can produce apparently smooth results from a messy control cage. This can lead to bad habits, or poor construction techniques. As long as the final model looks smooth, who cares how the mesh appears, right? Wrong. It may be fine while static, but if it's deformed through bones or morph targets (such as facial expressions), the model may pinch or crease in undesirable ways.

Counting on the subdivision routine of your software to "clean up" the model isn't the best way to approach modeling. Good control meshes are clean and allow you to easily make out what proportions the polygons define. They also make rigging or setting up the skeleton for animation easier when the cage is neat. In 3D programs, each bone often has influence over a specified area of vertices defined by the user. When the model's geometry is cleanly laid out, it is not a problem to determine what vertices each individual bone should affect. (Chapter 10 will go into more detail on this subject.)

If you pass on the task of rigging (setting up) the skeleton to another member of the production team, he will especially appreciate that the meshes are clean.

How many polygons should a good control cage have? That depends on the model, but it's usually as many as are needed to define the forms. All the polygons should help define a shape on the model. If you can lose some polygons and still have the model look the same, then get rid of them. Building efficient models with the right amount of concentrated detail takes practice, but that's what this book is for!

What are some of these techniques? Before we go there, let's go back to how a polygon subdivides. Make a basic cube and then copy and subdivide it once. In the wire-frame, notice how for every one face there now are four. Also notice how the corners have pulled in, becoming slightly rounder. This effect is what will ultimately produce a smooth model. If you subdivide again, then the polygons will increase and the edges will be even smoother. See Figure 2.1.

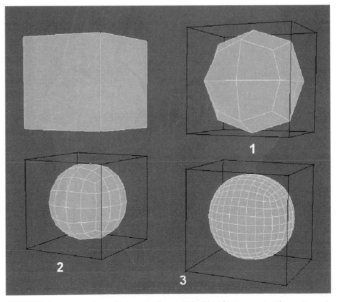

FIGURE 2.1   Examples of how a cube subdivides from one to three iterations.

Now observe what happens to the subdivided version when another row of polygons is introduced close to the top edge of the cube. See how that edge becomes sharper and the top flatter, as in Figure 2.2a.

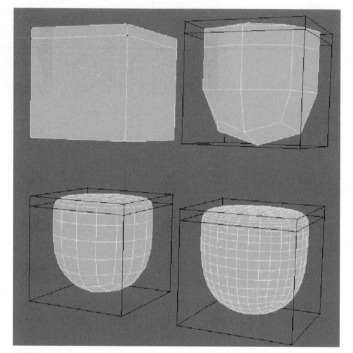

FIGURE 2.2a   Add another row of faces to produce sharper edges.

More polygons are being divided in a tighter space. We'll take advantage of this effect when creating harder edges or creases on the models since smoothing operations can tend to soften the model too much if there isn't enough polygonal detail. On the flip side, this crease effect is another reason why you shouldn't make your control cages too dense. You'll end up with unwanted edges and you'll have difficulty smoothing them out. Just remember that when the polygons are close together, you can achieve tighter edges and creases. Some 3D software allows you to set edge hardness or tension. This involves selecting vertices or edges on the cage object and assigning to them a value that either softens or creates a sharper edge, or crease, of the subdivided model. This technique cuts down on the number of polygons needed to create a tight edge. You can use this method sparingly in select areas, such as in the brows in Figure 2.2b.

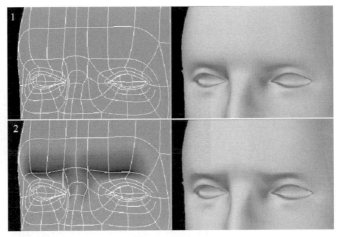

FIGURE 2.2b You can use vertex tension or weighting to create sharper edges without the need for extra geometry.

Another factor that affects how polygons subdivide is the number of sides. The above examples all contained four-sided polygons or quads. But your software's subdivision algorithm might be able to smooth a face with more than four sides. First, not all 3D software can subdivide more than four-sided polygons. Being able to work with programs that subdivide *N*-sided polygons is a plus, as long as you understand the outcome. For example, observe how a simple shape subdivides when a five-sided face is introduced. A five-sided face subdivides into five separate quad faces. This may or may not produce undesirable results in the smoothed model. Experimentation will tell. See Figure 2.3a.

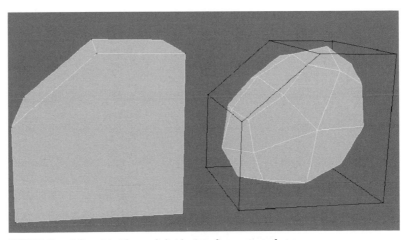

FIGURE 2.3a A five-sided face subdivides into five separate faces.

So, how many faces should you work with? It's easiest to predict how a four-sided polygon will subdivide, so working with all quads and triangles (three-sided faces) is a decent practice to get into.

As far as subdivision algorithms, you may have more than one to choose from. Two common routines are Catmull-Clark and Doo-Sabin. See Figure 2.3b.

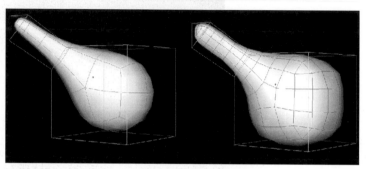

FIGURE 2.3b   Catmull-Clark and Doo-Sabin subdivision routines.

Each produces different polygon configurations in the smoothed model. Notice that the Catmull-Clark routine rounds out the forms more than the other. It also produces only quads. The examples in this book are subdivided with a Catmull-Clark routine. Spend some time getting to know your software's subdivision with simple models such as primitives, and you'll be more in control of the final results.

How many times should you subdivide the final model? That depends on the output and how close to the camera, or far away from it, your model will be. For broadcast television, subdividing two or three times is probably enough. Film resolution can be higher. A good rule is that if you notice faceted edges in your final output, then you should up the subdivisions. Some programs allow you to set the subdivisions automatically based on how near or far the object is from the camera. Some algorithms, such as Maya's Subdivision Surfaces feature, produce an infinitely smooth surface as soon as the algorithm is applied to the model.

COMMON MODELING TOOLS

For the exercises in this book, we'll use modeling tools that are found in just about all polygonal software packages in some form or another. They might go under different names, or may have more or fewer variables in your particular software, but the base functions are the same.

Lathe

The Lathe function has been found since the beginning of 3D software. Using it involves creating a profile outline and then sweeping it around an axis, usually in 360 degrees. Wineglasses and vases are made this way. See Figure 2.4.

FIGURE 2.4   Use the Lathe operation to turn a simple polygon into a wineglass.

Extrude

Extrusion is performed on a polygon face or a collection of faces. The selection is moved out at a user-defined distance and direction. New polygons are created along the edges, creating a thickness. Multi-selected faces can be extruded as a whole or group, or individually. Extrusions can also be performed along a spline path or a curve as a guide and with multiple curves as guides. See Figure 2.5.

Cut, Split, or Connect

This function comes in numerous forms, but it essentially involves increasing detail by splitting or dividing polygons. You select edges or faces and perform the operation. Some programs allow you to draw across the screen a line that represents the projected cutting line, which is infinite along the axis perpendicular to the view initially dragged in. Other

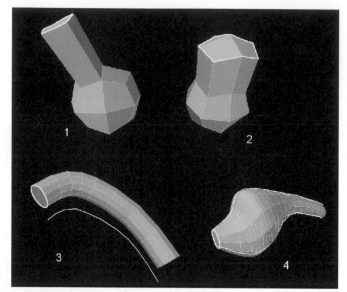

FIGURE 2.5   Drawing 1 shows an example of single-face extrusion; drawing 2 shows an example of multi-face extrusion; drawing 3 shows an example of single-rail extrusion; drawing 4 shows an example of multi-rail extrusion.

options automatically cut through a contiguous band of polygons. The reverse of this command allows you to erase a loop of edges to minimize detail. This is sometimes called Dissolve. See Figure 2.6.

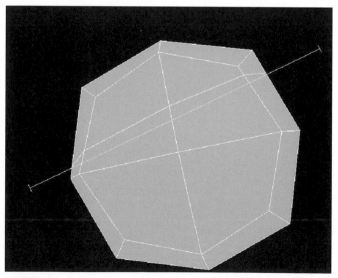

FIGURE 2.6   Use a cutting operation to cut new faces into the model by drawing the cutting plane on the screen.

Join, Weld, or Merge

These operations are performed on vertices, usually to connect separate faces together. If you want a mesh to subdivide and render properly, you must ensure that it does not contain any holes that might come from un-welded vertices. See Figure 2.7.

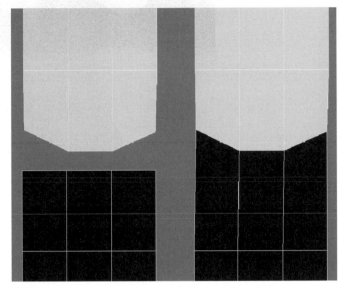

FIGURE 2.7   An example of faces welded or joined together.

Point-by-Point Polygon Creation

Individual points, or vertices, are laid down in 3D space and then connected to form a new polygon. You can also use this technique to connect separate parts together or fill in holes in the model. See Figure 2.8.

Mirror and Symmetry Function

It makes sense to try and cut your work in half when you can. Therefore, it is a common practice to build half the model and then mirror the rest when you're done. However, working on half a model is not the best choice for doing the entire modeling process since you will not be seeing the whole picture. Proportions can be off, and the model may look strange when mirrored back. You should get into the habit of viewing the model as a whole as often as you can. Some programs may allow a simple mirror along an axis, while others may require you to duplicate and scale

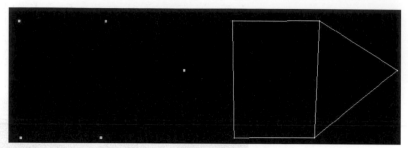

FIGURE 2.8   Individual points are connected to form polygons.

the faces with a negative value (–1 or –100%). The faces may then need to be flipped or inverted.

Another useful feature that some programs have is to create a virtual or instanced copy of one half of the model. This will let you see the model as a whole, although the virtual or instanced half is not a true copy of the original half. They usually cannot have their own unique material or surface properties, or may not let the model subdivide as a whole. When finished modeling, you would turn off the instance and mirror the true geometry over.

The Symmetry feature is another variation. Programs with this feature allow the user to work on one half of the model, while a user-defined symmetry axis automatically updates the other half.

Magnet, Soft Selection, and Proportional Tools

These tools are handy for moving, scaling, or rotating areas of polygons smoothly in given directions. A radial area of falloff is defined, and all geometry within that range is affected. Magnet features add a very clay- or taffy-like feeling to the modeling process, which is desirable for organic modeling. See Figure 2.9a.

Lattice and Cage Tools

An alternative to the magnet-type deformation tools we have mentioned, the Lattice and Cage tools involve setting up a simple box-like cage around the object. As the vertices of the cage are moved, the whole model that it surrounds deforms smoothly. The more subdivisions there are in the cage, the more control you have over area changes. See Figure 2.9b.

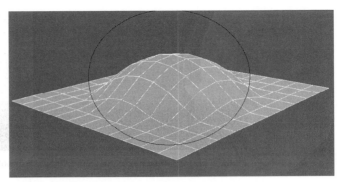

FIGURE 2.9a   Use a Magnet operation to quickly add a bulge to a flat grid.

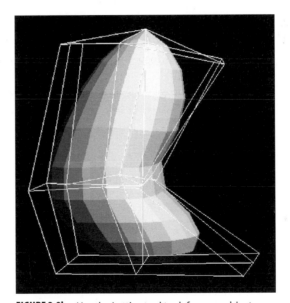

FIGURE 2.9b   Use the Lattice tool to deform an object.

Smooth or Tighten

This Smooth tool is not to be confused with the subdivision smooth. Smoothing helps smooth out rough or jagged surfaces or points without adding extra faces. If this needs to be done manually, it can be time consuming. See Figure 2.10.

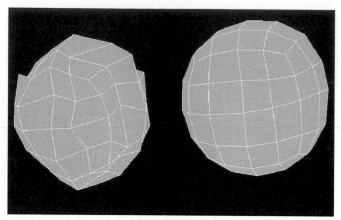

FIGURE 2.10   Use the Smooth or Tighten command to smooth out irregular or jagged surfaces without adding extra faces.

POLYGONAL TEXTURE MAPPING

Unless you have no plans for a model beyond viewing the raw geometry, you will want texture maps on it for rendering. These determine such qualities such as skin color, specularity, and smaller details such as pores and wrinkles. Specularity is a highlight that occurs on the surface of smooth or shiny objects and indicates where the light is reflecting from.

Although texturing is technically not modeling, it is important to think about how you will texture a model as you're working on it. And in the case of UV mapping, texturing can be a step in the modeling process. But we're getting ahead of ourselves. First, let's look at the different mapping types available in the software packages.

Image Map Projection Types

Your texture maps will appear to wrap and conform to the 3D shape of your model, but in reality the actual maps are just rectangular or square 2D images that are projected onto it in various ways. Choosing the proper mapping type that works for the shape of the model and its parts is important. Often, it will take a combination of several maps and projection types to properly cover a model.

Planar

Planar mapping projects an image onto a surface through a selected axis as if shown through a slide projector. This obviously works best for flat surfaces such as walls, but you can use this technique on curved surfaces to a certain extent. After the angle of the surface becomes too great, the image map will streak. See Figure 2.11.

FIGURE 2.11   An example of planar mapping on a flat grid (left) and the streaking that occurs when it's applied to a curved surface (right).

Cylindrical

Cylindrical mapping wraps an image around the geometry in the same manner in which a soup label fits on the can. This can also be on any axis. This method works well for can-type objects, as well as limbs and even heads. If you use this technique alone, you will notice pinching at the top and bottom of the map. See Figure 2.12.

Spherical

Spherical mapping wraps the image in a ball-shaped fashion on a selected axis. This technique is useful when you are creating round shapes such as planets or eyes. There will eventually be pinching at the poles. See Figure 2.13.

Box

Box mapping automatically breaks the model up into essentially a series of planar maps that eliminate any stretching. That's one problem solved, but another problem that arises in its place is that the map becomes flattened when viewed in the UV editing window. The geometric specifics become virtually indiscernible due to the scattered planar maps, so it's nearly impossible to use it as a painting template. See Figure 2.14.

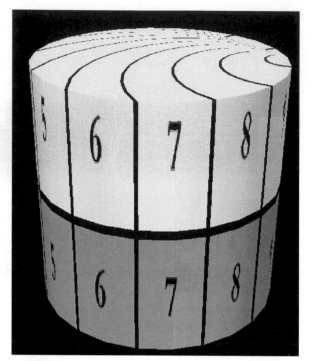

FIGURE 2.12   The cylindrical map works well on the sides of a can-shaped object, but reveals stretching on top.

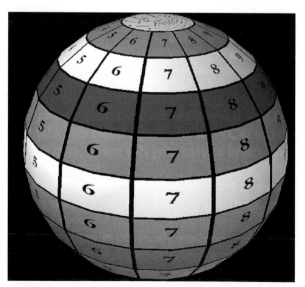

FIGURE 2.13   The spherical map works well on round shapes but has pinching at the poles.

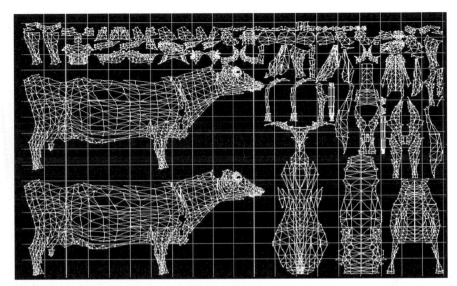

FIGURE 2.14   A box map of a cow model reveals some discernible geometry, but most of the geometry is a disparate mess.

Some 3D paint programs will let you paint across a box map in the 3D window, which will allow you to take advantage of the box method, but 2D editing of the map is still difficult.

UV Mapping

When you apply an image to a model, the faces are automatically assigned UV coordinates. The geometry is locked onto the image so that any topological changes will be reflected in relation to that image. The *U* and *V* refer to the 2D texture map coordinates' axis much like the 3D coordinates of your modeling windows.

Additionally, most software that supports UV mapping also allows you to edit the UV coordinates in their own window or module. Other programs offer plug-ins that allow you access to UV editing tools. In addition, some third-party software is dedicated to UV editing. One good freeware program is UV Mapper, available at *www.uvmapper.com*.

Most UV-editing interfaces have similar features. The interface can display a representation of your mesh, in the chosen mapping method (cylindrical, planar, and so on), as well as the texture map image. You can then move the vertices or faces around, and the relationship of the texture image to the model will change. Remember that any of this editing is not actually changing the shape of your model.

However, when you change the shape of the geometry, the texture will conform to the shape as it was when the map was assigned to it. Figure 2.15 shows a cylinder that was assigned a cylindrical map and a texture. When the cylinder is bent, the texture conforms nicely. The UV map layout will look the same as when the texture was first assigned.

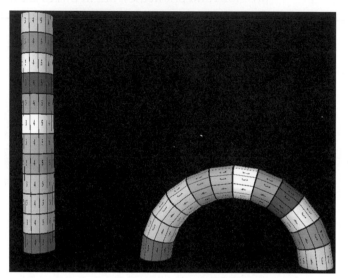

FIGURE 2.15   When the UV mapping is assigned before major deformations of the geometry, the texture conforms to the altered geometry.

This is also another example of the importance of thinking about your mapping methods as you model. If the final shape of a model piece was a bent cylinder similar to the example in Figure 2.15 (such as snaking tubes or wires) but you waited until after it was all modeled to texture it, you'd have a rough time even with UV mapping because of the odd shape. However, if you set up the UV mapping while the cylinder was still in its straight position, you could then continue modeling it into more complex shapes without worrying about the map conforming properly to it. Also, you don't even need to have a texture map painted to apply it at this stage. Setting up the coordinates is good enough.

The bent cylinder example is simple, but you can apply the same principles to modeling organic creatures. For instance, you can model a body; cylindrically map it while it's still in the most neutral, conductive position; and then continue to model it into a more "natural" position. You can also perform the reverse; build your model into whatever position suits your eye, decide on a mapping method, make another copy of the model but then remodel it to best suit the mapping method, assign the map(s), and then morph the "UV model" back to the original. Be careful not to delete any points or to cut and paste. Doing so will change the point order, which needs to be the same for morphing. Some programs will let you create morph states that are saved as part of the model and can be called up through a requester list. These are usually facial expressions and phonemes, but in this case can be the UV state. Examples of these techniques will be covered in Chapter 8.

GOOD WORK HABITS

We now need to mention some good work habits that you should incorporate into your hardwiring as soon as you can. Whether you're working for yourself as a hobby or in a production environment, these simple tips can save hours of headaches down the road.

Build to Scale

This means that if your model is six real-world feet tall, then build it to that scale in your software. A scale issue might never come into play, but then again, it could.

Name Surfaces and Parts as You Model

You will find that naming groups of polygons for selection or texturing is very helpful. So, another good habit is to name these parts as you model, not when the model is finished. You should do so because a completed model is going to be more complex than it was in the earlier stages, and because it will be harder to make all the selections at a later stage.

The second part of this habit is to name the parts and surfaces *clearly*. When you are first building a model, most of it will be fresh in your head, so the attitude might be, "Oh, I'll know what that naming convention is." But what if you load the model sometime later or along with other models? Will you know what the part "Leg" refers to? Whose leg? A better name might be "Frank_Leg_L." That's pretty clear. (The "L" means left in this case.)

Lastly, be consistent with your naming conventions. If you've named the left leg "Frank_Leg_L," then don't name the right one "Frank_R_Leg." Software can list the parts or surfaces alphabetically, and it's much easier to track down or decipher names when they appear logically close together. If you name numerous parts, then your eyes will be glad you've made it easier on them.

Move the Camera Often While You're Modeling

The camera can refer to the modeling view in this case. We all have our "good sides"—angles we look best photographed in—and so will our models. But you should always keep the model moving around while you are working on it so you can make the model the best it can be from as many angles as possible. Don't lock onto that favorite good side and model it that way. Work in a perspective view often, and utilize the front, top, and side views simultaneously if your software allows this. Keep the virtual sculpture stand spinning.

Move Lights While You're Modeling

Another bad habit you may fall into is to never adjust the light while modeling. Don't keep the default "head-on" camera light as your only source. If you succumb to this habit, when you do eventually load the model in a scene and set lights, you might suddenly notice undesirable shadows or surfaces. By moving your light or lights around while modeling, you'll be able to watch how the light plays over the surface, and you can judge from there whether you need to adjust the geometry, etc. If your modeling package doesn't support lights, then periodically load the model into your rendering software and check it there.

Save Often and Incrementally

This is perhaps the most important. Nothing can fix lost work. Software crashes, hard drives fail, files get corrupted. These are all unfortunate realities. To prevent that horrid realization of having to redo hours of lost work, train your fingers to save often. Don't be lazy about it; a gesture that takes a second can save days of work.

Also, save the files incrementally—such as "Man_01," "Man_02," and "Man_03." This has to do with the naming convention and has a number of purposes. You can experiment while modeling and save out different versions. If you end up not liking one, then you can go back to a previous version. It is a form of backup as well. It can help you keep track of the latest version. When you are done modeling, you can delete or move the earlier versions (so as to avoid confusion) and then rename the final model. Or you can create a "work in progress" folder where you keep all your incremental versions, and then move the final version to a more root directory.

Back up Often

Along with saving often, back up your files often. All kinds of storage devices are available. Read/Write CD-ROM drives are fairly inexpensive now, and CD-ROM disks are very cheap. Many models, minus textures, can even fit on a floppy disk. So, there's no reason to lose data.

SUMMARY

This chapter covers the very basics of modeling and texturing polygonals. As you can see, most 3D software contains various tools that vary by name from program to program. Become familiar with the tools your software offers. You can do this by practicing on simple primitive objects. You will feel much more comfortable when proceeding to the following chapters, which will get us started on the basics of constructing a digital human.

BUILDING A DIGITAL HUMAN

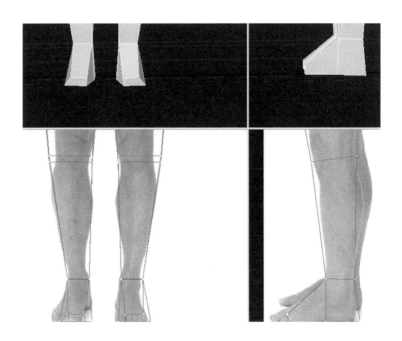

BLOCKING OUT THE FORMS

ON THE CD

If you have all your reference photos in order, it is time to get started in 3D. If you are using the model from this book, open the Reference folder and load in Front.jpg into the front view of your modeler, and Side.jpg into the right-side view. You can also load Top.jpg into the top view. Make sure the images are all the same size and in a real-world scale. Frank is 5′8″. Use the grid option in your software to help you with scaling. It is also important that the midpoint of the front view lie on the X axis as much as possible. See Figure 3.1.

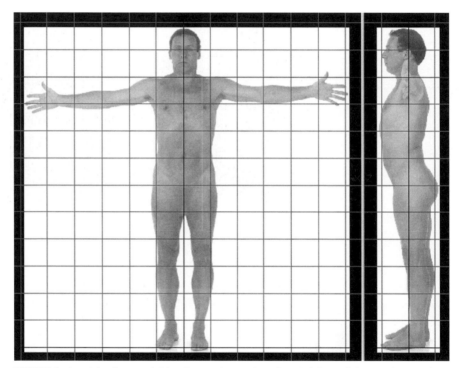

FIGURE 3.1   Load the front and side reference images into the modeler and then package and scale them appropriately.

ON THE CD

The figures supplied on the CD-ROM are in the .tiff format. Converting them to a compressed .jpeg format will save memory with a minimal loss in detail. The models and reference files are already in .jpg format.

Before we get down to some hard-core modeling, we will build a simple box model so that we can understand the broadest volume, proportions, and forms, which are the basis of a well-done model. Well-modeled specific surface details, such as the features of the face, will not save a model with poor proportions, so it is important to establish a good model early.

This is a simple exercise—so simple, in fact, that it might not even seem worth taking the time to do it. Herein lies its value: you will train your eye to view the body in basic shapes and will reproduce them with easy modeling techniques. The understanding you gain here will help you all the way down the road.

To begin with, make a box that roughly surrounds the shape of the head. Do not perform any individual vertex editing. See Figure 3.2.

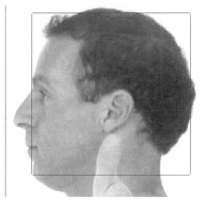

FIGURE 3.2   The head box.

Next, we are going to make a box for the neck. Do the same as with the head; create a box that simply approximates the shape of the neck. However, instead of leaving the box straight, rotate it a little on the X axis so that it is angling forward. It does not matter if it intersects with the head box. This angling is in keeping with the natural slant our necks have. It is subtle but important. See Figure 3.3.

Moving on down, we will create the chest box. This will approximate the volume and angle of the chest cavity. Make the box, and angle it slightly on the X axis, as seen in Figure 3.4.

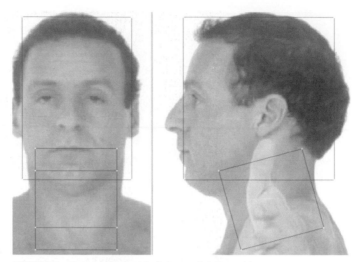

FIGURE 3.3 The neck box with slight angling forward.

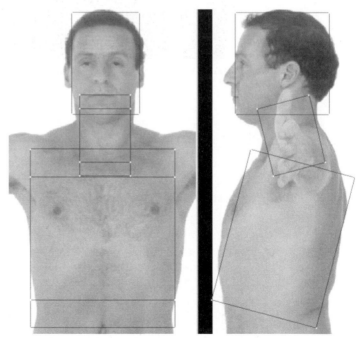

FIGURE 3.4 The chest box.

As with every step in reproducing a digital human, try to envision the underlying anatomy. Figure 3.5 shows how the rib cage fits into the chest box volume.

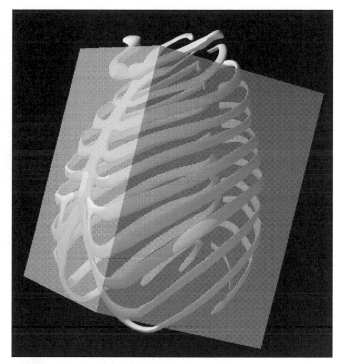

FIGURE 3.5   The rib cage and how it fits into the chest box volume.

The next major torso mass is the pelvic region. Make a box to fit this, as seen in Figure 3.6.

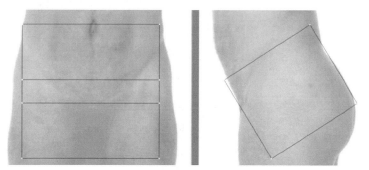

FIGURE 3.6   The pelvis box.

The driving anatomy for the angle and shape is the pelvis and gluteus muscles, as seen in Figure 3.7.

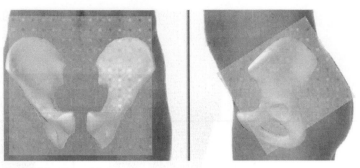

FIGURE 3.7   The pelvic bone and its volume.

In continuing with our descent down the body, we will make the upper leg box. Make one that starts at the hip and ends around the knee. This will be given two rotations: one along the X axis, angling it backwards, and one along the Y axis, angling it inwards towards the center line, as seen in Figure 3.8.

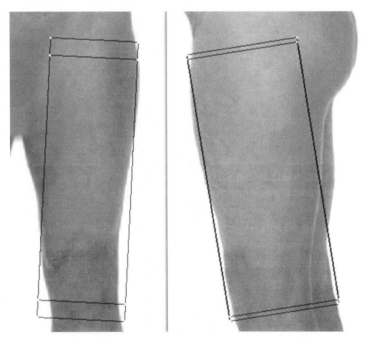

FIGURE 3.8   The upper leg box.

If we view the femur inside the upper leg, we can see how its angle affects the entire mass and shape of the upper leg. See Figure 3.9.

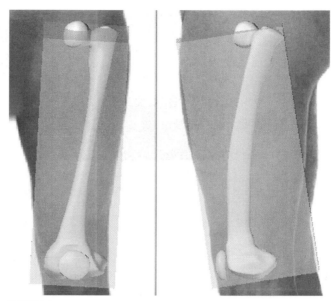

FIGURE 3.9 The femur and how it shapes the upper leg.

Next comes the lower leg. This has the same rotations as the upper leg but to a lesser degree. See Figure 3.10.

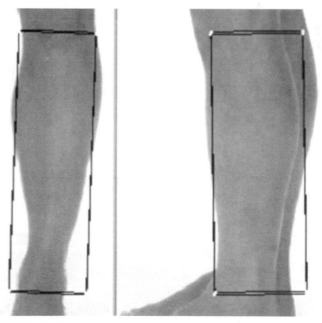

FIGURE 3.10 The lower leg box.

While we are here, take a look at the tibia and fibula inside the lower leg. See Figure 3.11.

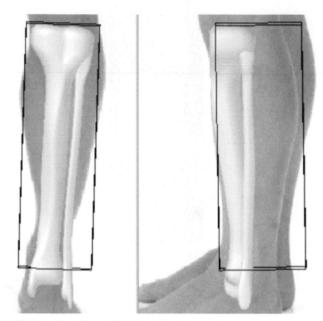

FIGURE 3.11 The tibia and fibula inside the lower leg.

Notice how the bone shapes the profile of the leg, especially in the shin.

The foot box is straightforward, as seen in Figure 3.12.

FIGURE 3.12 The foot box form.

Now let's see what the box man looks like so far, as shown in Figure 3.13. Notice how, with these most basic of unaltered shapes, we can get the sense of the human posture and form.

When viewing the profile, notice how the spine works into the flow of the block forms. See Figure 3.14.

FIGURE 3.13   How the box man looks so far.

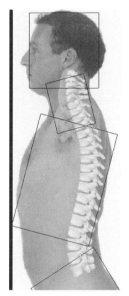

FIGURE 3.14   The spine seen against the figure and box forms.

By now, you should have a feel for blocking out the forms. We will now work on the arms.

Rotate the upper arm slightly on the *X* axis. This represents the angle that the top surface of the biceps is facing. See Figure 3.15.

FIGURE 3.15   The biceps box.

Figure 3.16 shows the shape of the forearm box and its relationship to the ulna and radius. The lower third of the arm is particularly affected by the shapes of these bones because they are close to the surface. Observe the reference photos and even your own arm, and you will see how square the wrist area is.

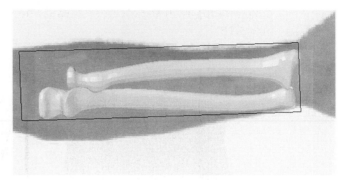

FIGURE 3.16 The forearm box and related bones.

The hand comes next. A box will represent the whole hand and fingers in this exercise. The important form to see here is the square shape of the palm area, and how it actually angles slightly downward in its natural position. See Figure 3.17.

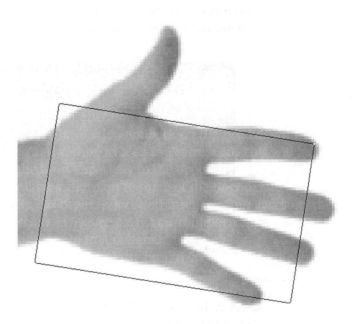

FIGURE 3.17 The hand box.

To make the box man appear as a more solid unit, we will add one more box in the midsection between the chest and pelvis. Angle this to follow along with the abdominal wall and back in profile, as seen in Figure 3.18.

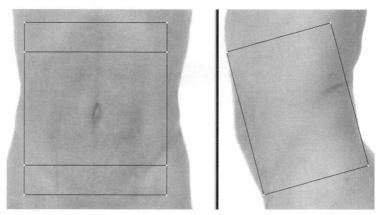

FIGURE 3.18   The abdominal box.

Step back and observe your box man in a shaded view. Rotate the model around and get a feel for the forms. See Figure 3.19.

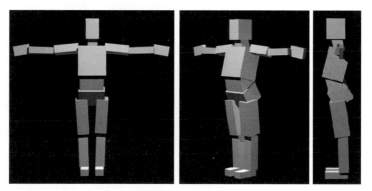

FIGURE 3.19   The completed box man.

Notice how, even in this blocky state, this model appears as a well-proportioned human form. This is the first and most important step in recreating the human form.

ON THE CD

You can load the support file, BoxMan.obj, from the models folder on the CD-ROM for study, but it is still recommended that you attempt this exercise yourself. You will be surprised how much you learn from observing the human form and recreating it in the most simplest of manners. You may even wish to return to our basic friend here for reference further down the modeling road.

Standards of Proportion

Since we are working from a live model, the proportions are already taken care of. It does help to understand what the standard of proportion is so that you may alter the proportions to suit your needs.

For instance, measurements for figures in art are usually in head lengths. The average male is around eight heads tall. Our model for this book measures in at approximately this. See Figure 3.20.

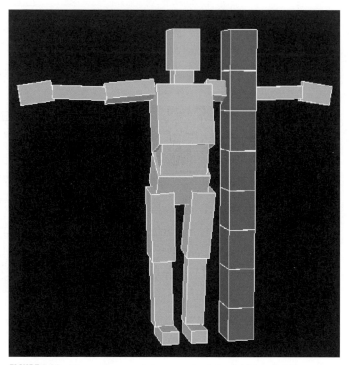

FIGURE 3.20   The average male is approximately eight heads tall.

What if you weren't planning on creating an average male? Many artists change the proportions of the head lengths to be nine or more. When you are creating a classic powerful male character, these proportions are usually referred to as the heroic scale. This scale works well for figures such as superheroes. Take a look at Figure 3.21. This shows a heroic-proportioned male, at 10 heads, compared with the average male.

FIGURE 3.21 The heroic proportions of a figure who is 10 head lengths tall.

Notice that the heroic figure wasn't just enlarged overall. His head remains of the same size at the average male's.

You can alter the head-length proportion, however, if you want to suggest youth. If you were going to construct a child character, you would not just scale down a full-grown human's proportion. A child's head is larger in proportion to its body. See Figure 3.22.

You can see by experimenting with our simple box man that we can quickly work out the proportions for different types of characters. Since we are dealing with an easily manipulated model, we can quickly establish the forms early on in the modeling process.

The One-Piece Mesh

Our digital human is going to be a one-piece mesh. It will not be segmented like a plastic toy doll or the box man from the previous exercise. One-piece-mesh vertices and polygons will all be connected, save for a few select areas such as the eyeballs or teeth.

To create a one-piece mesh, we will start in much the same way as with the box man—with a simple cube. However, instead of adding the rest of the body in pieces, we will extrude and split the geometry to form the necessary anatomy. This will start simply, and the detail will emerge as the forms are refined. Our toolset will be simple as well, with the core tools being Split, Cut, or Connect, depending on your software's naming. Using the one-piece-mesh method is akin to carving a figure out of a

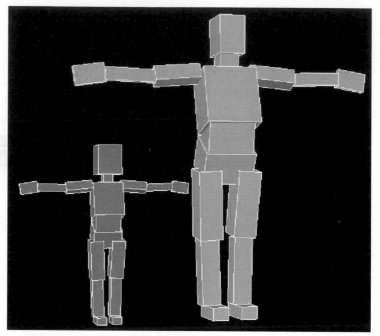

FIGURE 3.22   A child's proportions.

block or stone; the broad shapes and forms are defined first, then the secondary forms, and finally the detail. Polygons are much more forgiving than stone, though.

Do not put away the box man, however; he will guide us in the following steps.

We will start with the head. Make a cube in roughly the volume of the head. Move the back vertices up to start the angle of the skull, as in Figure 3.23.

Select the face on the bottom of the cube and extrude it downwards. This represents the neck. Pull the vertices to roughly conform to the shape of the live model, but obviously there is only so much you can do at this stage. See Figure 3.24.

Continue with the process of extruding the bottom face. This time, bring it to mid-chest, as in Figure 3.25.

One more big extrusion will bring the new bottom face to the crotch, as in Figure 3.26.

Move back to the upper chest area and, this time, select the two faces on the sides of the body. Extrude and scale them to approximately where the shoulder is on the live model. Move these new faces closer to the rear of the model and then to the front. See Figure 3.27.

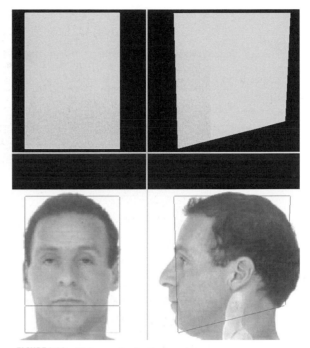

FIGURE 3.23   Make a cube for the head.

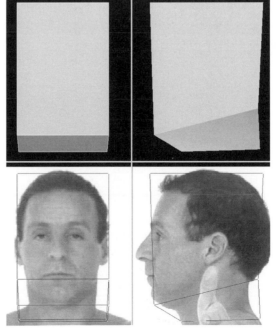

FIGURE 3.24   Extrude the bottom face for the neck.

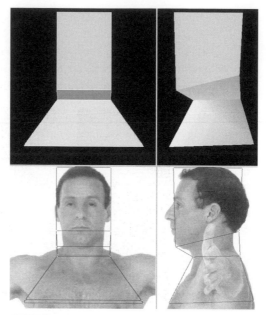

FIGURE 3.25   Extrude the bottom face to mid-chest.

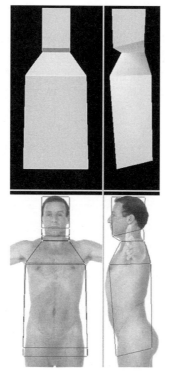

FIGURE 3.26   Do the extrusion for the body.

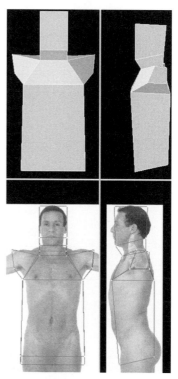

FIGURE 3.27   Start the extrusion for the arms.

If you have a Symmetry Mode in your modeler, this is a good time to use it. If not, then work on one half. We will mirror the second half later.

Continuing with the arms, perform another extrusion to the elbow. This is the upper arm. Give this a slight twist on the *X* axis so that the forward face angles upwards a bit. See Figure 3.28.

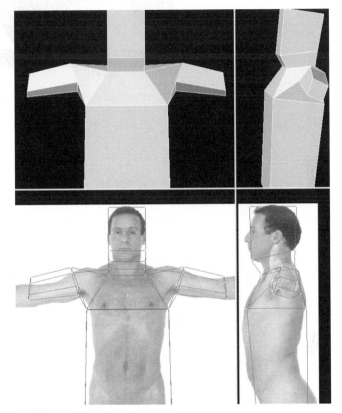

FIGURE 3.28   Extrude the upper arm.

The next two extrusions are easy to figure out. There's one for the forearm and one for the hand. Doing this is simple, but remember to view the geometry from all angles to make sure the arm is the proper thickness as it gradually tapers down to the hand. See Figure 3.29.

The next step is to divide the model in half with a large cut or split down the middle. See Figure 3.30.

This will help you easily make an instance of the model half, or, for simplicity, just work on the half alone. This will also set us up in preparation for the legs.

Make another division line, this one close to the midpoint line we just made, as seen in Figure 3.31.

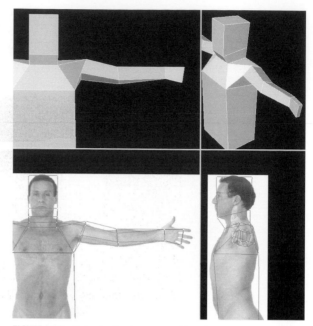

FIGURE 3.29   Extrude the forearm and hand.

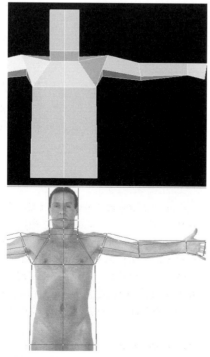

FIGURE 3.30   Divide the model in half.

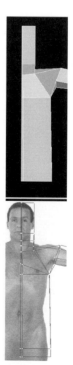

FIGURE 3.31   Make another division line.

We can now get going on the legs. Select the bottom face at the base of the thigh, being careful not to select the very inner faces towards the midline. Extrude that to the knee, and then to the ankle. Scale these new faces appropriately to taper near the ankle, as seen in Figure 3.32.

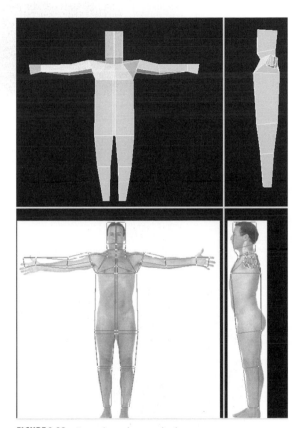

FIGURE 3.32   Extrude and taper the leg geometry.

To complete the leg, make an extrusion to the bottom of the heel, then forwards to the start of the toes, as seen in Figure 3.33.

A small operation comes next: Eliminate the midline split that travels around the body. If your software allows you to select a loop of edges, you could Dissolve or delete the edges. You could also combine the faces down the middle. Be sure and delete any stray points that may have been left behind. Whatever method you use, the results should resemble Figure 3.34.

This midline will come back in a few steps, as you'll soon see. For now, it is important to keep the geometry as light as possible.

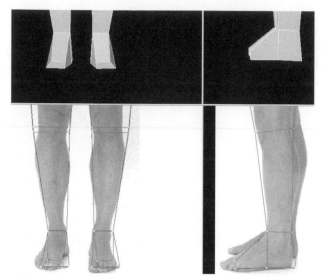

FIGURE 3.33   Do the basic foot geometry.

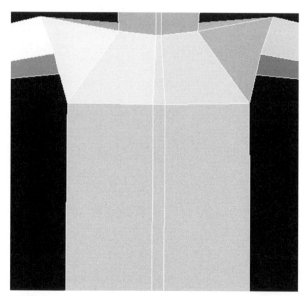

FIGURE 3.34   Delete the midline edges.

We will eventually get into shaping the body, but first we need more geometry to help with that. Make an angled horizontal slice that is level with the hip, as seen in Figure 3.35.

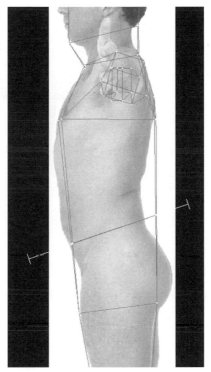

FIGURE 3.35   Add a horizontal slice that is level with the hip.

With the help of the new geometry, give the torso a more natural position and gesture by indicating the curvature of the back. You should do this in the profile view. You should also narrow in the hips from the front view. See Figure 3.36.

This is about as far as we can go with the amount of geometry we have. It's time to add more. We can continue to cut slices where we need them to build geometry, but there is a quicker way: Subdivide the model once. This will nicely give us more geometry to work with while rounding out any square corners. If you were working on a half or instanced model, mirror back the other half for this step. Figure 3.37 shows the model subdivided once.

You will also notice that our midline came back during the subdivision. This is a good method of adding geometry quickly to a model, but you must use it judiciously, since it can make a model too dense too fast. That is why we kept the geometry light from the start.

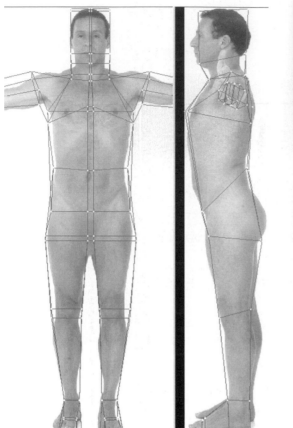

FIGURE 3.36 Shape the body further.

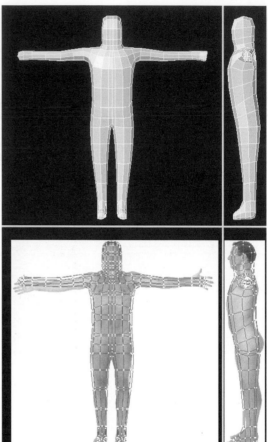

FIGURE 3.37 The model is subdivided once to add geometry.

Now that we have this extra geometry, we can do something with it. Figure 3.38 shows the full figure with adjustments, such as a more distinct curve to the back, a narrowing of the waist and neck, an indication of the calf and triceps, and a more defined cranial shape. The feet are elongated but stop at the toes; they will be added later. Notice how we can get a better profile for the chest and back, and how the shoulders are established. Also note that there is a definite indication as to the lower outline of the ribcage. This will be valuable down the road.

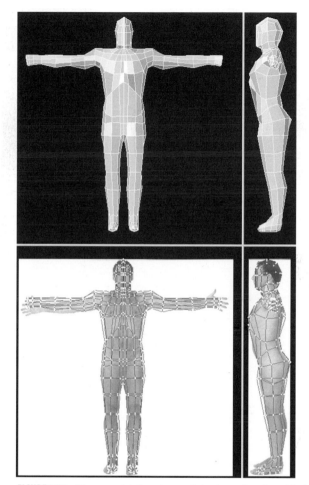

FIGURE 3.38   Shape and define the mesh further using the added detail.

Figure 3.39 shows the back of the mesh. At this stage, you should be able to notice the difference between the front and back.

Figure 3.40 shows what was done with the face's geometry. The jaw line, as well as a line running through what will be the center of the eyes, is established.

This is as far as we will take the whole mesh for now. Subsequent chapters will tackle the detailed modeling of the various major anatomical parts (such as the head, arms, legs, and torso) separately. Yet, all these body parts will still remain a part of this one-piece mesh, which will act as a framework and guide for the proportions so that we do not go astray.

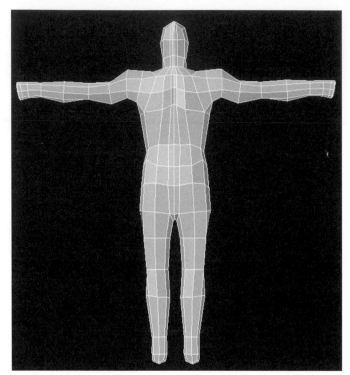

FIGURE 3.39 The back of the mesh.

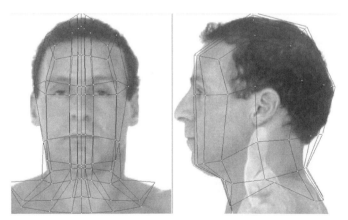

FIGURE 3.40 Set up the head geometry.

SUMMARY

In this chapter, we used simple box models to illustrate the importance of establishing and understanding proper proportions early in the modeling process. We also set up the first stages of the one-piece mesh. When we make the final model, we will build all the detail and refinement onto this one-piece mesh. These first steps are deceptively simple, yet they are crucial. Now we can narrow our focus. Our first stop is the head.

4

MODELING THE HEAD

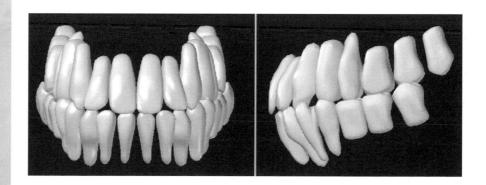

REFINING AND DEFINING THE HEAD

The human head is certainly one of the most challenging features to model. Within the confined volume of the head are many characteristics that make us unique. It can be overwhelming to look at a human head and to try to figure out where to begin. To help with this, the tutorials in this book follow the process of defining the broadest forms first and then gradually adding and refining detail. This allows you to work the model while the geometry is still light before you proceed to the next level of detail. If you completely model the individual features, such as the eyes or mouth, first, their geometry may get misshapen as you adjust the whole head—and this inevitably needs to happen during the modeling process.

The toolset needed here is light: split or connect edges are predominantly used to add detail. Simple face, edge, and vertices moves are used to shape it. Magnet or Soft Selection moves are good for smoothly adjusting larger areas while retaining the proportions. The Smooth command is used to smooth out areas that have become too uneven or lumpy.

Beyond these tools, the most important tool is your observation skills. Your ability to observe the human form will be your best asset. And do not forget to keep an anatomical reference handy.

If you are following along with the live model example from this book, load HeadFnt.jpg and HeadSid.jpg from the reference folder into the respective modeling view ports, as seen in Figure 4.1.

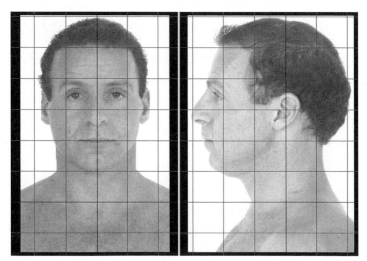

FIGURE 4.1   The front and side head images loaded into the modeler for reference.

You could use the full-figure Frank images, but the close-up head shots have more detail. Do make sure the images are in the same scale and proportion to the full-body shots in your modeler. A grid option can help with this task. In addition, make sure the front and side shots line up with one another.

Load the model you created from Chapter 3. The head should line up to the reference images. Now is a good time to name parts or surfaces of the model for easy reference. Select the faces from the top of the head down to the collar bone area and name them "Head." Now you can hide the rest of the body geometry. This will keep the screen much less cluttered while you are working. See Figure 4.2.

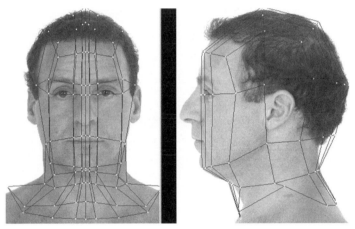

FIGURE 4.2   Define the head geometry and hide the body.

Now we can get into it. Make three horizontal splits across the whole head, as seen in Figure 4.3.

Use the new geometry to shape the head more. For instance, now you can pull the bridge of the nose area out and pull the eye area in. Align the line of the lips with the newly made vertices by the chin in the front. Do not forget to compare the back of the head and the front view against the reference images. See Figure 4.4.

Make another horizontal split that travels from underneath the nose to the back of the head, as in Figure 4.5.

We will now make our first oddly shaped split. It will travel from the top of the forehead, down the temple, and along the jaw line and will then turn, ending under the chin, as in Figure 4.6.

However, this will give us an undesirable face configuration: the triangle next to a pentagon located at the jaw corner. To correct this, we need to turn this into a quad configuration. To do so, split the triangle in

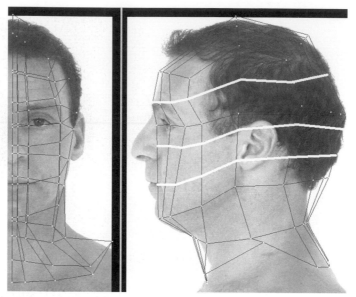

FIGURE 4.3 Three horizontal splits add geometry.

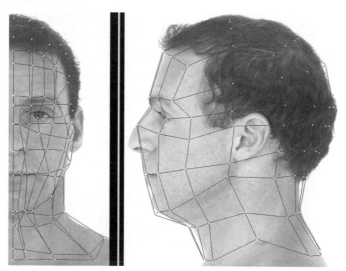

FIGURE 4.4 Use the new geometry to shape the head by comparing the background reference images.

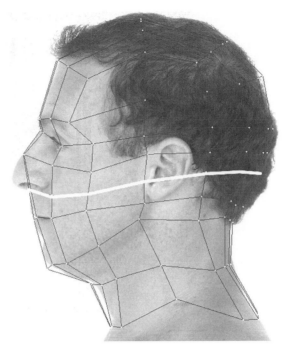

FIGURE 4.5   Make another horizontal split.

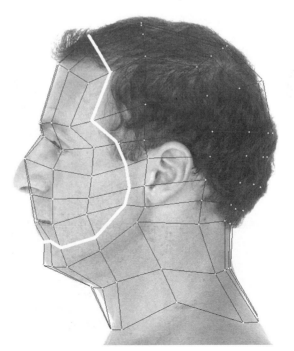

FIGURE 4.6   Make a large L-shaped split along the head and jaw line.

the middle (or divide its edge in two), and connect it to the lower, middle vertices on the pentagon, as seen in Figure 4.7.

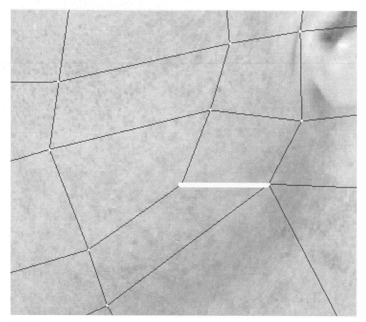

FIGURE 4.7   Split the triangle and pentagon into quads.

You can use this technique anywhere that you create a triangle and a five-sided face next to each other.

Now it's time for a couple more simple splits: first, horizontally from across the nose to the back of the head, as seen in Figure 4.8.

If you haven't already, shape the geometry in the other views such as the perspective. Establish the major planes of the head, such as the sides and front. Granted, there is only so much you can do with the limited geometry at this point, but think only in the broadest terms and forms at this stage. See Figure 4.9.

It is time to add some vertical cuts. The first one will divide the second vertical row of faces, located at the center of the head. However, this time the split will not continue all the way around the head. It will start from the collar bone/lower neck area and will end in a triangle approximately midway on top of the head. Why not continue it all the way around? As you will see, performing contiguous cuts completely around a model will quickly increase detail. While you may be building up detail in areas you desire, there will also be extra geometry in areas that don't need it. This

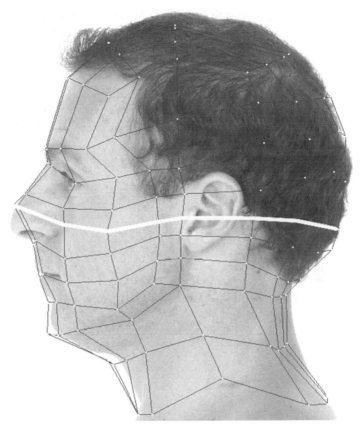

FIGURE 4.8   Make a horizontal split across the head.

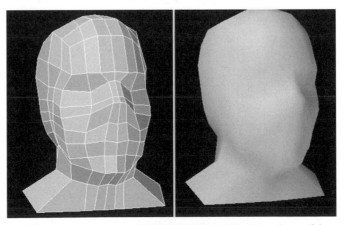

FIGURE 4.9   Shape the light geometry to capture the major planes of the head.

will lead to heavier models. Areas such as the top and back of the head do not require as much geometry to define their forms as other parts of the head, especially if they will be covered by hair. You shouldn't terminate the geometry everywhere, but you can do so safely here. See Figure 4.10.

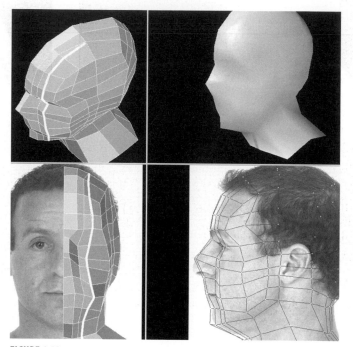

FIGURE 4.10   Make a vertical split terminated at the top of the head.

From here on out, we will be adding detail with an eye towards localizing it, as we did in the above example. The next example involves creating a circular-type division. This one will be in the mouth and nose area. Starting at the tip of the nose, go across one row, and then down to the corner of the mouth; then split across and end under the lip, as in Figure 4.11.

You can use the new-found detail to further add definition to the nose. You may have noticed that we created a couple of triangle/pentagon combinations in our last operation. Eliminate these as shown earlier. Turn the offending areas into quads, and further shape the geometry, rounding it out as in Figure 4.12.

At this stage, we are making the model ready for future operations. The circular split we have just made is set up to follow the face's folds and anatomy—mainly, the area that is the nasallabial fold. This is the crease that occurs from the corners of the nostrils to the corner of the mouth

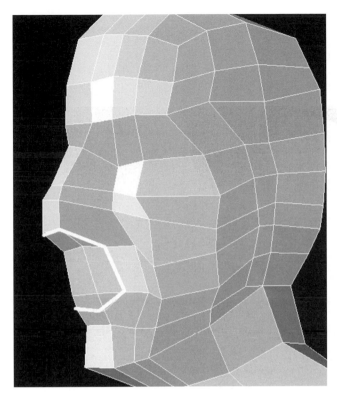

FIGURE 4.11   Use a circular type split to localize detail around the nose and mouth.

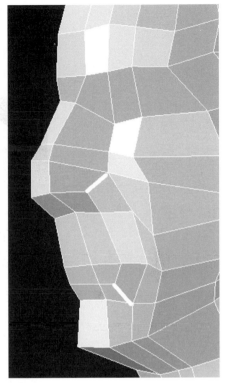

FIGURE 4.12   Turn the three- and five-sided faces into quads.

and is most evident when you smile. Take a look in a mirror and smile, or look at our model Frank smiling. See Figure 4.13.

As you get older, this fold of skin will become more prominent even when you're not smiling, but young and old alike display it when making expressions such as a smile. Since everyone makes this expression, it's important to set up the geometry to accommodate this should you decide to create expression morphs for your character.

Look again at the live model's front view (see Figure 4.14). Can you see the nasal labial fold now? Move the geometry to help capture the flow. It does not need to lie perfectly on the line at this stage. The detail that will come later will define this more.

Add another split across the upper lip area, but terminate it in a triangle, as in Figure 4.15.

This triangle will not remain there for long, however, as you will soon see.

FIGURE 4.13   The smile brings out the nasallabial fold around the mouth and nose.

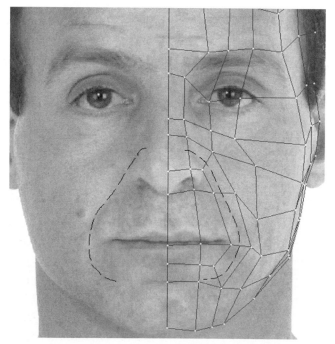

FIGURE 4.14   Configure the geometry to follow the nasallabial line.

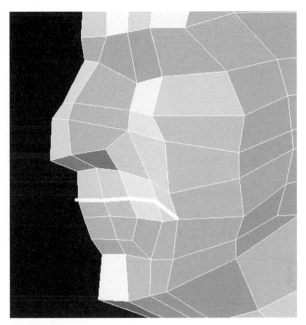

FIGURE 4.15   Add another split across the upper lip.

Now add a vertical split up the front of the face that ends at the triangle we created a few steps back. We will rearrange this undesirable configuration of triangles later. But for now, it is fine. See Figure 4.16.

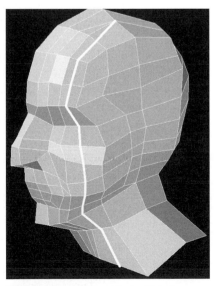

FIGURE 4.16   Make a vertical split that terminates at the top of the head.

Getting back to the mouth area, we will add another circular split along it and the nose, as seen in Figure 4.17.

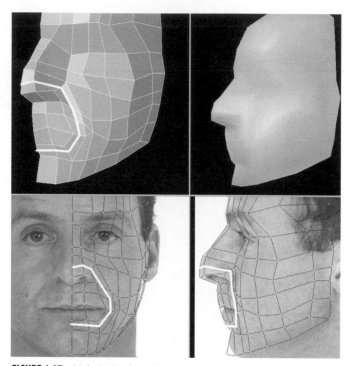

FIGURE 4.17   Make a circular split around the mouth and nose.

Continue splitting faces around the mouth in a circular manner. Make two more cuts, as seen in Figure 4.18.

As you create new geometry, continue to model with it. In this case, move the vertices so that they start to create the outline of the lips.

Break up the five-sided face that we created in the previous step by cutting through it, as seen in Figure 4.19.

Split another contiguous ring of faces in the nasal labial ring that goes through to the underside of the chin. See Figure 4.20.

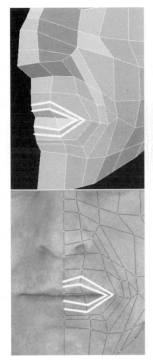

FIGURE 4.18   Make two more circular cuts around the mouth.

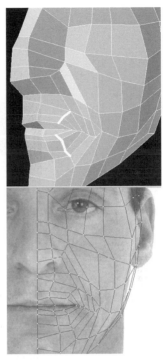

FIGURE 4.19   Break up the five-sided face.

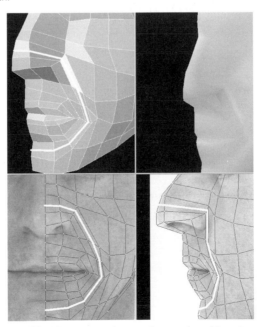

FIGURE 4.20   Split another contiguous ring of faces in the nasal labial ring.

Then, make two short cuts from the corner of the mouth, as in Figure 4.21. The extra faces here will help create a tighter lip corner. Also notice how we turned that one triangle into a quad.

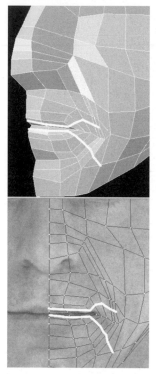

FIGURE 4.21 Make two short cuts from the corner of the mouth.

Move up to the eye area and make a long horizontal split from the bridge of the nose that terminates in a triangle towards the back of the head, as in Figure 4.22.

We will now make one of those L-shaped, or corner, cuts that travels from the front of the chin, along the jaw line, and up the head until it reaches the triangle that we created earlier. By splitting the triangle with this split, we now have a desirable quad. See Figure 4.23.

We will now make a split that makes a couple of turns. However, when we do this, we'll create a three-/five-sided face combo that you should eliminate, as illustrated earlier in the chapter. This split will start at the triangle created in Figure 4.22 towards the back of the head, will travel to the inside of the bridge of the nose and down to the nostril area, and will turn to end under the nose. See Figure 4.24.

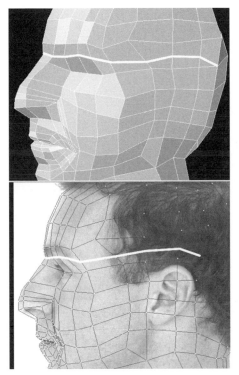

FIGURE 4.22   Make a long horizontal split from the bridge of the nose.

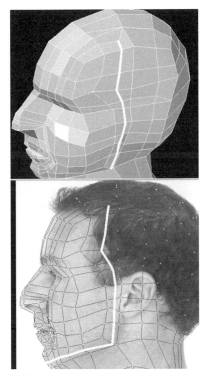

FIGURE 4.23   Make a split that travels along the jaw line and up the head.

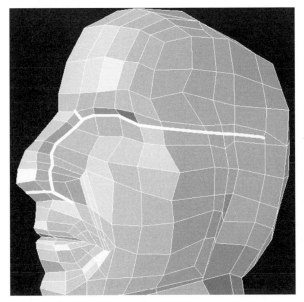

FIGURE 4.24   Make a long split with two turns.

Now we will define the eye area. Make a split as in Figure 4.25. Make it curved while imagining the eye socket underneath. You can see this subtly on Frank's face.

Perform a split from under the nose and end it as a triangle on the forehead, as in Figure 4.26.

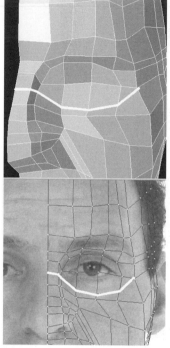

FIGURE 4.25   Make a split that defines the eye area.

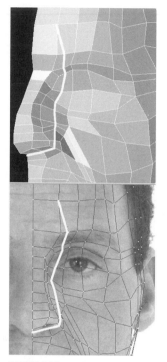

FIGURE 4.26   Make a split from under the nose to the forehead.

As with the mouth area, the eyes work best if you model them in a radial fashion. Make two radial cuts in the socket, as in Figure 4.27.

While you are here, shape this geometry to better resemble the eyelid outline. See Figure 4.28.

It is the perfect time to make a pair of stand-in eyeballs. These will help guide you in shaping the lids. Later in the chapter, we will make a more realistic set of eyes.

The shape of the eyes is obviously nothing more than spherical, so make one sphere with 24 sides and 12 segments. Make sure to keep it evenly proportional on all axes, and keep the poles (the area where the faces converge) facing forward. The average human eye is 24mm big, so size your sphere with the help of your software's Grid feature. Name the

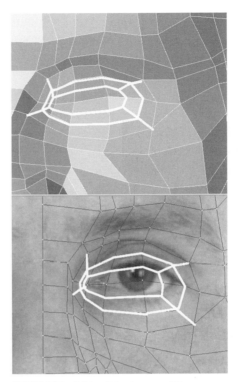

FIGURE 4.27   Add radial cuts around the eyes.

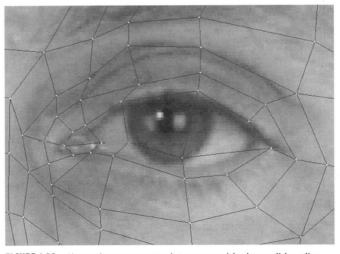

FIGURE 4.28   Shape the geometry to better resemble the eyelid outline.

surface "Eye" and keep it light and shiny. The extra geometry at the rear half of the eye will never be seen, so delete it. See Figure 4.29.

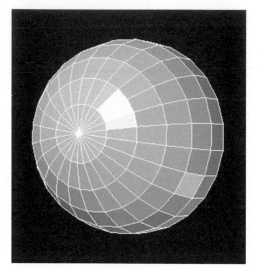

FIGURE 4.29   Start the stand-in eye.

The available geometry can be used to create quick surface qualities, such as the iris and pupil. Use the image of the live model for the proper iris size. See Figure 4.30.

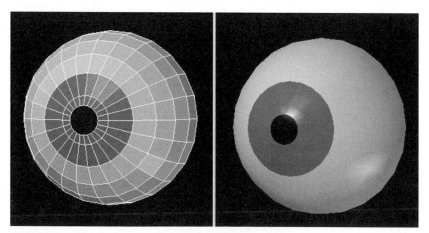

FIGURE 4.30   The stand-in eye.

Shape the rest of the lid to better conform to the eyeball. Do not forget to work from all views. See Figure 4.31.

We still need more geometry around the eye area to define the lids. Make one more radial split around the eye socket, as in Figure 4.32. This will help you get a better crease between the upper lid and the bone.

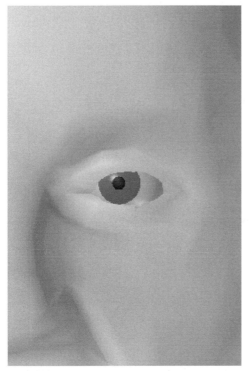

FIGURE 4.31   Shape the eyelid around the eyeball.

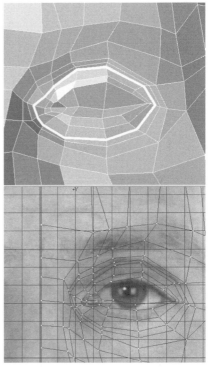

FIGURE 4.32   Make a radial split to help define the lids.

We will pay some attention to the neck now. It needs geometry so that we can do some further modeling. To begin with, make three horizontal cuts along the neck similar to those in Figure 4.33.

Once you have the extra geometry, shape it to the live model.

We have created the general shape of the neck, but the current face configuration does not optimally capture some of the muscle forms. The most prominent muscle that artists reproduce is the sternocleidomastoid. This muscle attaches to the skull behind the ears. It then extends down the neck, ending with two attachments at the collar bone: The main part attaches at the sternum, and a flatter, usually less visible, head attaches at the clavicle. When you view a subject head on, this muscle forms a V shape. See Figure 4.34.

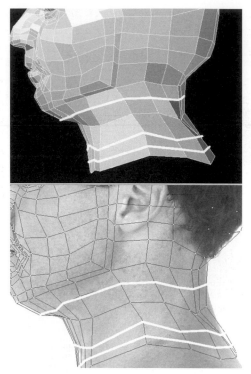

FIGURE 4.33. Add horizontal cuts along the neck.

FIGURE 4.34. The sternocleidomastoid muscle.

Rather than trying to force the neck geometry that we have now into these shapes, we will rearrange the shapes so they naturally follow the shape of the sternocleidomastoid muscle.

There are several ways to rearrange faces without spending much effort. If your program supports a Spin or Rotate Faces feature, then using it is obviously the easiest route. This feature takes two faces and rotates their configuration while keeping the same number of faces. Another technique is to delete the faces, then rebuild them in the configuration you want. Yet another method is to combine or merge faces together into one, then split them into a new configuration. Choose whichever technique is best for you. The final face arrangement is what matters.

To begin, rearrange the two faces at the corner of the jaw, as shown in Figure 4.35.

Perform the same operation on the next two set of faces to the right, behind the jaw line, as in Figure 4.36.

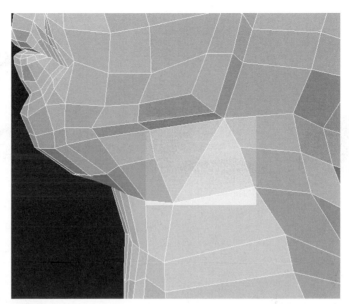

FIGURE 4.35   Rearrange the two faces at the corner of the jaw.

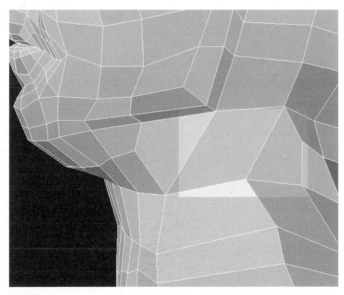

FIGURE 4.36   Rearrange the next two faces behind the jaw line.

Delete the face, as shown in Figure 4.37.

Then, weld the two open points to close the hole. See Figure 4.38.

Make a vertical split up to eye level and terminate in a triangle, as in Figure 4.39.

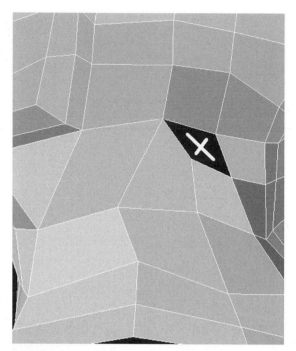

FIGURE 4.37 Delete this face.

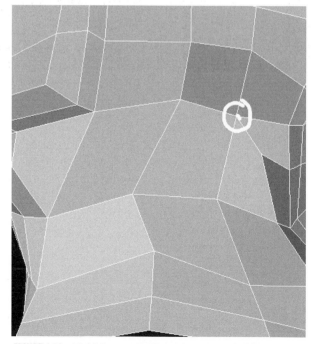

FIGURE 4.38 Weld the two open points to close the hole.

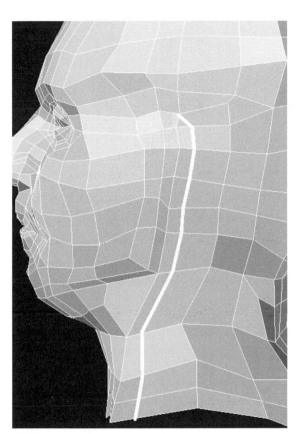

FIGURE 4.39 Make a long, vertical split.

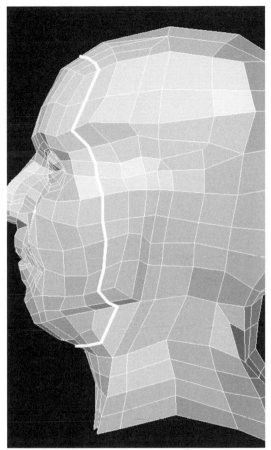

FIGURE 4.40 Two more cuts will yield more geometry to work with.

To get a decent amount of geometry to work with for the neck, we need to make just two more cuts: one horizontal across the neck, and one that travels from under the chin, across the side of the face, and over the forehead. See Figure 4.40.

Spin, rotate, or rearrange the two faces on the neck so that they resemble Figure 4.41.

Then rotate the two faces at the base of the neck, as in Figure 4.42.

We will leave the neck for now and return to the eye area. At this point, we will create depth for the inner eye. To begin, select the eight faces that make up this region, as seen in Figure 4.43.

We will perform three extrusions in the Z axis to create the socket. The first will be close behind the edge of the lid, the second will be close

FIGURE 4.41 Spin two more faces.

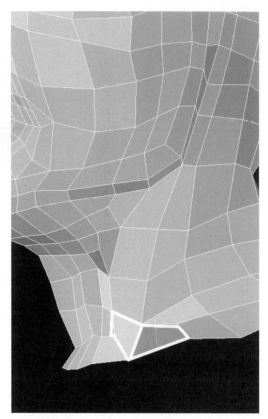

FIGURE 4.42 Rotate the two faces at the base of the neck.

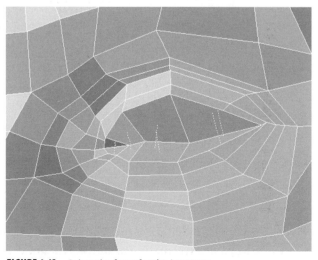

FIGURE 4.43 Select the faces for the inner eye.

behind that, and the third will be brought deeper into the head as in Figure 4.44.

FIGURE 4.44   Make the extrusions for the inner eye.

The original eight faces can be pulled back into the head and scaled smaller. The eyeball will block this geometry. In fact, you could even delete the eight faces in the back of the eye socket, or weld them together into a single-point. Scale the second row of edges so they disappear behind the upper and lower lids. This will give the eyelid more of an edge. See Figure 4.45.

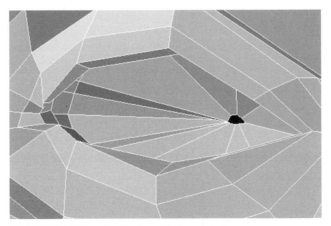

FIGURE 4.45   Pull and scale down the inner eye faces.

Continue to shape and model areas such as the eyelids using the stand-in eyeball we made earlier. It is a good practice to evaluate, and reevaluate, the model as you work on it against the live model images.

The head we are modeling would still benefit from more geometry to model with. Move down the face, split a new row of faces from the tip of the nose to behind the ear, terminating in a triangle, as seen in Figure 4.46.

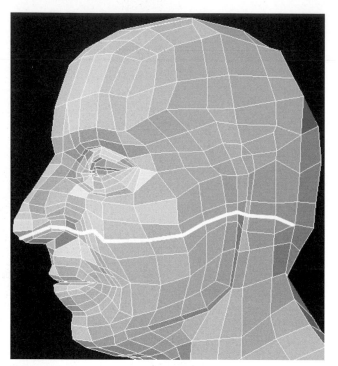

FIGURE 4.46 Create a new row of faces from the tip of the nose to behind the ear.

The next split will be vertical. Start at the base of the neck, two rows in from the centerline. Continue the split up the neck, and through the chin, lips, and nose. See Figure 4.47.

Here comes a tricky part. This split will continue to the top of the nostril and will then loop around the edge of the nostril and back under it to the centerline of the face. See Figure 4.48.

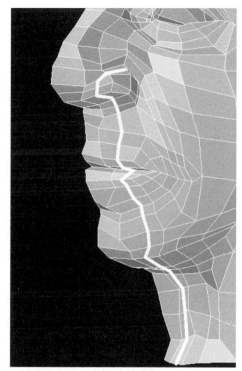

FIGURE 4.47   Make a vertical split up the lower portion of the face.

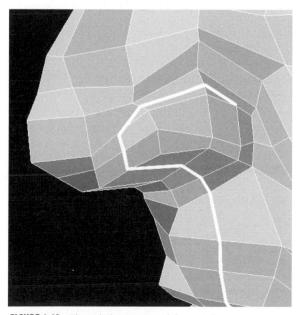

FIGURE 4.48   The split loops around the nostril.

This loop split has left us with a geometrical-face configuration that is generally undesirable. By cutting across a face to alter the direction of the edge flow, we have created a five-sided face next to a three-sided face. Figure 4.49 shows an example of this on a simpler surface of a grid.

Most subdivision routines can handle this configuration, but look at what happens to the faces when you perform a subdivision (see Figure 4.50). The corner of the five- and three-sided faces has subdivided into an awkward arrangement.

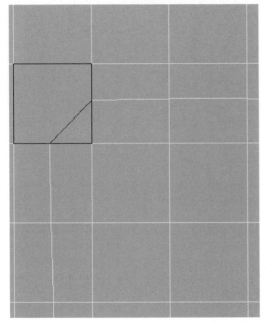

FIGURE 4.49 Cutting at an angle across a face creates a five-sided face next to a three-sided one.

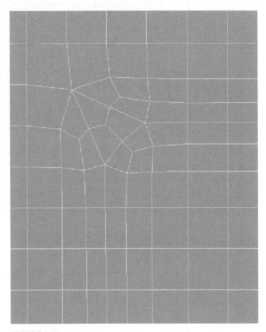

FIGURE 4.50 The five- and three-sided faces have subdivided into an awkward arrangement.

On a flat plane such as this, the results might not be noticeable on the smooth, shaded model. But on the contours of a more complicated surface such as the human face, this configuration could cause shading artifacts or surface pinching, especially if it is in an area that will bend during animation.

The quickest way to eliminate this undesirable combo is to split the five-sided face in two, thus turning it into two quads and the triangle into one. See Figure 4.51.

Subdivide this arrangement and notice in Figure 4.52 how much cleaner the flow of the faces is.

The lesson here is that it you should try to keep as many faces as possible in a quad configuration.

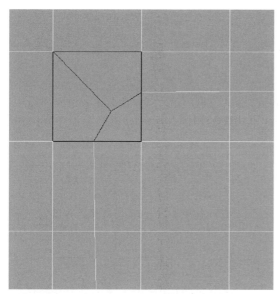

FIGURE 4.51   Split the five- and three-sided faces to make quads.

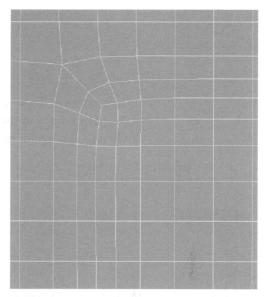

FIGURE 4.52   This arrangement subdivides very cleanly.

Applying this lesson to the model, split the five-/three-sided combo that occurred at the corners of the nostrils, as seen in Figure 4.53.

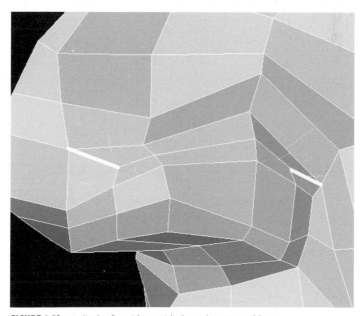

FIGURE 4.53   Split the five-/three-sided combination of faces.

Organic modeling such as this requires you to think and plan on several different levels. The most obvious focal point is the likeness or final appearance of the character. However, below the surface are the polygons, which you need to arrange in the most efficient manner so that you can define the character's secondary forms. These should not be laid out in a haphazard manner. Yet another level of thought has to be directed at how the forms will bend if animated. The flow and direction of the polygons are important aspects to consider when you are creating facial morph shapes for lip sync and expressions. Reworking faces to meet all the needs is an ongoing process.

We will now rearrange some of the faces of the character's face. Move to the cheek area, underneath the eye. Spin, reconstruct, or flip the direction of the two faces seen in Figure 4.54.

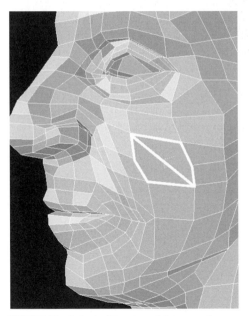

FIGURE 4.54   Spin the direction of these two faces.

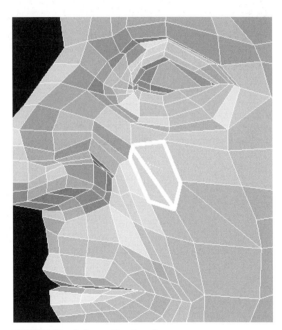

FIGURE 4.55   Spin another two faces.

Next, spin the two faces slightly above, as in Figure 4.55.

Spin the next two faces, as seen in Figure 4.56.

Lastly, spin another two faces below the last, as in Figure 4.57.

Things are looking pretty good. We can further clean up the lower cheek area by deleting a face, as seen in Figure 4.58. This face was not causing any problems, but it wasn't helping any geometry either. There will be spots on the model when you can safely eliminate faces here and

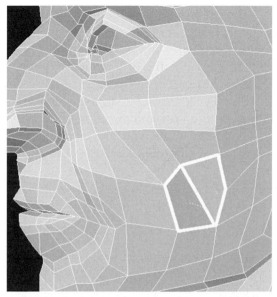

FIGURE 4.56   Spin two more faces.

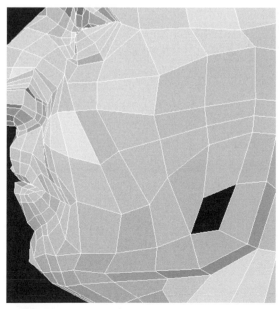

FIGURE 4.57   Spin yet two more faces.

there. These usually appear in the form of "diamond-shaped" quads. Test whether these faces will be missed by deleting them and welding the hole closed. If it causes the surrounding geometry to stretch too much to fill the gap, put the face back in (or press undo).

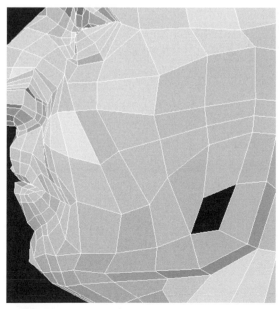

FIGURE 4.58   Delete this face.

Finally, weld the two points to close the hole. See Figure 4.59.

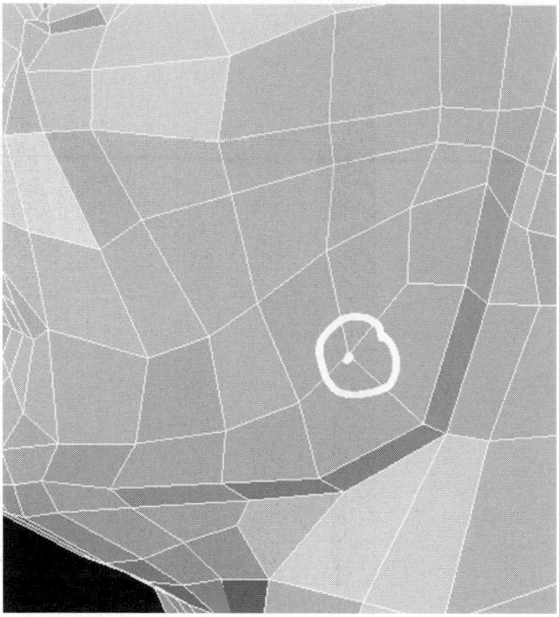

FIGURE 4.59   Weld the two points to close the hole resulting from the deleted face.

Next turn your attention to the center of the head. Split a new vertical row of faces from midpoint back on the head down through the nose and ending at the chin, as seen in Figure 4.60. This will help us add definition to the form, especially to the upper lip.

We will now move on to some of the finer details in the face such as the nostrils. To begin, select and inset the four faces on the underside of the nose, as in Figure 4.61. You could accomplish the same thing by splitting the faces in that pattern.

Extrude those up into the nose twice. Spend a little time shaping the nose and nostrils, as seen in Figure 4.62.

During the modeling process, it is important to view a subdivided version of the model. Take a moment to view the head and specific features, such as the nose, from many angles to see if they look natural and resemble the live model. How does light play across the surface? This is where viewing the model under different lighting conditions can help. Are there any harsh shadows or creases? The nasallabial fold is a common area to overdo. Unless the subject is very old, this fold will not be too deep. On the flip side, even younger people have this fold. It may not

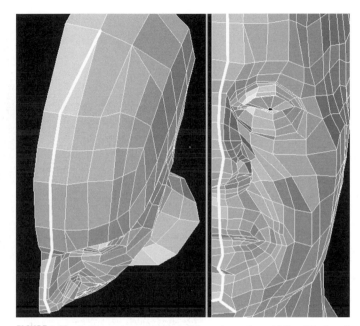

FIGURE 4.60   Split a new vertical row of faces down the middle of the head.

FIGURE 4.61   Inset the faces for the nostrils.

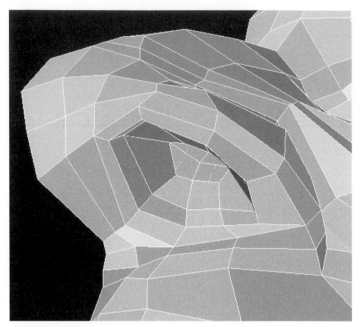

FIGURE 4.62   Extrude the faces into the nose to make the nostrils.

be pronounced in a neutral face, but it will be there in varying degrees and will definitely show up in all ages during expressions such as smiling. Another subtle feature of the nose area that most people share is that the nostrils are higher than the bottom of the septum. See Figure 4.63.

Figure 4.64 shows another rows of faces split around the lips. Notice that the newly created faces, which are a result of the split operation, are close to the edge of the lips. If you remember the properties of subdividing polygons, faces close together will help create a sharper edge or crease. The upper lip, especially, tends to have a sharper ridge than the lower lip along its edge.

You may have noticed that Frank doesn't have his ears yet. We will tackle them shortly, but first we should prep the area where they will be attached. This is easy enough. Make a split similar to the one in Figure 4.65. This will eliminate the two triangles in those spots and will give us a five-/three-sided combo, which we will eliminate shortly.

To get rid of the five-/three-sided combo, make a split, as in Figure 4.66.

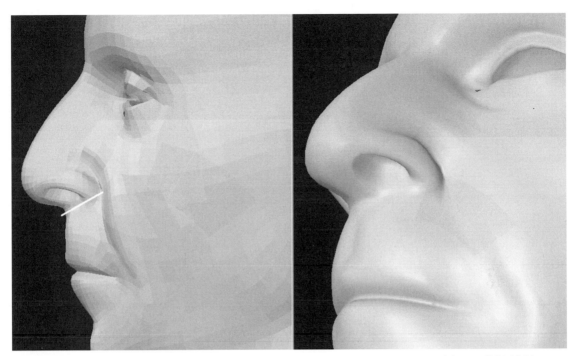

FIGURE 4.63   Review the model from numerous angles to check the features such as the nose and the nasallabial fold.

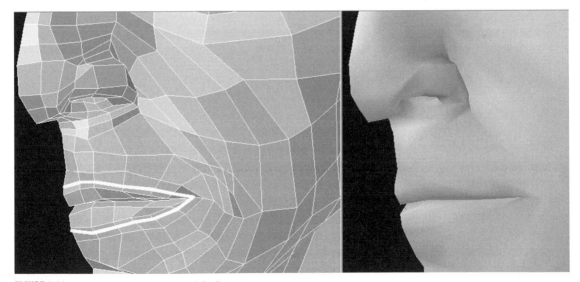

FIGURE 4.64   Split a loop of faces around the lips.

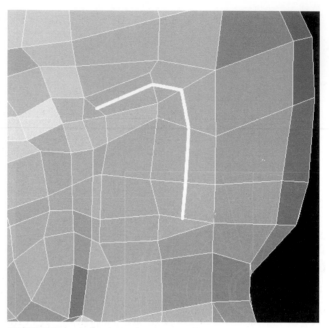

FIGURE 4.65 Prep the ear area.

FIGURE 4.66 Get rid of the five-/three-sided combo.

Next, move the vertices to make a rounder arrangement of faces, as in Figure 4.67.

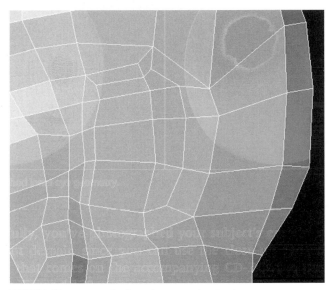

FIGURE 4.67   Arrange the faces in preparation for the ear.

THE EARS

This small arrangement of skin-covered cartilage on our heads is one of the toughest features to model in 3D. Seemingly simple at first glance, the ear is quite complex in the twisty forms it contains. More than ever, it pays to plan ahead when tackling the ears.

As with any modeling project, it helps to break down and understand the forms you want to re-create. Therefore, spend some time looking at ears—yours, those of others, or those of the live model images provided in the reference folder of the CD-ROM included with this book. Get a feel for the shapes from all angles.

ON THE CD

For the ear, we will make a flat template with most of the geometry mapped out, and then we will pull form and life from that. You could start with a cube and add detail into that, but with the complexity of the ear, you may soon find yourself trapped in a corner, modeling-wise. The template method allows you to take your time and plot the specific features carefully, before the model becomes too complex.

If you are working from photos of your own design or model, zoom into the side view and frame the ear. Even better is to have specific close-ups of the ear itself. This will allow you a higher resolution and detail to work with. See Figure 4.68.

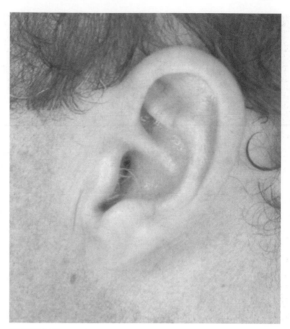

FIGURE 4.68   A close-up of the ear.

ON THE CD

The template method involves plotting out where the faces of the form will go. This is just kept to one axis initially. Figure 4.69 shows the template made for the ear shown in this book. You may copy this template, or load the EarTemp.obj file from the models folder on the CD-ROM.

This still may appear to you as a mess of polygons. Therefore, it is important that you take the time to try and understand the shapes you are re-creating. Figure 4.70 shows the ear broken down into different colors for clarification. It's not necessary to know the anatomical terms for each area of the ear (yes, there are terms for these forms) as long as you see these forms when you look at an ear.

Ears are not flat, so we will give our ear some depth. Extrude out the ear faces as a group. Do not make the extrusion too thick. Delete the faces at the rear of the ear, except for the rim. See Figure 4.71.

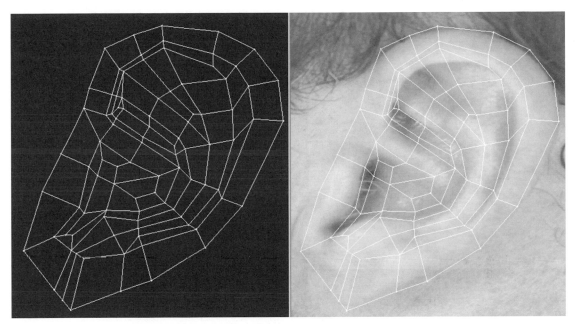

FIGURE 4.69   The ear template.

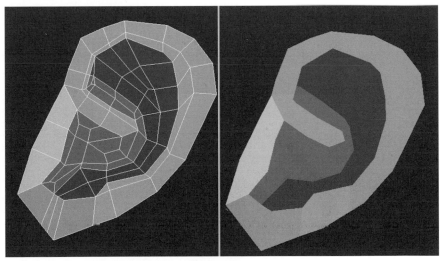

FIGURE 4.70   The ear broken down into different colors for form clarification.

Give the inner forms depth by pulling faces back into the ear. There are several levels to concentrate on, from the rim down to the ear canal. Notice how the outer rim winds back into the ear too. See Figure 4.72.

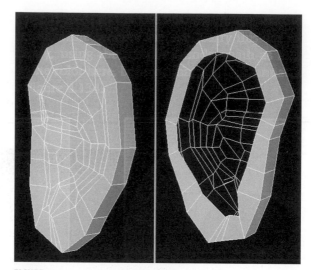

FIGURE 4.71   Extrude out the ear faces.

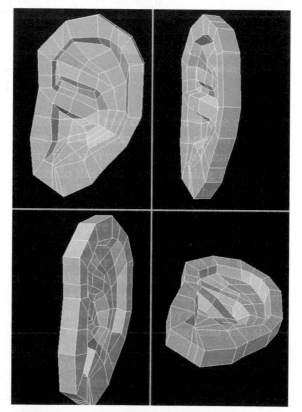

FIGURE 4.72   Give the ear forms some depth.

Continue to refine the shapes. Also, give the whole ear form a slight bend. The curve will vary in person to person, but it is never a flat plane. See Figure 4.73.

Move the ear into position by the head. Be sure to turn it outwards a bit. Delete the eight faces on the head to make a hole to attach the ear to, as in Figure 4.74. Get the position as good as you can while the geometry is still loose from the head.

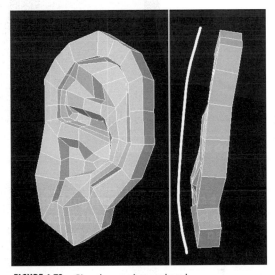

FIGURE 4.73   Give the ear shape a bend.

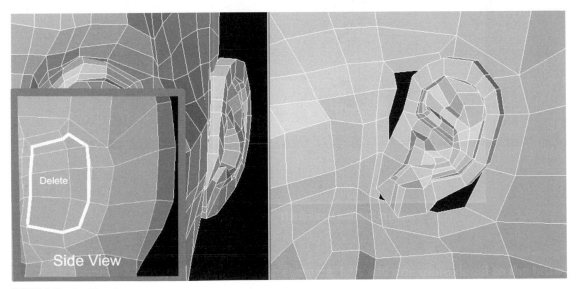

FIGURE 4.74   Position the ear.

We will need to delete some of the front faces of the ear object in order to get it to fit. See Figure 4.75a.

To create the back of the ear, create a new partial ring of faces using the existing geometry. If your software allows you to extrude new faces from points or edges, that would be a solution. Otherwise, it is a matter of building the new faces one at a time. Figure 4.75b shows the new faces created at the back of the ear.

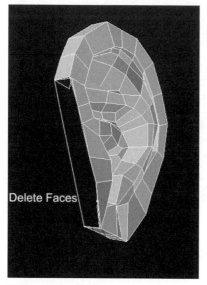

FIGURE 4.75a   Delete faces on the ear in preparation for attaching it to the head.

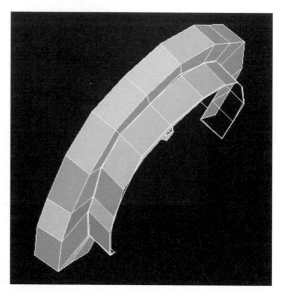

FIGURE 4.75b   The new faces created at the back of the ear.

Attaching the ear to the head involves a combination of welding and creating some more new faces. This process can quickly become visually confusing, so hide as much of the unneeded geometry as possible. The welding will be done mostly at the front. Creating new faces is reserved for the rear, behind the ear. Every vertex of the ear might not line up with those of the head, but you can "tie" them off with a diamond-shaped quad. This type of face is illustrated in Figure 4.76. It may not be the prettiest arrangement, but since it is in an unseen area and will not animate, it will be fine. Figure 4.76 shows how the ear was attached with the newly created faces and highlighted welded areas.

Figure 4.77 shows the subdivided head with the attached ear. The ear was tough, to be sure, but now that it is complete, the rest will seem much easier. A poorly made ear can diminish an otherwise well-done model. The added bonus of this step is that you will have an ear model you can re-use on any future heads you build.

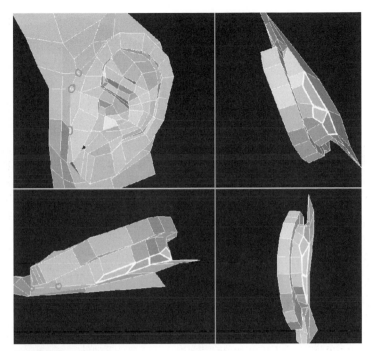

FIGURE 4.76 The attached ear.

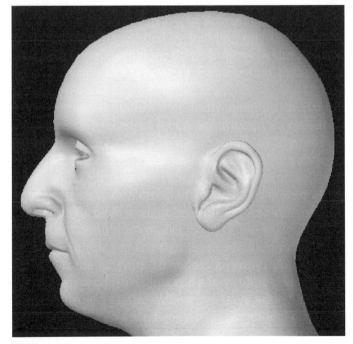

FIGURE 4.77 The subdivided head with the attached ear.

REFINING THE HEAD

Move now to the brow area. Create a split that turns that triangle over the brow into a quad, and terminate it as a triangle at the temple, as seen in Figure 4.78. This will help us form an eyebrow ridge.

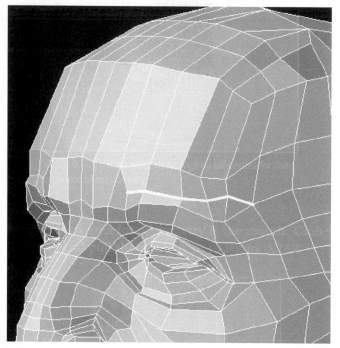

FIGURE 4.78   Add detail to the brow.

Add another row of faces across the forehead, but terminate it halfway back on the head, as in Figure 4.79.

Move down to the mouth area. Although the face at the corner of the nasallabial fold, as seen in Figure 4.80, is a quad, it does not help define the line of that area optimally since its edge is split. This could cause shading issues if the face is animated.

We will therefore rework it. To do so, split a new row of faces from the quad's corner to behind the ear, as seen in Figure 4.81.

Combine the quad and triangle at that spot into one face. See Figure 4.82.

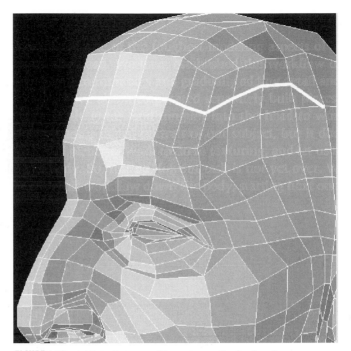

FIGURE 4.79   Add another row of faces across the forehead.

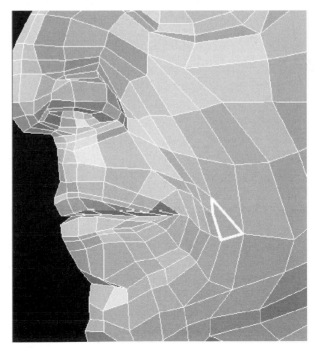

FIGURE 4.80   This face, while a quad, does not help define the form optimally.

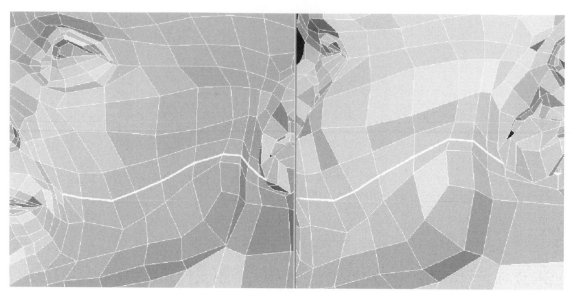

FIGURE 4.81   Split a new row of faces from the quad's corner to behind the ear.

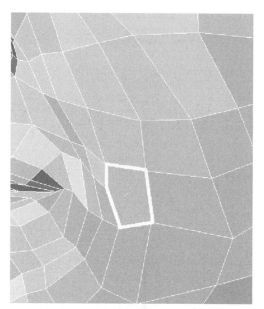

FIGURE 4.82   Combine the quad and triangle at that spot into one face.

This will create a five-sided face, which we will now get rid of by splitting. Also, continue the split across the cheek and end in the same area behind the ear, as in Figure 4.83a.

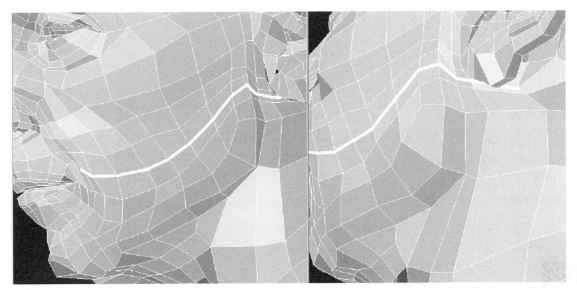

FIGURE 4.83a   Continue the split across the cheek and end behind the ear.

THE MOUTH

One common mistake made while modeling mouths is to make them straight slits across the face. Bear in mind the anatomy behind the mouth and surrounding area; namely the skull and teeth. See Figure 4.83b.

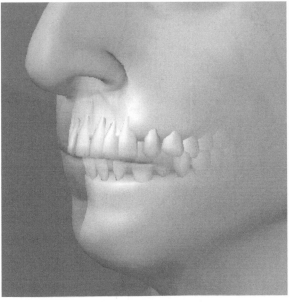

FIGURE 4.83b   The skull and teeth affect the shape of the mouth.

To break the underlying forms down into a simple shape, imagine a cylinder behind the mouth, the lips conforming to its contour. See Figure 4.83c.

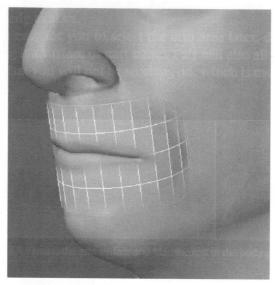

FIGURE 4.83c Imagine a cylinder behind the mouth to understand the shape.

Unless this character is going to be mute, or will never open his mouth, we will need to make other arrangements. The first step would be to separate where his lower and upper lips connect. Un-weld or disconnect the eight faces where the lips meet and create a space there. If necessary, weld back together any vertices that may have been disconnected during this process. See Figure 4.84.

Depending on your modeling software, you will have different options for creating the inside of the mouth. One method would be to create a large polygon in the space created in the previous step. Collect the points in the space to make the polygon. See Figure 4.85.

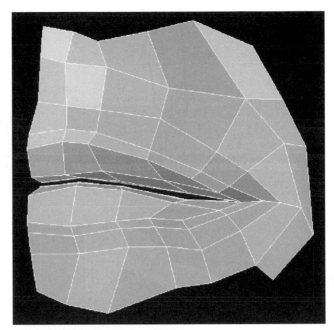

FIGURE 4.84   Create a space for the inner mouth (the other face geometry is hidden for clarity).

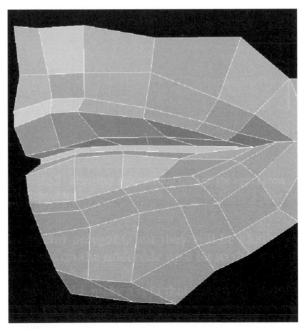

FIGURE 4.85   Create a large polygon in the space created between the lips.

Do not be concerned that this is a large, awkward face; we will divide or delete it later. We are going to use it to extrude back to make the inner mouth. Start by making a couple of extrusions to give a thickness to the lower lips. See Figure 4.86.

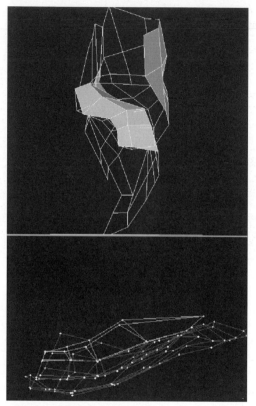

FIGURE 4.86   Make a couple of extrusions to give a thickness to the lower lips.

Make another extrusion. This time, enlarge the extruded face in the *Y* axis. This will be the beginning of the mouth cavity. See Figure 4.87.

Now it is just a matter of making another four or five extrusions back into the mouth and throat. Get rid of that large extrusion polygon by either breaking up the faces into smaller quads and triangles, or by deleting it altogether. If you delete it, make sure that it is deep enough into the throat so that the hole will not be seen when the character opens his mouth. Figure 4.88 shows the extruded inner mouth and throat.

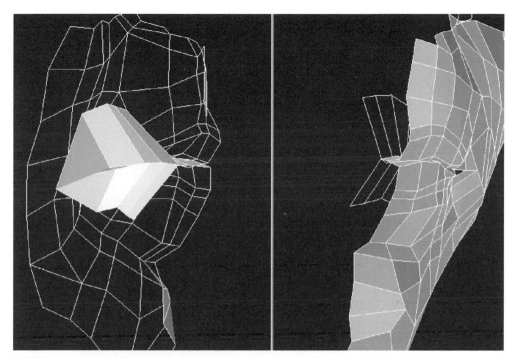

FIGURE 4.87   Make another extrusion and enlarge the face.

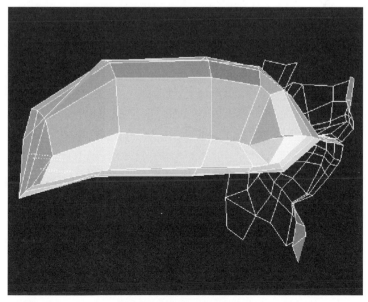

FIGURE 4.88   The extruded inner mouth and throat.

INSIDE THE MOUTH

If you have come this far in modeling the head, then you will want to have some geometry to put in the mouth. The teeth, gums, and tongue are the logical choices.

As with every other part of the human form, it is beneficial to study the forms you want to re-create. Anatomy books and photos of your live model will help with that. If your live model has a distinctive bite, be sure and photograph it. See Figure 4.89.

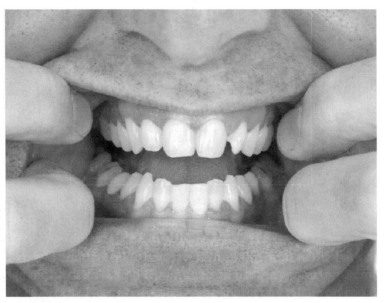

FIGURE 4.89   A photo of the live model's teeth.

The teeth can be broken down into three categories: the incisors (flat and in front of the mouth), canines (pointed), and molars (short, square, and in the rear). You can model one of each and replicate it, with some variances, throughout the mouth.

Starting with the incisor, make a box three segments along the Y axis, two on the *X*, and two along the *Z*, as in Figure 4.90. Name the surface "Teeth."

Shape this geometry so that the cutting edge is thin and it tapers towards the root, as in Figure 4.91.

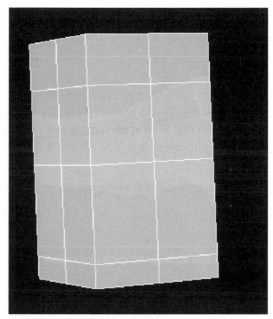

FIGURE 4.90   Make a box with three segments along the *Y* axis, two on the *X*, and two on the *Z*.

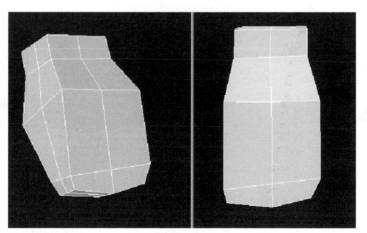

FIGURE 4.91   Shape the incisor.

Figure 4.92 shows further shaping of the geometry.

Figure 4.93 shows the subdivided incisor.

The canine is created in much the same way. First, make a box with three segments on the *Y* axis and two on the *X*, as in Figure 4.94.

Shape this tooth, but make it pointier at the tip than the incisor. See Figure 4.95.

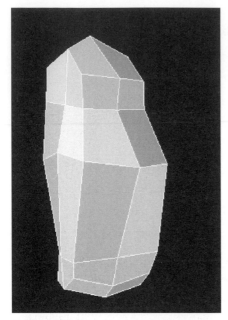

FIGURE 4.92 Shape the geometry further.

FIGURE 4.93 The subdivided incisor.

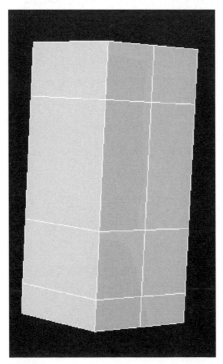

FIGURE 4.94 The start of the canine.

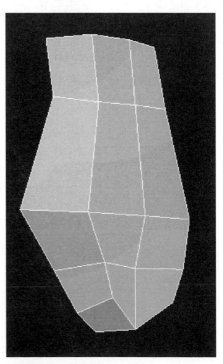

FIGURE 4.95 Shape the canine.

Give the canine a little extra point by extruding the four faces at the tip. Shape them so they flow with the form of the tooth, as in Figure 4.96. Figure 4.97 shows the subdivided canine.

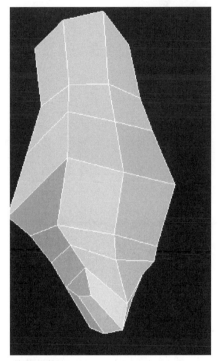

FIGURE 4.96   Give the canine a little extra point by extruding the four faces at the tip.

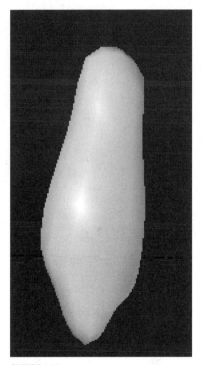

FIGURE 4.97   The subdivided canine.

By now, you should have a good feel for how the teeth are made. Figure 4.98 shows the basic shape for the molar. You can see the main difference between it and the other teeth at the top, where there is the inset of faces. This will help create the groove and indentation found in molars.

This geometry can now be pulled into shape. Figure 4.99 shows the subdivided molar.

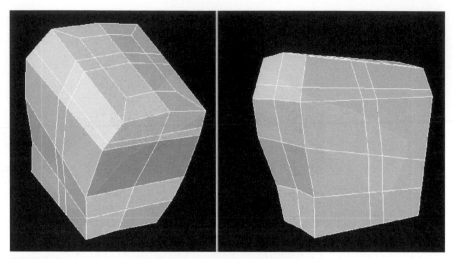

FIGURE 4.98 The basic molar geometry.

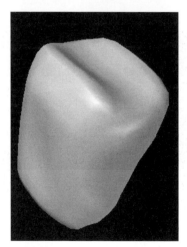

FIGURE 4.99 The subdivided molar.

We can fill a mouth with these three basic teeth types. Turn to your photo reference and images of skulls for areas that can't be seen in the live photo. See Figure 4.100.

Here are some basic guidelines for arranging the teeth (see Figure 4.101):

- Most upper teeth are larger than the lower ones. This is mainly noticeable in the front incisors. Notice how much wider they are than the lower ones.
- The upper teeth overbite the lower ones.

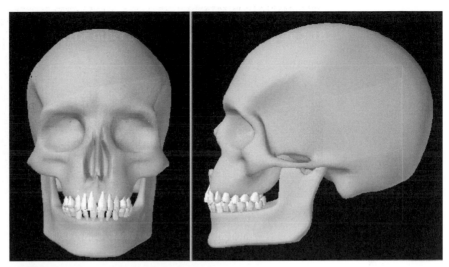

FIGURE 4.100   The teeth in the skull.

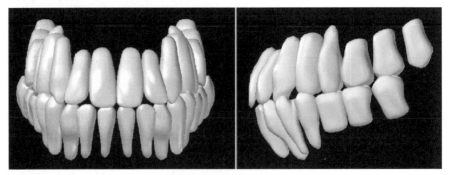

FIGURE 4.101   The basic teeth arrangement.

Of course, there are many variations depending on the individual. The condition of the teeth can add much to the character. Unless you are planning to have an entire animated sequence take place inside a character's mouth, there is no need to get too detailed with the teeth geometry. What we have done here is fine for most cases.

We have teeth. Now we just need something to set them into. Gums will do just fine. Begin the gums by making a box with eight segments, as seen in Figure 4.102.

Bend the box into a horseshoe-like shape. If your modeler does not have a Bend command, select sections of the geometry and rotate them until the shape is achieved. See Figure 4.103.

FIGURE 4.102 Begin the gums by making a box with eight segments.

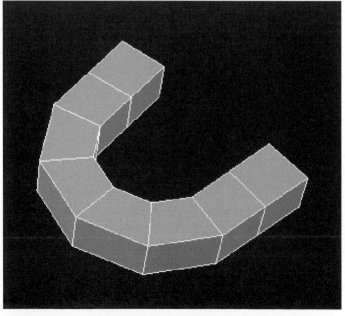

FIGURE 4.103 Bend the box into a horseshoe-like shape.

Next, angle and shape the gums. If you find it helpful, use the teeth you modeled in a background layer. See Figure 4.104.

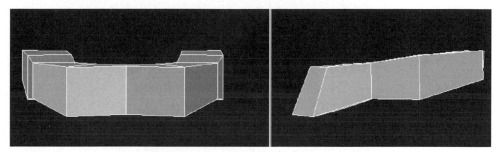

FIGURE 4.104   Angle and shape the gums.

We will need more geometry to model this further. Make new cuts in between the existing faces, as seen in Figure 4.105. (The gum object was cut in half here.)

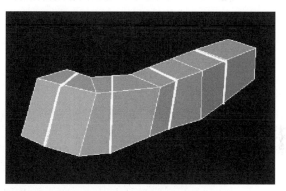

FIGURE 4.105   Make new cuts in between the existing faces.

Continue to make more cuts of the same nature. This will provide vertices that you can pull down between the teeth, which will simulate the tight fit between gum and tooth. See Figure 4.106.

Figure 4.107 shows the vertices pulled to create the indentations for the teeth.

Next, we want to add geometry to help hold the shape when it subdivides. We can accomplish this by adding two horizontal cuts: one at the top edge of the gums, and one along the bottom near the teeth. See Figure 4.108.

The lower gums can be created in the same way. In fact, you can rework the upper gums into lower by flipping them and moving vertices. Figure 4.109 shows the completed gums and teeth.

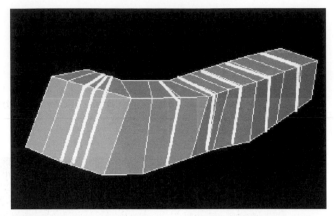

FIGURE 4.106 Continue to make cuts between existing faces.

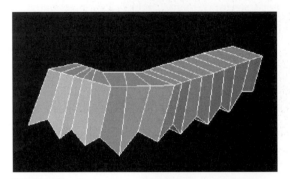

FIGURE 4.107 The vertices pulled to create the indentations for the teeth.

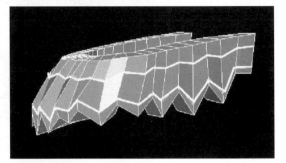

FIGURE 4.108 Add two horizontal cuts to help hold the gum's shape when the model subdivides.

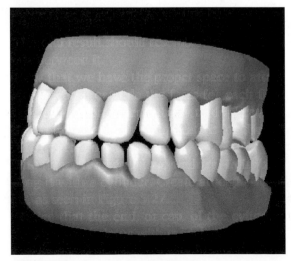

FIGURE 4.109 The finished teeth and gums.

Since the gums will be buried in the mouth, it is safe for you to delete the top row of polygons. Doing so cuts down on the number of faces in the final subdivided model. You should delete unseen faces anywhere you can. An extra face or two here or there might not seem like a big deal, but they quickly add up over a whole model. You can also delete faces on the portion of the teeth that are hidden by the gums. See Figure 4.110.

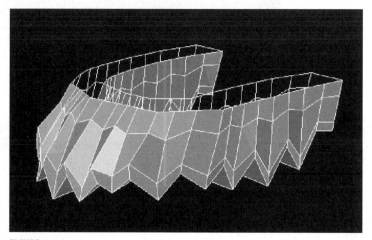

FIGURE 4.110   Delete unseen faces on the gums.

If our character is going to open his mouth and speak, then it would make sense to give him a tongue. Luckily, this is very simple. Make a flat, segmented box, as in Figure 4.111.

Pull the corners back, as in Figure 4.112.

Add new faces on the top and underside to help the tongue hold its shape during subdivision, as seen in Figure 4.113.

Then, split two new rows of faces close to the center, as in Figure 4.114.

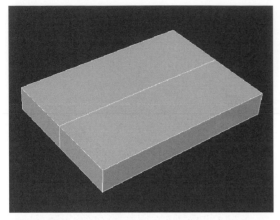

FIGURE 4.111 To start the tongue, make a flat, segmented box.

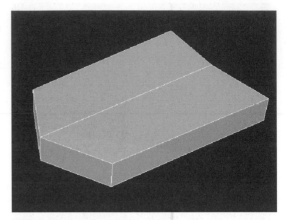

FIGURE 4.112 Pull the corners back.

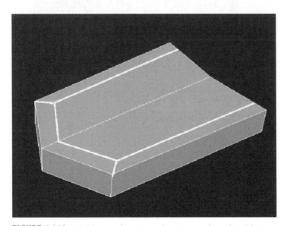

FIGURE 4.113 Add new faces on the top and underside.

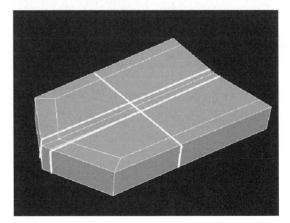

FIGURE 4.114 Split two new rows of faces close to the center.

We have enough geometry, but now we need to give a little life to this board. Give the tip a slight curve. Pull down the center points on the top and even further down on the underside, as in Figure 4.115.

Subdivide the tongue and view the results, as in Figure 4.116.

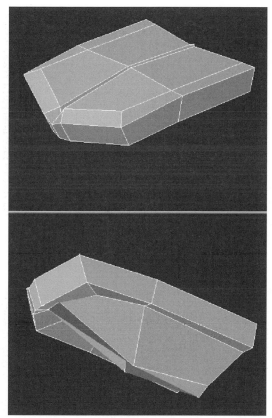

FIGURE 4.115   Give the tongue shape.

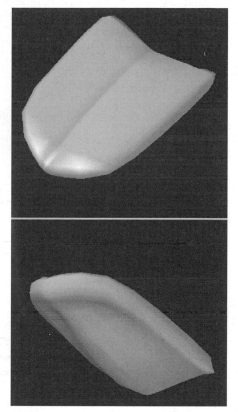

FIGURE 4.116   Subdivide the tongue.

Now that you have the inner mouth details, you should set them into the head. Remember that the teeth will not extend to the edge of the cheeks, so do not make the teeth too wide. Also, leave some thickness for the lips. Figure 4.117 shows the teeth and gums and their position inside the head.

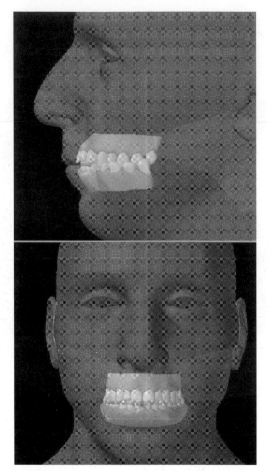

FIGURE 4.117 The teeth and gums set inside the head.

THE EYES

Earlier in the chapter, we made a simple eye form to help us model the lids. This was fine for those purposes, but you will most likely want to put more realistic eyes in your model. This involves a few extra steps, but the results are dramatically different and well worth the time.

We will be making a more involved eye model than we did for the stand-in eye. This will include two spheres for each eye: a smaller one set inside a slightly larger one. The larger, or outer, sphere will represent the cornea. It will be given transparent material settings. The inner sphere will be for the colors that we expect to see in an eye. Both of these spheres will be given subtle geometric alterations beyond their perfectly round beginnings.

To start, create a 24mm-large sphere with 24 sides and 12 segments. Name this surface "Cornea" and give it a high specularity setting. If your modeling software allows you to assign transparency at this point, you can do so. It should be close to 100 percent. See Figure 4.118.

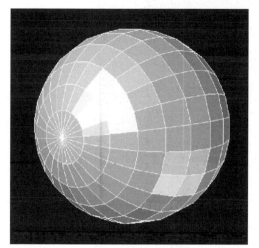

FIGURE 4.118   Start the eyeball by making the outer cornea sphere.

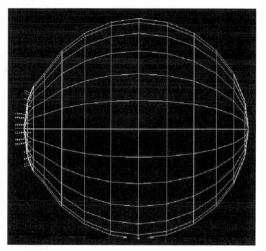

FIGURE 4.119   Pull the faces out for the corneal bulge.

We are going to add the corneal bulge, a slightly convex area at the center of the cornea. Select the front two rows of faces and pull them out slightly, as in Figure 4.119.

Next, add a new row of faces in the third row from the front edge, as seen in Figure 4.120a.

That is it for the outer eye. It's pretty simple, but this little detail will add a good deal of realism to the eye, as you will see later.

We will now create the inner sphere. This will represent the white, or sclera, and the iris of the eye. Start by making another sphere with the same dimensions and face count as for the cornea. The scale of this sphere is just slightly smaller than that of the cornea sphere. Make sure it fits inside the larger sphere. Name the surface "White" or "Inner Eye." See Figure 4.120b.

Next, split two new rows of faces through the second center ring of faces, as seen in Figure 4.121.

The next step is to pull these center faces to make a shallow, concave area. This will be where the iris is mapped to, and its shape will catch light differently than the cornea. A Magnet tool will help achieve a soft fall-off for the movement. See Figure 4.122.

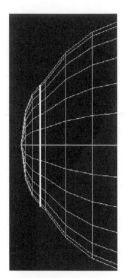

FIGURE 4.120a Split a new row of faces.

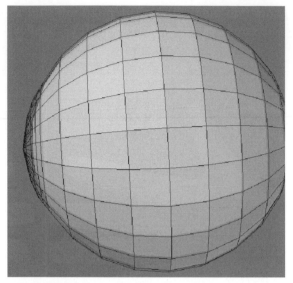

FIGURE 4.120b Place another, slightly smaller, sphere inside the first one.

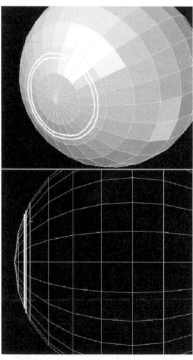

FIGURE 4.121 Split two new rows of faces through the second center ring.

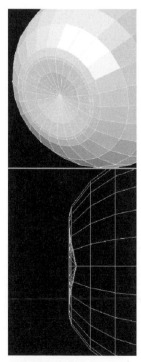

FIGURE 4.122 Pull the center faces to make a shallow, concave area for the iris.

Combine the center group of triangle faces into a single polygon, as in Figure 4.123.

Scale this center polygon smaller, give it the surface name "Pupil," and color it black. Remove any specularity from the pupil surface. See Figure 4.124.

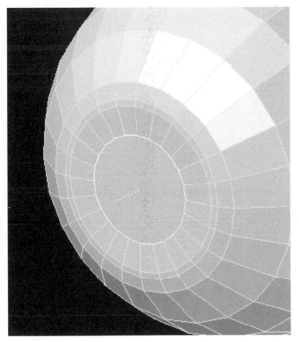

FIGURE 4.123   Combine the center group of triangle faces into a single polygon.

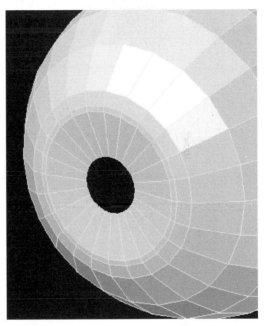

FIGURE 4.124   Scale this center polygon smaller and give it the surface name "Pupil."

Extrude the pupil surface face back into the eye, as in Figure 4.125.

Now, split a new ring of faces close to the edge of the pupil, as in Figure 4.126.

We are just about done with modeling the eyes. The last step is to subdivide them once. This will make a smoother surface. Once you have done that, delete the back half of the eye spheres because they will never be seen. Figure 4.127 shows the finished cornea geometry.

Figure 4.128 shows the finished inner eye geometry.

To fully see the results of this work, we should apply a texture to the eye and render it. We will texture the rest of the head in Chapter 8, but we will texture the eye here.

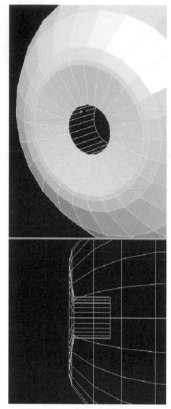

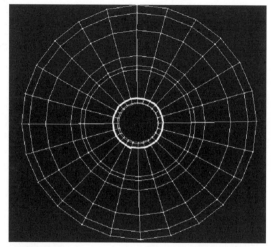

FIGURE 4.125 Extrude the pupil
surface face back into the eye.

FIGURE 4.126 Split a new ring of faces close to the edge
of the pupil.

FIGURE 4.127 The finished cornea geometry.

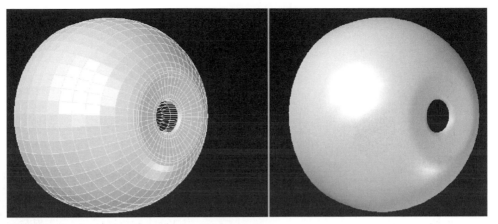

FIGURE 4.128   The finished inner eye geometry.

ON THE CD

Hopefully, you've photographed your subject's eyes in close-up. If not, do not despair, since you can use the close-up eye image (Eye-Close.jpg) that comes on the accompanying CD-ROM in the reference folder. See Figure 4.129.

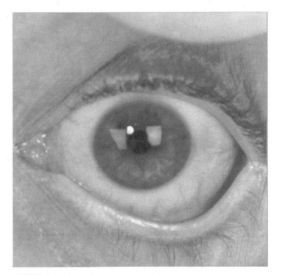

FIGURE 4.129   A close-up eye photo.

We are going to use this eye image as the basis for the texture map on the eye model. It will need some work before we can use it as a texture. For instance, we will want to remove the eyelid, reflections, and highlights as well as make the iris centered.

Before we alter the original image, we will make a painting template of the eye. This will allow us to scale and fit the eye image precisely. The painting template is derived from the UV map. Where does the UV map come from? Well, we have to make one.

In your modeling package, assign to the inner eye sphere a planar UV map along the Z axis. Export out an image of this template (if your software supports this), or perform a screen capture of the UV map. Either way, you should end up with a template that resembles Figure 4.130.

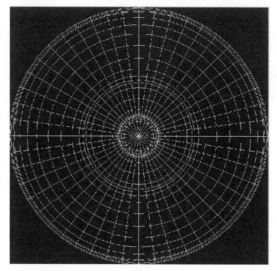

FIGURE 4.130   The eye painting template.

For this exercise, the template image was 1,024 × 1,024. You can scale the image down later to conserve memory, if you like.

Load the eye template image and the eye photo into your favorite paint program. Copy the eye photo image and paste it into the eye template image. The new copy should be on a new layer. You may need to scale the eye photo layer to get it to fit properly. The best way to do this is to turn the opacity of that layer down so that you can see the template underneath. Size and fit the iris to the iris geometry in the template. See Figure 4.131.

The first alteration we will do is mirror one half of the eye. This will help eliminate some of the distortion in the original photo. In this case, the lower half of the image was mirrored to the upper half. You can do this with the help of the paint program's Grid feature. You should end up with something like Figure 4.132.

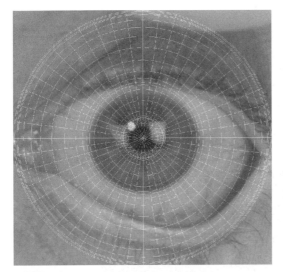

FIGURE 4.131   Scale and fit the eye photo layer.

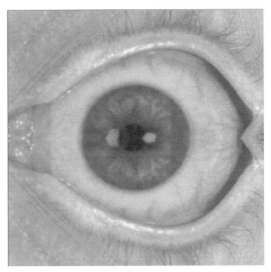

FIGURE 4.132   Mirror the eye half.

Next, we will paint out the pupil, highlights, and reflections. We will create the pupil on our eye model with the geometry. We will get highlights in the eye when we render the model, so we need to get rid of these elements in the eye photo. To do this, use the Clone or Stamp tool to sample areas that don't have these unwanted features onto the spots that do. See Figure 4.133.

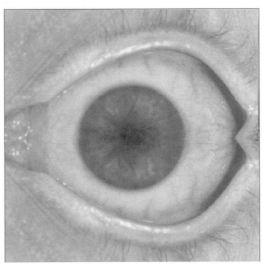

FIGURE 4.133   Paint out the pupil, highlights, and reflections.

The next step is to paint out the lids. Again, use the Clone or Stamp tool to sample the white spots of the eye. Carry this out to the edges of the eye geometry, using the template underneath as a guide. Do not paint a pure white color here, because that will look unnatural when you render it. See Figure 4.134.

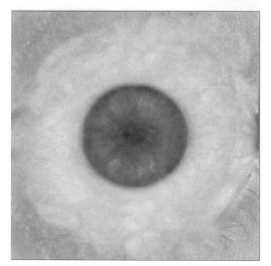

FIGURE 4.134   Paint out the lids.

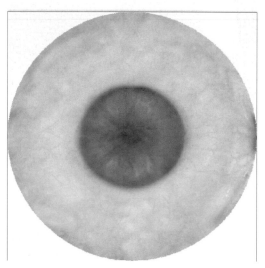

FIGURE 4.135   Add a white circular border.

To clean up the image, you can add a white circular border around the eye image. Use the Layers feature to paint in new veins, if you like. Also, try to eliminate any repeating patterns that were created with the Clone tool. You can do this with more cloning, or by hand painting little bits of color here and there. The white of the eye may look unusually splotchy, but that will actually render more natural looking than if it were a pure color. See Figure 4.135.

Save this eye image with an appropriate name, such as "Eyecolor." Now you just have to apply this texture to the UV map on your eye geometry. Make sure the cornea is transparent. You can even add a slight refraction to it, which will control the bending of light through the transparency. A low amount of reflection may be useful as well. Perform test renders to tweak the values to your liking, and you should have something similar to Figure 4.136.

One last modeling detail for the eye area that will add a nice bit of realism is the tear ducts. Observe the inner corner of your eye. Notice that the corner extends beyond the edge of the eyeball itself. Instead of having a space there, model a simple shape to represent the tear duct. This

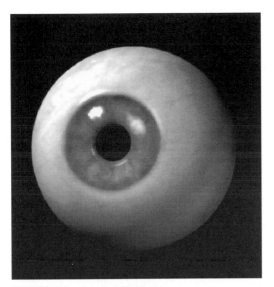

FIGURE 4.136   The rendered eye.

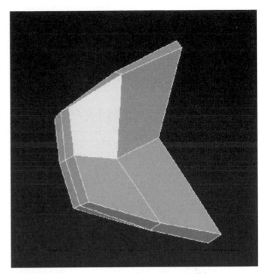

FIGURE 4.137   The tear duct geometry.

doesn't have to be anything more complex than a slightly modified cube. See Figure 4.137 for an example of the tear duct geometry.

Give the tear duct an appropriate surface name, and move it into place in the corner of the eye. Adjust it and/or the lids until they meet up tightly with one another. See Figure 4.138.

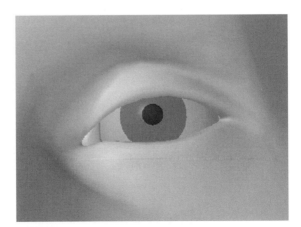

FIGURE 4.138   The finished tear duct in place.

While we are in the eye area, let's add one more detail to the brow. Although we will not be modeling in the actual eyebrows, giving the geometry a little ridge will help when we apply the image maps later. To do this, simply split a new row of faces from the triangle by the temple across the brow, as in Figure 4.139.

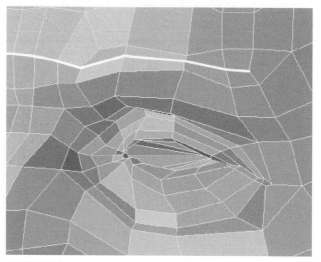

FIGURE 4.139 Split a new row of faces across the brow.

GETTING THE LIKENESS

We have gone over numerous modeling steps to create a head. Background image templates have helped us place the geometry so that our digital human resembles the live character. There will be a point where you will have to abandon following the background templates strictly and will have to rely more on using your eyes. One reason is that there will always be some distortion in the template photos, and following them slavishly will just cause you to chase your tail. You should study photos of the live model (or the actual person) outside of the 3D program used to create it. Then, observe the head you are creating. Does it capture the person's likeness? What seems "off" to you? This is why it is helpful to have good photo coverage of the live model. View photos that aren't head- or side-on. Three-quarter angles will reveal a great deal. Compare your model to these photo angles. Make adjustments. Most likely, you will need to do a fair amount of tweaking. Keep at it until you are happy and you've captured the essence of the person. Figure 4.140 shows the live model compared with the model we made.

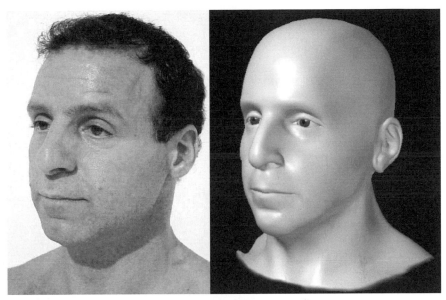

FIGURE 4.140   The live model compared to the 3D replica.

ASYMMETRY

One of the great features of modeling in the computer is that you can reduce the amount of work needed by building one half of a model, and then mirroring the rest. Until now, this is how we've been working. Mirroring and/or utilizing the symmetry features just makes sense when you're working on a head.

However, nothing in nature is perfectly symmetrical. In fact, perfect symmetry will work against us when we attempt to capture a natural head. Our facial features are a prime example of asymmetry. Take a closer look at the live model's face and you will notice subtle differences from one side of the face to the other. This can come in the form of a slightly higher eyebrow, or a droop of an eyelid or corner of the mouth. Even the nose might have a slight bend. It is these differences that will help add to a more natural 3D model.

Even if you don't notice any significant symmetry differences on the live model, put some in your 3D model anyway. You do not need to make the face Quasimodo-like; just add a few subtle changes on one side. For example, Figure 4.141 shows how we have added a subtle bend to the nose. Do this once you are happy with the model and once you do not plan to alter it in any major way.

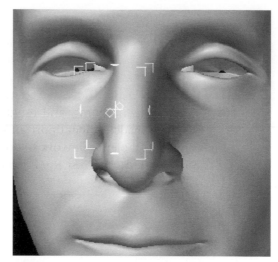

FIGURE 4.141 Tweak the nose slightly off-center for the purposes of asymmetry.

Another common area for asymmetry is the mouth. Grab some vertices in the corner and pull them down, as in Figure 4.142.

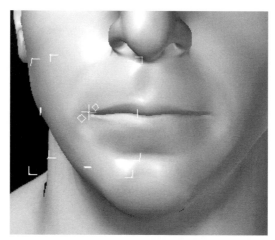

FIGURE 4.142 Add asymmetry to the mouth.

You will be surprised at how these subtle alterations can go a long way to making a model look much more natural.

SUMMARY

We have completed one of the toughest modeling aspects of building a digital human: the head. We have established the workflow of starting with a low polygon count model and gradually adding detail and refining as we work. We have also incorporated separately built pieces (such as the eyes, ears, teeth, gums, and tongue) into the head to work as one unit. We have made a digital portrait of our subject, but it doesn't stop here. There is still plenty of work to do in texturing, and let us not forget the rest of the body. So, rest up, for our task is not yet over. We will be continuing with this workflow down the body, starting next on the arms.

REFINING AND DEFINING THE ARMS, HANDS, AND FINGERS

The next body parts we will model are the arms, hands, and fingers. We will also include the shoulders. Make sure you have the reference images loaded and aligned in your modeler. Load the body you have made so far, and you are ready to start.

To make it easy for you to select the arm area later, define it on the model by giving it a surface or part name. This will also allow you to hide the geometry that you will not be working on, which is most of the body. See Figure 5.1.

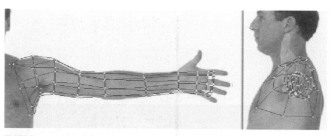

FIGURE 5.1   Name the arm surface and hide the rest of the body geometry.

As in the previous (and following) chapters, we will use a small toolset to create and shape the geometry: Split, Connect, or Divide; Extrude, simple vertex; and face manipulation.

Get in the habit of refining the model as you work. Shape the geometry as far as it can go, and until it looks correct, before you add more detail.

We will start by adding detail to work with. Make two vertical splits on either side of the elbow, as in Figure 5.2. Use the extra vertices to widen out the forearm.

Now, make four more vertical splits on the upper arms and shoulder. This will give you more geometry so that you can shape it closer to the arm using the background image as a guide. See Figure 5.3.

Next, make two lengthwise splits—one on top and one underneath—from the base of the forearm to the edge of the selected geometry. This

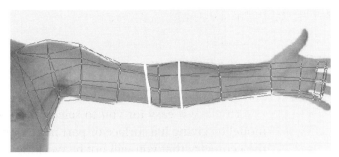

FIGURE 5.2   Make two vertical splits on either side of the elbow.

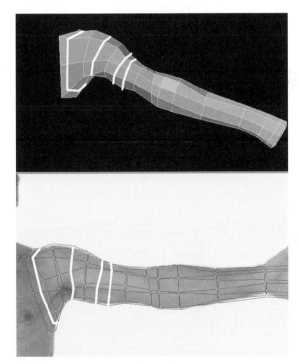

FIGURE 5.3   Make four more vertical splits on the upper arms and shoulder.

will create five-point polygons, but they will be eliminated later. Pull some of the vertices on the underside up a bit so that you start to define the biceps. See Figure 5.4.

To define the deltoid, make a split that travels around the top portion of the arm to the rear, as in Figure 5.5.

Add more faces for shaping to the deltoid with a circular split, as in Figure 5.6.

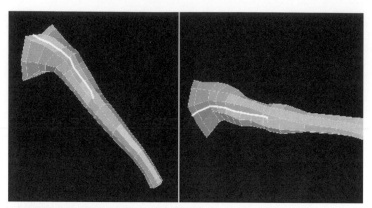

FIGURE 5.4   Make two lengthwise splits.

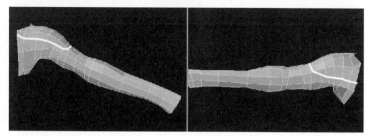

FIGURE 5.5   Define the deltoid.

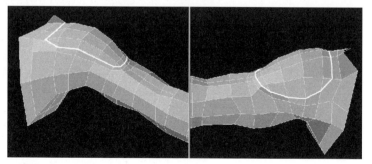

FIGURE 5.6   Add further detail to the deltoid.

Again, do not be concerned with the five-sided faces at this point.

To define the pectoral muscle's connection to the arm, make a split as in Figure 5.7.

Continue the connection, eliminating one five-side face in the process, as in Figure 5.8.

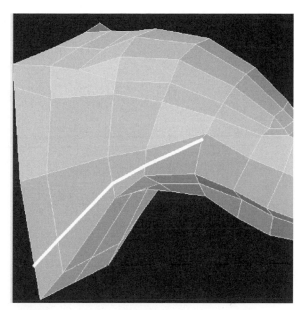

FIGURE 5.7   Define the pectoral muscle's connection.

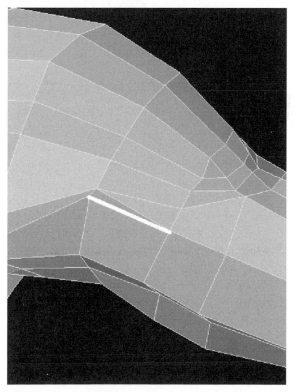

FIGURE 5.8   Continue the connection to eliminate the five-sided face.

We are left with a couple of triangles next to each other. They can be neatly merged or combined into one quad, as in Figure 5.9.

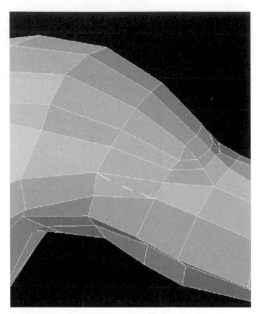

FIGURE 5.9   Merge the two triangles.

Next, add another split that travels from the front to the back around the edge of the deltoid, and continue to adjust the geometry. Remember that the closer the faces are together, the sharper an edge you can define. This is desirable where muscles meet up against each other. If you are making a less-muscular character, you may want to leave some areas "softer." See Figure 5.10.

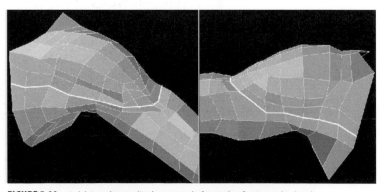

FIGURE 5.10   Add another split that travels from the front to the back.

Next, make another split along the top of the upper arm and deltoid, towards the back, and end it (for now) at the forearm, as in Figure 5.11.

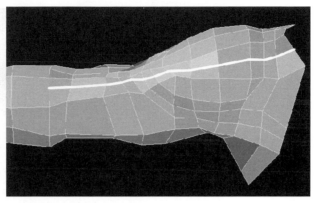

FIGURE 5.11   Make a split along the top of the upper arm and deltoid.

Now make two more vertical splits towards the forearm joint area. It is a good idea to have enough geometry around this joint so that it will bend during animation. If geometry is lacking, you could run into bad deformations and texture stretching, since the geometry is stressed during movement. See Figure 5.12.

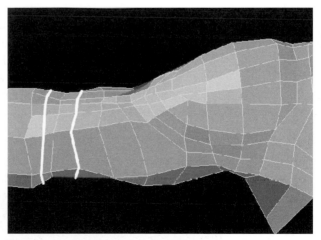

FIGURE 5.12   Make two more vertical splits.

Next, make a longer length-wise split from the end of the hand, down the forearm, and terminating at the deltoid, as in Figure 5.13. Notice that this also turned a triangle into a quad.

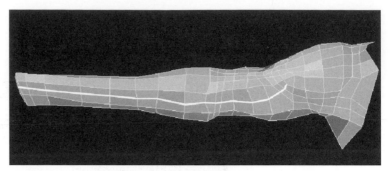

FIGURE 5.13   Make a longer length-wise split down the arm.

Use this geometry to define the triceps. This is the large muscle located at the back of the upper arm. The overall shape is a diamond-like configuration, with the widest portion high on the upper arm. When one thinks of strong, muscular arms, the biceps first come to mind and is usually over-exaggerated when reproduced in art. However, the triceps are the larger muscle group on the upper arm. Do not forget to pay attention to them. See Figure 5.14a.

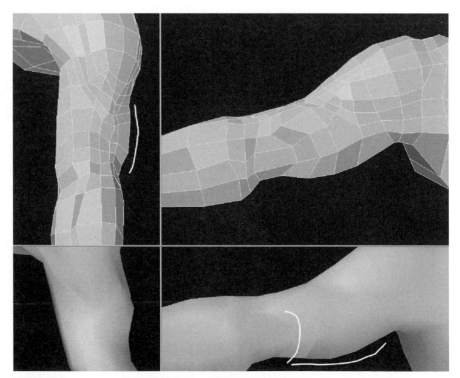

FIGURE 5.14a   Use the geometry to define the triceps.

Now let's move down to the forearm, where we will define the bulk of the muscles. Although the muscles obviously travel all down the arm to the hand, the major mass will be noticeable at the upper half of the forearm. It will appear rounder in contrast than closer to the wrist, which will be squarer due to the ulna and radius bones. See Figure 5.14b.

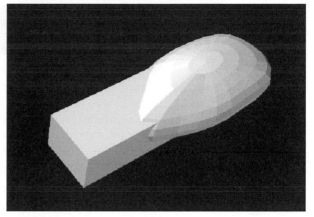

FIGURE 5.14b   The forearm's basic shapes.

To begin defining muscles here, make a partial circular split, as in Figure 5.15.

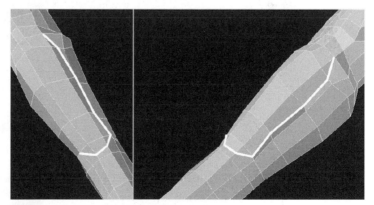

FIGURE 5.15   Define the muscles of the forearm.

Carry another split from the mid-forearm across and around the hand, and ending in the palm, as seen in Figure 5.16.

Shape the geometry to resemble the major portion of the hand, minus the fingers, as seen in Figure 5.17. Notice that we are preparing the geometry with the proper spacing for the fingers.

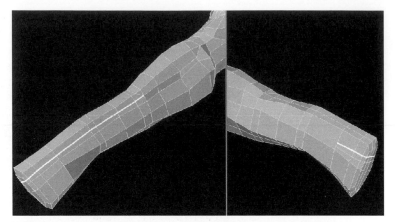

FIGURE 5.16   Carry another split from the mid-forearm across the hand.

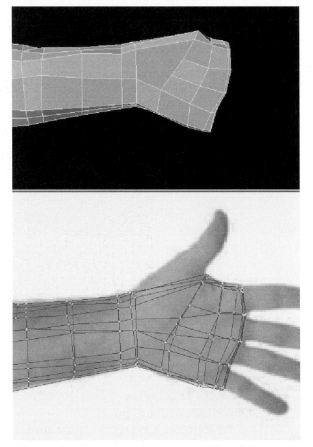

FIGURE 5.17   Shape the geometry to resemble the major portion of the hand.

We will now concentrate on the hand. Make two splits: one at the wrist and the other across the palm, as in Figure 5.18.

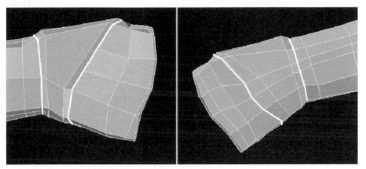

FIGURE 5.18   Make two splits across the hand.

It is time to give Frank some fingers. Starting with the thumb, collect the three faces in that area, as seen in Figure 5.19.

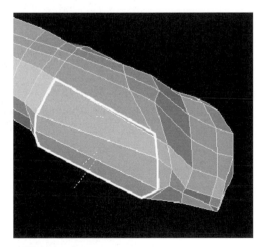

FIGURE 5.19   Collect the three faces for the thumb.

Extrude these faces four times, shaping and tapering them as you go. Keep each segment at the joints. The live model in these images curved his thumb slightly backwards. Do not replicate this because it is not completely natural. See Figure 5.20.

Make three new splits on the thumb, as seen in Figure 5.21. As with the elbow joint, we will want to have enough geometry in the finger's joints for bending.

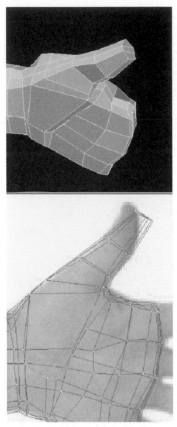

FIGURE 5.20 Extrude these faces four times, shaping them as you go.

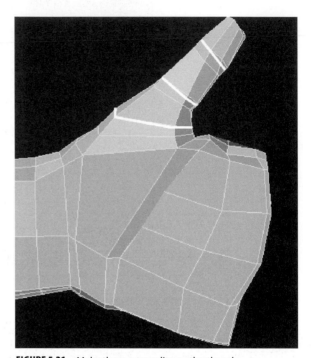

FIGURE 5.21 Make three new splits on the thumb.

To get a better crease in between the joints, add four additional splits, as seen in Figure 5.22.

Add a split across the palm of the hand, close to where the fingers will be. See Figure 5.23.

We want to set up the geometry to make it easier to attach the fingers to the hand. This involves spacing the faces at the end of the hand so that they are more or less even. We could extrude the finger geometry now, but it would be better to have a little space between each finger because that will allow for better definition when it subdivides. You can accomplish this in a couple ways. You can split the new faces, or if your pro-

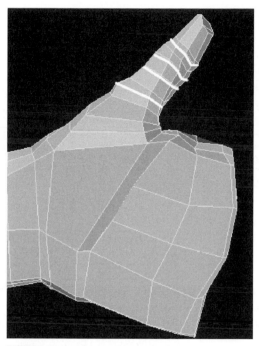

FIGURE 5.22   Add four additional splits.

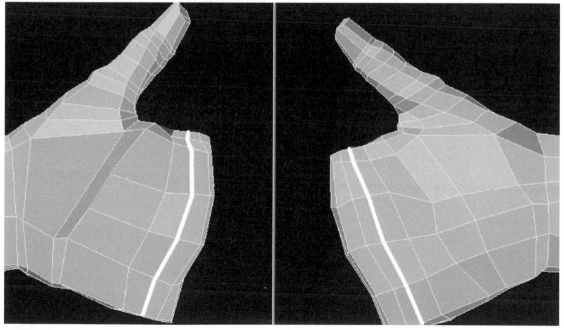

FIGURE 5.23   Add a split across the palm of the hand.

gram has the Bevel feature, bevel the edges between the fingers. The results should be the same as in Figure 5.24.

You can leave this space as is, or you can add extra control faces, as in Figure 5.25.

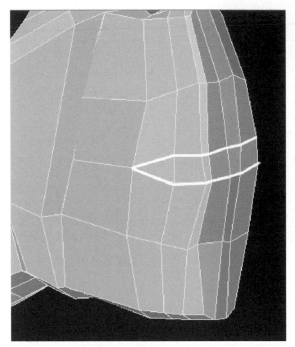

FIGURE 5.24 Create a space between each finger.

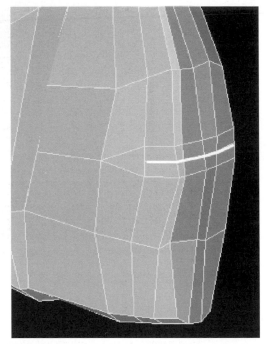

FIGURE 5.25 Further split extra control faces.

The end result should resemble Figure 5.26. Each finger should have a space between it.

Now that we have the proper space to attach the fingers, let's create them. We could extrude the faces for each finger, but we will take advantage of the computer's ability to duplicate data. In this case, we will build one finger and then duplicate it for the others. After that, you can size the fingers accordingly.

The finger is essentially cylindrical in its basic shape, so we will start building it with a cylinder. Create an eight-sided cylinder with four segments, as seen in Figure 5.27.

Notice that the end, or cap, of the cylinder has been split into two quads. This will help us with modeling and the eventual subdivision. For now, you can work the finger in a separate layer, or with the rest of the arm geometry hidden for ease of viewing.

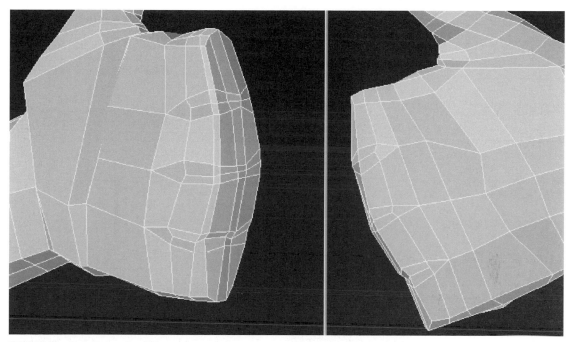

FIGURE 5.26   Each finger should have a space between it for better separation.

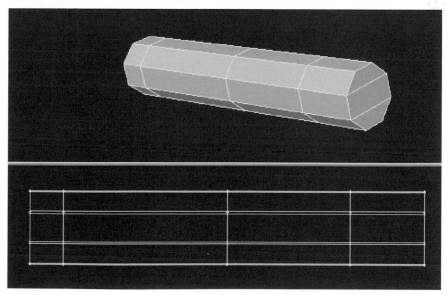

FIGURE 5.27   Start the finger with a cylinder.

The first modeling step is to give the finger a slight taper towards the tip, as seen in Figure 5.28.

We can add more geometry now. Make new vertical splits at each end, and create two around each joint, as seen in Figure 5.29.

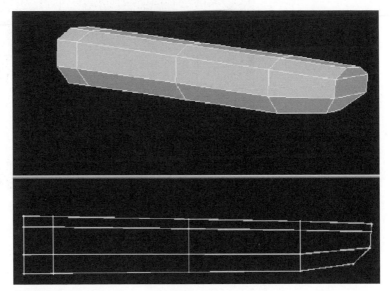

FIGURE 5.28   Give the finger a slight taper towards the tip.

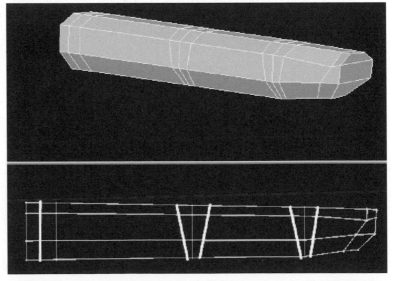

FIGURE 5.29   Add more geometry to the finger.

We can now begin to shape this geometry. First, add two more verti-cal splits. Then stretch the top vertices to add a slight bulge at the joints, and pull them up to make creases underneath. See Figure 5.30.

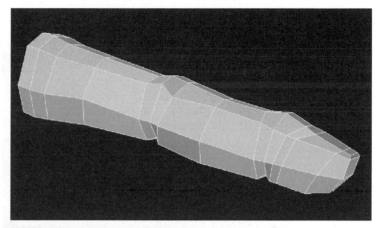

FIGURE 5.30   Shape the finger geometry.

We will create an indentation for the fingernail to sit in. To do this, select the top two faces at the tip and extrude/scale them a small amount. See Figure 5.31.

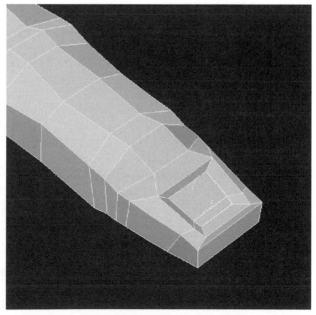

FIGURE 5.31   Create an indentation for the fingernail.

Now that we have the indentation, we will make a nail to put there. This is simply a flat, segmented box with some geometry tweaks such as a slight pointing of the tip and a curve, as seen in Figure 5.32.

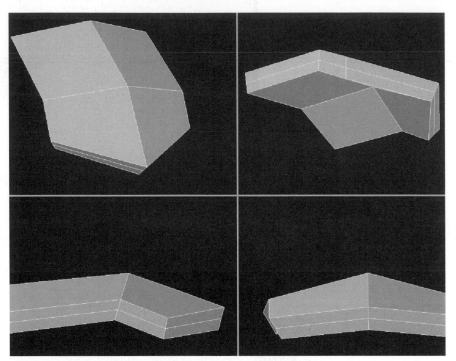

FIGURE 5.32   The fingernail geometry.

Give it a part of surface name such as "Fingernail." While we are at it, surface the finger if you haven't already. Figure 5.33 shows the nail inserted into the finger. An alternative method of creating the nail would be to extrude the geometry out of the finger itself. The advantage of keeping the nail separate is that it will be easy to modify and will keep a sharp edge since it is not subdividing with the rest of the finger geometry. Do not forget to create a nail depression and nail for the thumb! You can just duplicate a fingernail for the thumbnail.

The next step is to duplicate and attach the fingers. Obviously, you need four fingers besides the thumb. Be sure to vary the sizes. The middle finger is the biggest. The ring finger is second largest. The pointer is third. The pinky is the smallest. Another detail concerns the direction they point; do not have them all face directly forward in the exact same line. There will be some subtle fanning out. If there is still a single capping face on the wide end of the finger, delete it. Also, delete the faces on the hand where the fingers will connect to it; there will be three faces per finger.

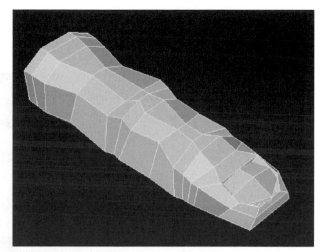

FIGURE 5.33   The nail is inserted into the finger.

Attaching the fingers is just a matter of welding the points around the edge of the fingers to the hand. They should match up nicely since the point number will be equal to that of the fingers. Figure 5.34 shows the fingers attached to the hand.

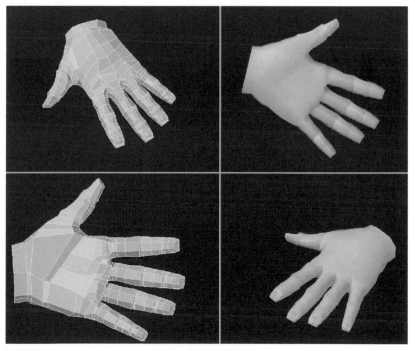

FIGURE 5.34   The fingers attached to the hand.

We will now work back into the hand again with more divisions. Make a loop split around the hand, in the palm between the thumb and fingers. See Figure 5.35.

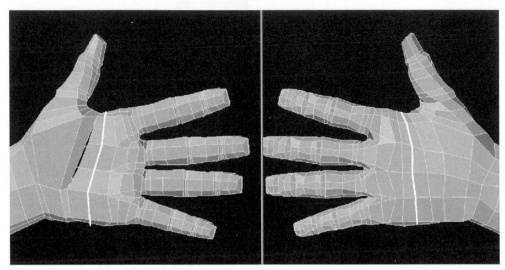

FIGURE 5.35   Make a loop split around the hand.

Now we will work on the lower palm, near the large face by the thumb. Make a split, continuing from the previous one in the hand, and around the wrist, as in Figure 5.36.

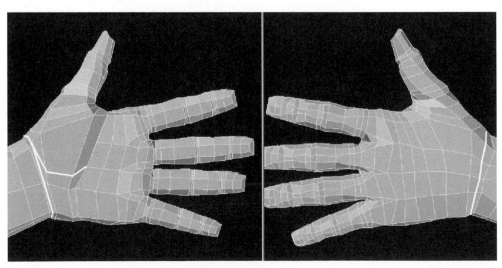

FIGURE 5.36   Continue with more splits on the hand.

To eliminate the *N*-sided face by the thumb, connect the line from the palm to the triangle created in the last step. This will create a nice quad. Adjust the geometry as in Figure 5.37.

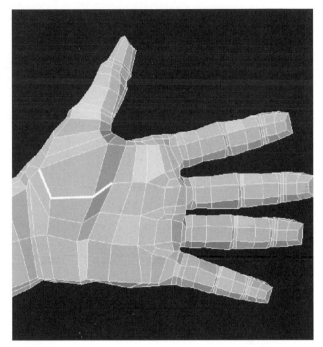

FIGURE 5.37   Continue to work and connect geometry in the palm.

Add another split across the palm, and end it halfway around the hand. This will allow for a good crease in the palm. Also, spin, rotate, or rebuild the two faces at the base of the thumb. This will define the form better. See Figure 5.38a.

Also, add another split across the base of the thumb, as in Figure 5.38b.

We will next turn our attention to the back of the hand. It looks pretty good but could use more geometry to pull some more anatomical touches out of it. We will split new faces down the middle of each finger and back of the hand. This will allow us to create the effect of the tendons under the skin by raising the vertices along them. We do not need to make the splits all the way around the fingers to the underside, so begin the split under the fingernail. Continue the split down the center of the finger and terminate it at the wrist. This will keep unneeded geometry from other areas of the arm. See Figure 5.39.

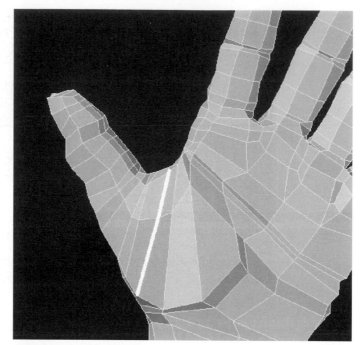

FIGURE 5.38a   Add another split across the palm.

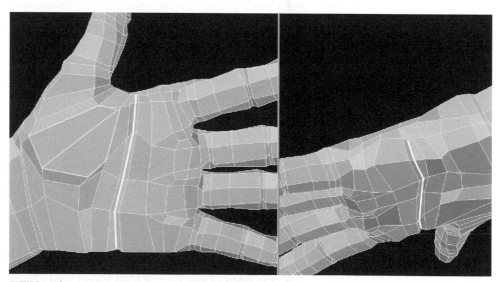

FIGURE 5.38b   Add another split across the base of the thumb.

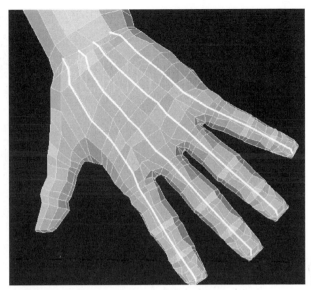

FIGURE 5.39   Split new geometry to make the tendons.

Perform a test subdivision to view the results of your efforts. Before continuing, tweak the geometry some more if you are not happy with it. See Figure 5.40.

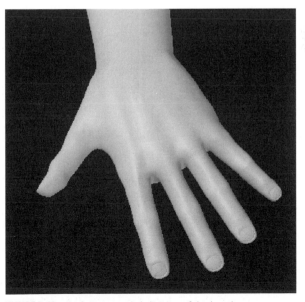

FIGURE 5.40   Perform a test subdivision of the hand.

We will now be working back down the arm. There are still some N-sided faces in there, so we need to clean them up. Make a split across the large face on the forearm and down to the wrist, ending at one of the triangles. Two triangles will form; you can then merge them into a quad. Also add a horizontal split closer to the wrist. See Figure 5.41.

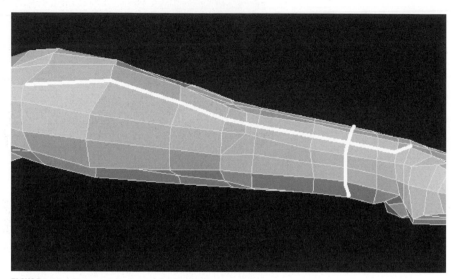

FIGURE 5.41   Make a split across the forearm.

To help give the forearm muscles more definition, split new faces, as in Figure 5.42.

This muscle line would look better if it extended higher into the upper arm a bit. This is because some of the actual forearm muscles attach at the upper arm bone, or humerus. To continue this in the geometry, make two more splits, as seen in Figure 5.43.

Then, make two more splits.

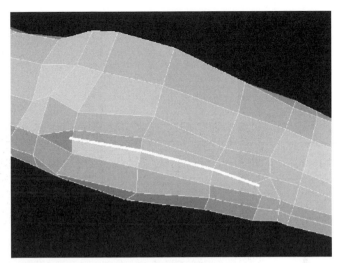

FIGURE 5.42   Give the forearm muscles more definition.

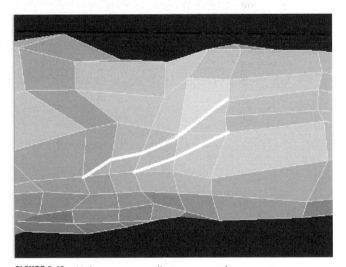

FIGURE 5.43   Make two more splits to connect the geometry.

Next, select the two adjacent triangles and combine or merge them into one face, as in Figure 5.44.

Finally, split that face and connect it to the triangle formed in the previous step. See Figure 5.45.

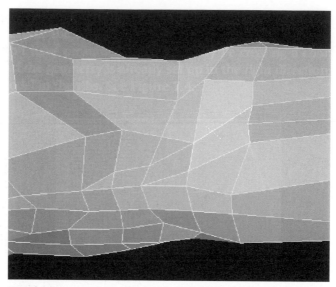

FIGURE 5.44 Combine or merge the two adjacent triangles into one face.

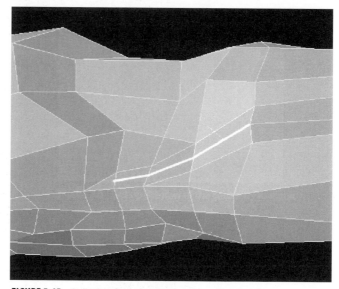

FIGURE 5.45 Split that face and connect it to the triangle.

Now, split a loop around the arm that connects the two triangles, as in Figure 5.46.

Moving up the arm again, we will add more definition under the biceps. Make a split that travels from under the arm and ends at the forearm joint, as in Figure 5.47.

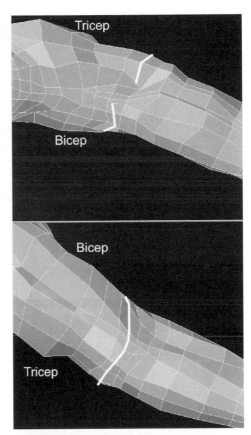

FIGURE 5.46   Split a loop around the arm that connects the two triangles.

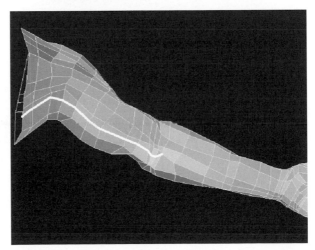

FIGURE 5.47   Make a long split that travels the length of the forearm joint.

We are almost done! For some extra modeling control, make two more loop splits, as in Figure 5.48.

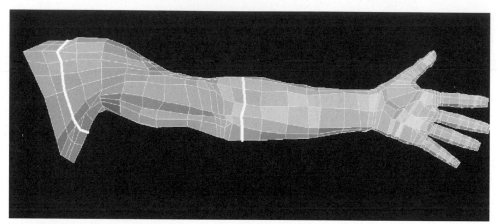

FIGURE 5.48   For extra modeling control, make two more loop splits.

Make a long split in the back, from the edge of the arm geometry to the wrist. See Figure 5.49.

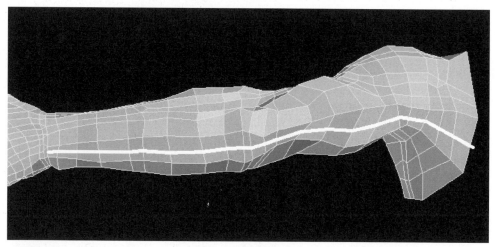

FIGURE 5.49   Make a long split across the back side of the arm.

Then, make a long split along the underside, from the edge of the arm geometry to the hand under the pinky. See Figure 5.50.

That is all the geometry we will add. The work is not done, though. Continue to adjust the geometry until it looks as good as you can make it. Check the 3D model against the live model reference images as well as in

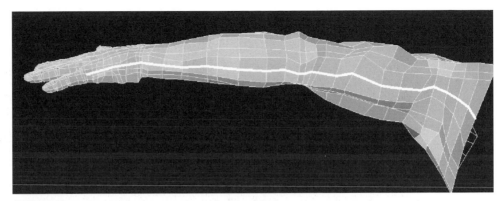

FIGURE 5.50   Make a long split across the underside of the arm.

a subdivided mode. Do not get too crazy if every joint angle doesn't match with the reference images since there are factors such as camera distortion and the live model not hitting the exact pose for each reference image. However, do be diligent in your study and observation of the reference material and apply that knowledge to the 3D model. See Figure 5.51.

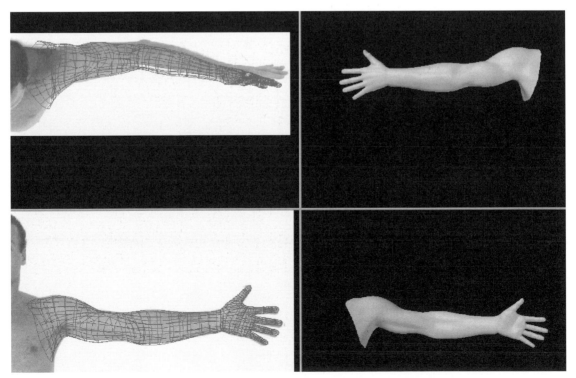

FIGURE 5.51   Check the 3D model against the live model reference.

SUMMARY

The arm, hand, and fingers presented several challenges. There are several complex muscular configurations in the arm. The hands are a very expressive body part that people are intimately familiar with. This makes accurate modeling especially important. In addition, we took advantage of duplicating geometry for the fingers. Doing this saved a good deal of work and will be applied to other areas of the body, as you will see. Now that we have conquered the arms, we will move on to the other limbs: the legs.

6

MODELING THE LEGS, FEET, AND TOES

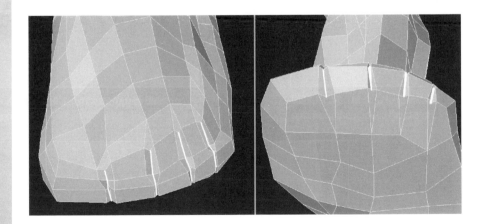

REFINING AND DEFINING THE LEGS, FEET, AND TOES

In this chapter, we will tackle modeling the legs, feet, and toes. If you've gone through Chapter 5, you will notice similarities in the process. In keeping with the workflow of the tutorials in the book, we will define the broad forms first with the low-geometry model, and then we will gradually add detail and refine the forms with a small toolset.

To begin, make sure you have the front and side view of the live model set up in your modeling package. Also, load in the 3D model that you have made so far. For viewing ease, you can hide the finished portions such as the arms and head. If you have not done so already, select and label (either through parts or surfaces) the leg geometry; this will make it easy for you to select these parts at any time. With the current geometry, shape it to best conform to the reference photos. Use the main cross sections of geometry to define the thigh, knee, and calf areas, as in Figure 6.1.

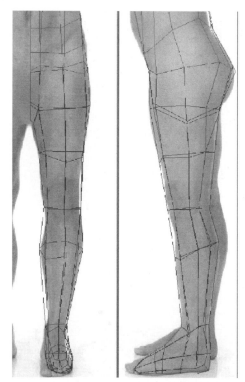

FIGURE 6.1 Shape the low-polygon geometry to broadly define the thigh, knee, and calf areas.

It is probably obvious that we do not have nearly enough detail to properly form all the subtleties of a leg, so it is time to split a bunch of new faces in there. We will start with the horizontal direction. Make 17 splits across the whole leg, starting above the hip and ending at the foot. This will give plenty of new geometry to shape the leg even further. Using the background reference images, adjust the geometry in the side and front views to better match the outer edges of the legs. See Figure 6.2.

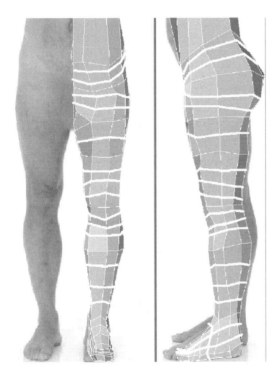

FIGURE 6.2   Make 17 splits across the whole leg, starting above the hip and ending at the foot.

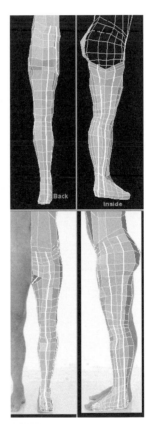

FIGURE 6.3   Add vertical splits to the legs.

We will now give ourselves some vertical geometry to work with. Make seven splits, two along the outside of the leg, and then continuing under the foot and up the inside of the leg. One split will travel up the front of the leg, under the foot, and around to the back. One more split will travel between the legs through the crotch. All splits should end at hip level. See Figure 6.3.

Now that we have a good amount of geometry to work with, we can concentrate on defining specific muscle forms. See Figure 6.4 for the muscles of the upper leg.

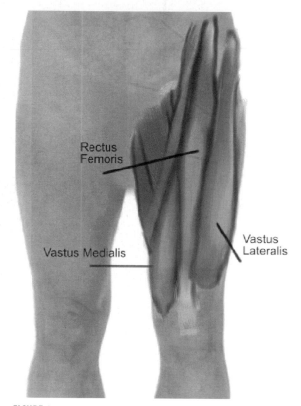

FIGURE 6.4   The muscles of the upper leg.

Starting with the muscles of the front upper thigh, we will model indications of three major muscles: vastus medialis, vastus lateralis, and rectus femoris. These are the most predominantly visible muscles on the average person, and our live model, Frank, has good definition here too. You may choose to accentuate or soften the effect of these muscles depending on the character you are creating.

We will start with the vastus medialis. (Don't worry—you will not be quizzed on the names later.) The visible portion of this muscle forms a teardrop-shaped bulge on the inside front of the leg, above the knee. We will create a split that travels across most of the leg horizontally but then turns upwards to help define the muscle. See Figure 6.5.

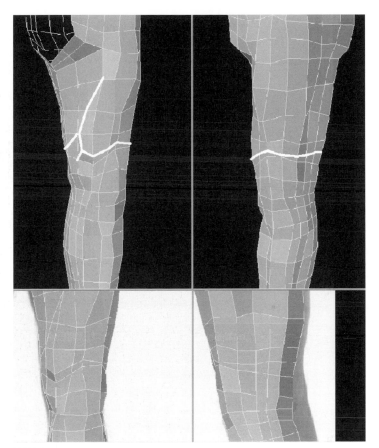

FIGURE 6.5   Define the vastus medialis.

If you end up with a three-sided face next to a five-sided one, as in this case, it would be best to split this combination to make them both quads.

Now we will move to the outside upper leg muscle, the vastus lateralis. This forms a larger bulge on the outer side of the leg, slightly higher than the vastus medialis. To define this, make a U-shaped split along the side and front of the leg, ending up at the hips, as in Figure 6.6.

Next, we will define the middle muscle, the rectus femoris. This runs down the middle front of the leg, angling towards the outside of the hip. To bring out this muscle definition, simply make a long split that goes from the top of the leg and ends mid-shin. The muscle doesn't really

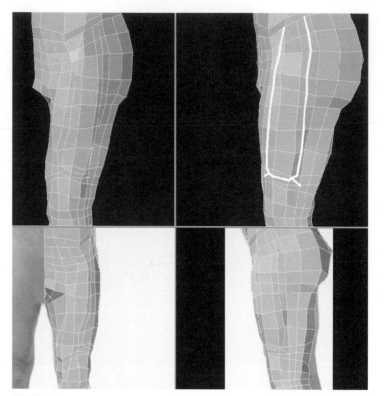

FIGURE 6.6   Define the vastus lateralis.

travel this far down the leg, but the extra geometry will help us out later. See Figure 6.7.

To help us define the inner thigh a bit, make a split down the middle that ends at the triangle formed a few steps back (in Figure 6.5). This will give us something to work with when we shape the leg in that area. See Figure 6.8.

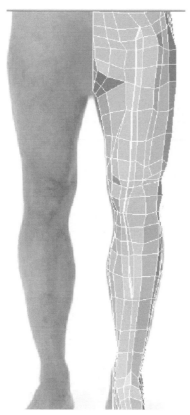

FIGURE 6.7　Defining the rectus femoris.

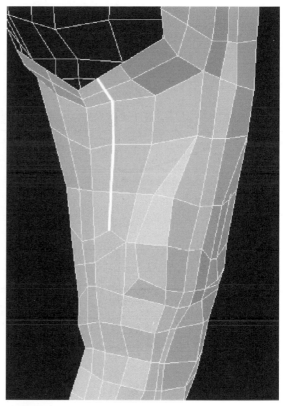

FIGURE 6.8　Add definition to the inner thigh.

Next, make a horizontal split all around the upper thigh, close to the crotch, as in Figure 6.9.

Before we proceed, we should work with the geometry to make sure we have established the leg's *chief lines*. These lines consist of distinct angles and forms on the leg. You will not actually model any lines, but make sure you can "see" them in the contours and forms. Figure 6.10 shows some examples of chief lines of the leg. In part A in Figure 6.10, the chief line is formed from the hip, along the satorius muscle and down the tibia. Chief lines to look for in the part B are the angle of the thigh and calf. The last part, C, shows a rear view. From behind, the calf should widen in its middle, with the outside peak being higher than the inside one. Also, the hamstring muscles form a slightly angled square form that tucks under the buttocks.

The leg is not yet done, and we haven't gotten to the foot at all, but take the time to work with what you have and make it feel as natural as

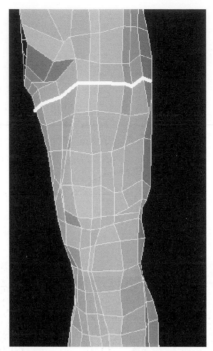

FIGURE 6.9 Make a horizontal split all around the upper thigh.

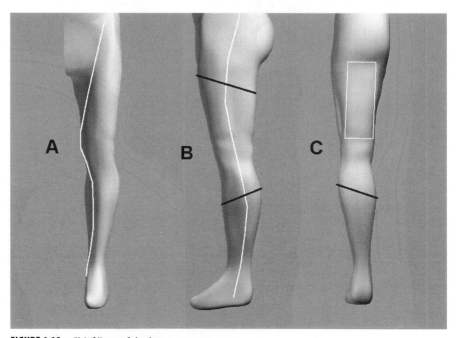

FIGURE 6.10 Chief lines of the leg.

possible. You will be able to do this mainly by establishing the chief lines and forms.

If you are ready to proceed, then we will concentrate on some smaller details such as the knee. To start, we need some more geometry at the joint, so make a horizontal split across, as in Figure 6.11.

The knee, or patella, is basically a disk that "floats" between the femur and tibia, held in place by a tendon and a ligament. To make the basic shape of the patella, collect the 12 faces around the knee area and extrude them slightly. Since you do not really want to make this person have too much of a knobby knee, scale in the sides of the new extrusion so that they flow off the surface of the leg naturally. You can also split a circular pattern around these 12 faces and shape those. Either way, you will end up with something similar to Figure 6.12.

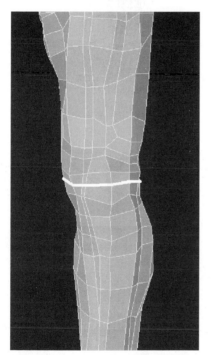

FIGURE 6.11   Add more geometry at the knee joint.

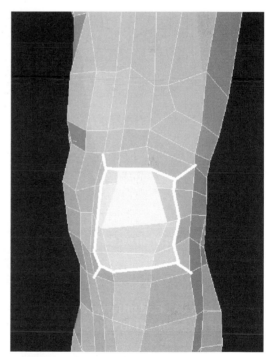

FIGURE 6.12   Form the knee.

Moving down the leg, we will concentrate on the foot and ankle region. For starters, add more geometry to work with by making three loop splits, as in Figure 6.13.

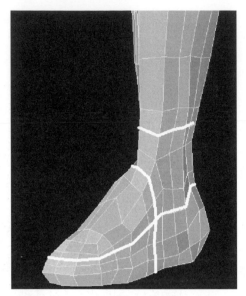

FIGURE 6.13   Add detail in the foot and ankle.

To add geometry to properly form the ankle bulges caused by the tibia and fibula, we will need to make two U-shaped splits on the inside and outside of the leg. See Figure 6.14.

Notice that the outside U is slightly higher than the inside one. Also notice that we have created three- and five-sided faces next to each other. We will eliminate those in the next step.

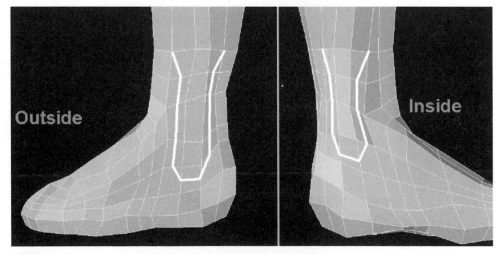

FIGURE 6.14   Make splits to add detail to the ankles.

Split the three- and five-sided faces on both ankles, and then pull out the geometry to form the bones' influence on the surface of the skin. See Figure 6.15.

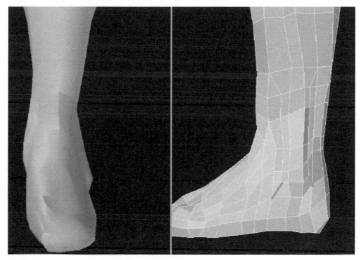

FIGURE 6.15   Define the ankle bones.

When you are content with the ankles, continue down the foot and make a loop split that travels around the foot, as in Figure 6.16. You should also be shaping the foot as you go. For instance, it gets very flat around where the toes will connect.

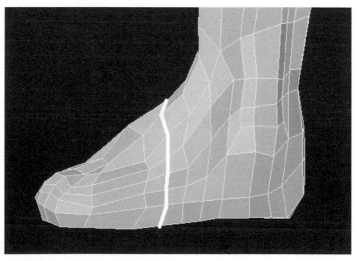

FIGURE 6.16   Add more detail for the foot.

A word about the reference images: due to the camera angle in the full-body live model shots, the foot isn't represented in the best way to model from. On the accompanying CD-ROM (in the reference folder), you will find close-up foot reference images that were taken at a much better angle for modeling over ("FootIn", "FootHeel", "FootOut").

We are close to giving this foot some toes. We must look at the geometry and judge what it would take to incorporate toes. As it stands now, the tip of the foot ends with four groups of faces that we could extrude toes out from. See Figure 6.17.

But, as you know, we have five toes. Where will we place this other toe? If we put it too much on the side, it would stick out at an odd angle, or it would take too much distortion of the geometry to get it to face forward. The solution is just to build out some more faces to place a toe.

Collect the 12 faces on the inside of the foot and extrude them out along the X axis, as in Figure 6.18.

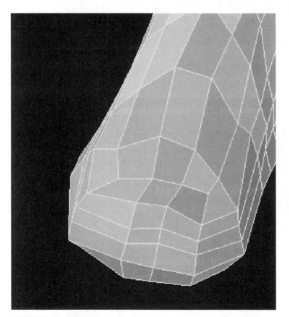

FIGURE 6.17   The tip of the foot in preparation for adding toes.

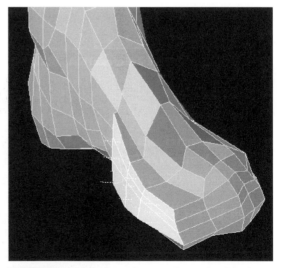

FIGURE 6.18   Collect the 12 faces on the inside of the foot and extrude them.

This gives us another "slot" to place a toe, but we will need to clean up the geometry a bit. First, collect the four faces that were created by the extrude along the inside edge, as in Figure 6.19.

Next, collapse or delete those faces. If you delete them, a hole will be left in the mesh, so weld the vertices to close it up, as in Figure 6.20.

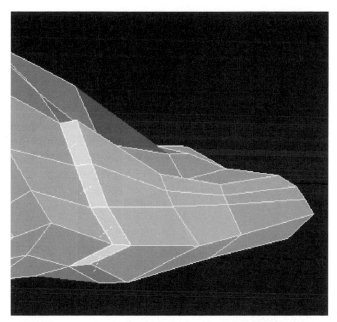

FIGURE 6.19   Collect the four faces that were created by the extrude.

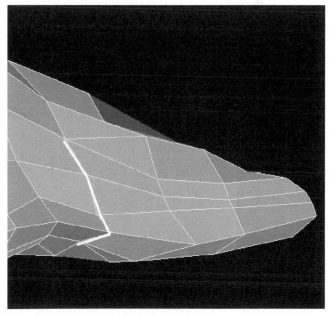

FIGURE 6.20   Collapse or delete the faces.

This will form a smooth transition from the foot out to the big toe.

Let's give ourselves a bit more geometry to shape with by adding two more loop splits around the foot, from the top, underneath, and connecting to the beginning, as in Figure 6.21. For future reference, a loop split will be one that forms a closed circle.

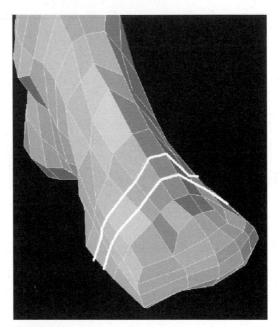

FIGURE 6.21 Add more geometry to the foot.

Now we should make the proper space for the toes; set up the geometry so that there is a larger space for the big toe, and smaller ones for the others, the pinky toe's space being the smallest. We could just attach the toes to the foot as it stands, but if we do a bit of extra work, this area will look even better. We need to create a small space between where each toe will go. This involves making a short split from the top of the foot around to underneath. Figure 6.22 shows how it was accomplished for the big toe.

Repeat this between each toe, as in Figure 6.23.

We can make the definition between the toes even more distinct by connecting each triangle that is formed when we split new faces. We can then adjust this geometry to create more of a crease, as in Figure 6.24.

It is finally time to tackle the toes. We will again take advantage of the computer's ability to duplicate data easily and model only one toe. Although there are small variances between the toes, we can still work

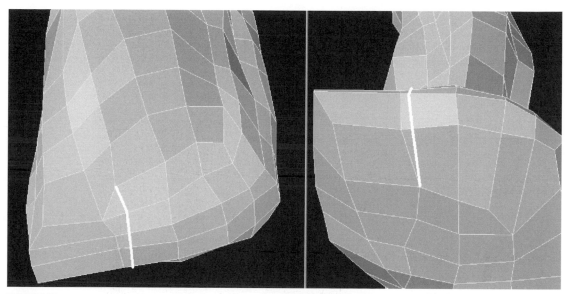

FIGURE 6.22   Add a space between the toes.

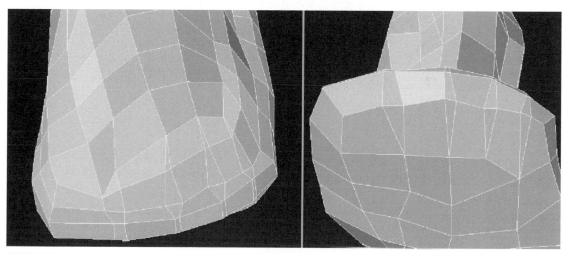

FIGURE 6.23   Create space between each toe.

with one main toe model. The big toe is the most distinct, but we can easily adapt it from our basic toe model.

Instead of extruding a toe out of the foot geometry, we should just make new, clean toe geometry and attach it to the foot later (it's easier that way). Begin by making an eight-sided cylinder with five segments or subdivisions with its center along the Z axis. Also, delete one end cap and

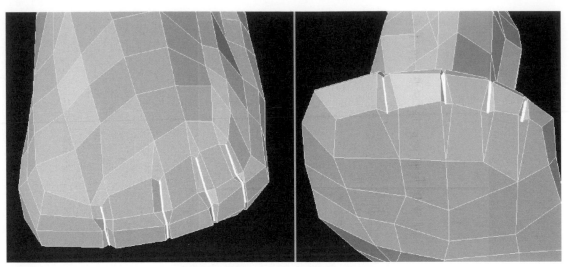

FIGURE 6.24 Create more definition between the toes.

change the other to three quads. Move the segments closer together, as in Figure 6.25. These will be the joints of the toe.

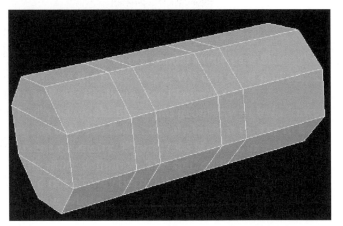

FIGURE 6.25 The toe begins as a cylinder.

Now, move the tip of the toe area down a little on the *Y* axis, as in Figure 6.26.

Round off the tip of the toe by adjusting the geometry, as in Figure 6.27.

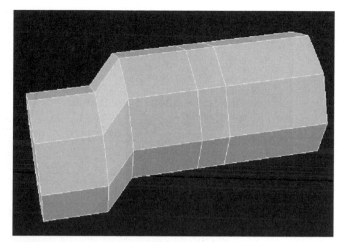

FIGURE 6.26   Move the tip of the toe area down.

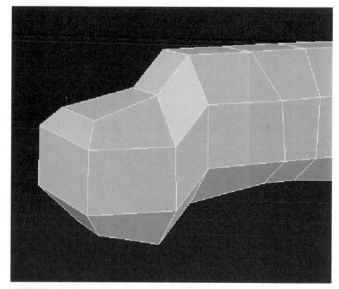

FIGURE 6.27   Round off the tip of the toe.

Make a couple of loop splits around the joint areas and adjust the geometry a little. Remember that you do not want to make the toe too knobby or overdone. Most toes have a smooth transition. See Figure 6.28.

Next, we will make a small depression in which to rest the toenail. Do this by collecting the top face at the tip of the toe and extruding down a small amount, as in Figure 6.29.

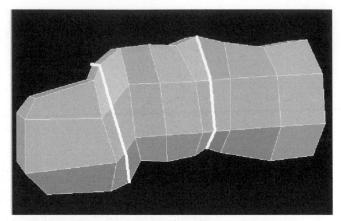

FIGURE 6.28   Make a couple of loop splits around the joint areas.

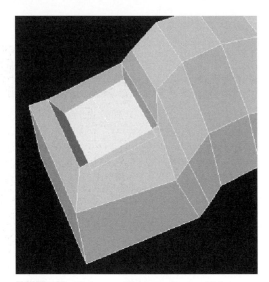

FIGURE 6.29   Make a small depression in which to rest the toenail.

Lastly, make another loop split around this area, and soften the front edge of the nail depression. Now, the basic toe model is done. See Figure 6.30.

We still need a toenail, though. Fingernails aren't too different in shape from toenails, so we can save a little work by copying one of the fingernails and repositioning it into the toe. This is another good skill to learn—when to reuse elements of geometry from your models. Figure 6.31 shows the toe with the nail inserted.

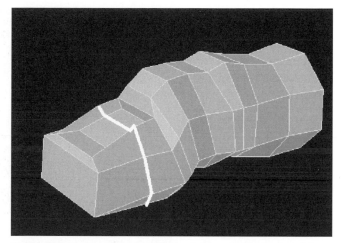

FIGURE 6.30   Make another loop split and soften the front edge of the nail.

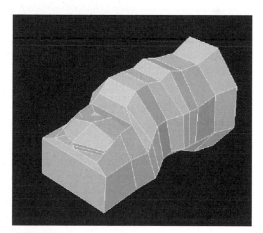

FIGURE 6.31   The toe with the nail inserted.

The next step is to duplicate this toe five times and move them all into position. You will also need to scale down the individual toes somewhat. Keep the toes facing forward as you position them. Figure 6.32 shows the five toes in place.

To attach the toes, you will need to delete the three faces at each toe "junction" at the tip of the foot. See Figure 6.33.

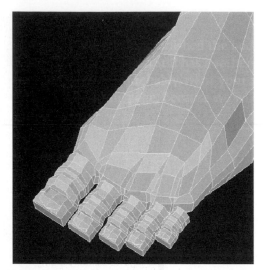

FIGURE 6.32   The five toes in place.

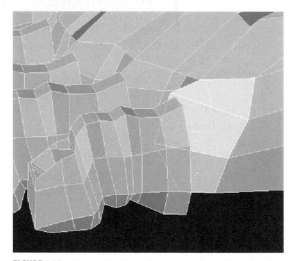

FIGURE 6.33   Delete the three faces at each toe "junction."

Then you will weld the faces of the toe and the foot together. This should go smoothly since the number of vertices around each is equal. When all the toes are attached, the foot should resemble Figure 6.34.

We are just about done here. Check the geometry to make sure that the faces are doing their best to help define the shapes. If you come across any that are very twisted, then do your best to smooth them out and still

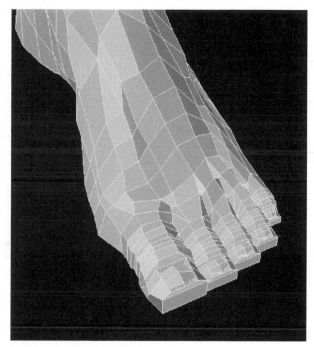

FIGURE 6.34   All the toes attached to the foot.

retain the form you are after. You can always split in more faces to help out, if need be.

Figure 6.35 shows an example of some slight face rearrangement on the top of the foot. The quad and triangle next to each other are re-worked to provide a better line to the big toe. This will also help us in the last bit of detail we are adding to the feet.

Another detail we can add is the suggestion of tendons under the skin. This is most predominant with the big toe. To create the tendon, we simply need to split a row of faces along the top of the foot and toe. See Figure 6.36. Then, end the split underneath the foot. Pull up on the newly created vertices to bring out the tendon.

We will stop here with the tendons, but you can choose to add them to the other toes using the techniques we have learned.

That completes the work on the foot. Before moving on, double check the forms on your foot. Make sure you have included important lines such as the arch. Define the rear tendon that attaches to the heel. Figure 6.37 shows the model foot with chief areas to pay attention to. In addition to the arch, make sure the other side, the blade of the foot, is resting on the ground and that it has a decently defined edge. The angle

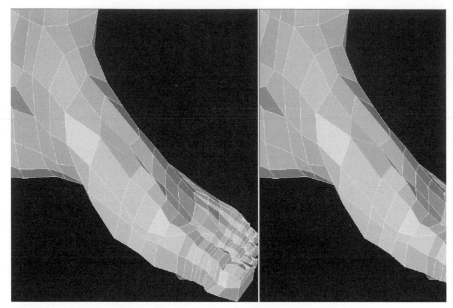

FIGURE 6.35 Rearrange the quad and triangle to provide a better flow of geometry.

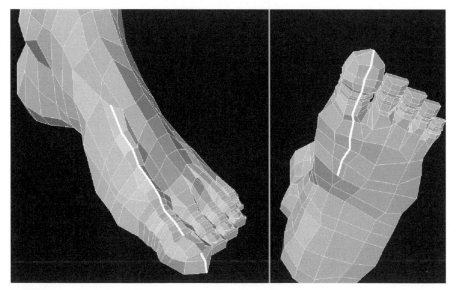

FIGURE 6.36 Create the tendon for the big toe.

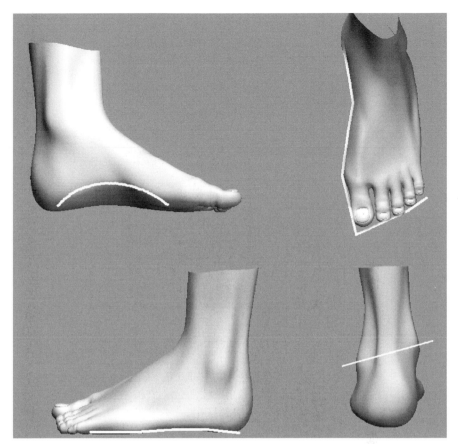

FIGURE 6.37   The foot with the chief areas you should pay attention to.

of the toes should be distinct, although some people's second toe is longer than their big toe. The big toe is still the most distinct. Lastly, the ankle bones are not at equal heights. (Look at the bottom portion of the tibia and fibula again on a skeleton reference.)

Jumping back up to the waist region, make sure that the middle vertices of the gluteus form a suitable division in between the cheeks. See Figure 6.38.

Guess what? That completes our modeling work on the legs. As always, take some time to review your work, and tweak where necessary. Tweak, tweak, tweak! That is what the majority of this type of modeling involves. View the model from every angle. There will be areas where the vertices do not match up with those of the body. We will wrap up all those loose ends when we complete the torso, which is the next chapter.

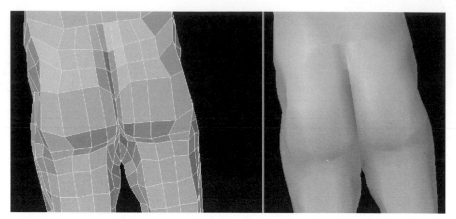

FIGURE 6.38   Mirror the model and form the crease between the gluteus muscles.

SUMMARY

With the completion of the legs, we are much closer to finishing the modeling portion of our digital human. By now, you should have a good feel for the workflow of blocking out the forms with low geometry and gradually adding and refining detail through splitting faces. When you are ready, turn the page and we will delve into finishing off the torso.

MODELING THE TORSO

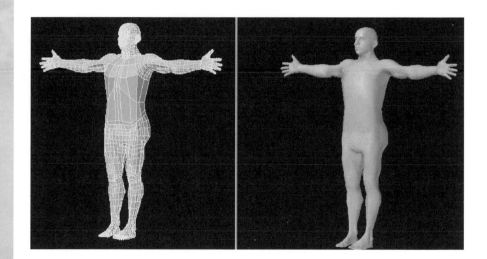

REFINING AND DEFINING THE TORSO

This is the chapter where we finish off the major modeling on our digital human. While the torso is a pretty simple tube in basic shape, much that plays out on the surface in many subtle ways is going on underneath. Our task is to bring these forms to believable life while cleanly connecting the torso up with the other parts of the body that we have completed.

Load the model that we have made so far. We can see that it is looking pretty close to a finished human. See Figure 7.1.

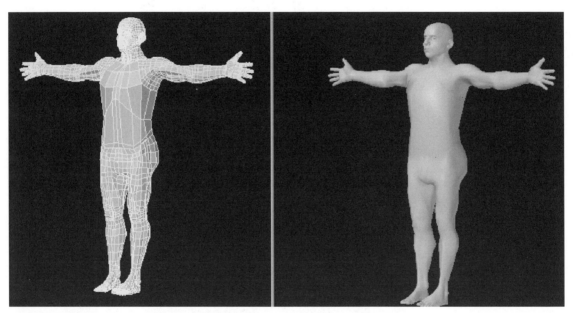

FIGURE 7.1   The model so far with the un-detailed torso.

Also, make sure your live model reference images are in place in your modeling package. If we take a look at the profile, we can see that we will need more geometry to properly form it. Starting in the midsection, make two loop splits all the way around and then pull the new vertices to more closely conform to the profile image. See Figure 7.2.

It is time to add detail to the upper torso. We will be making more loop splits, but it is important to carefully place their angle as we do so. For instance, Figure 7.3 shows four new splits made, but look at how they are angled.

FIGURE 7.2   Make two splits and adjust the geometry to the profile image.

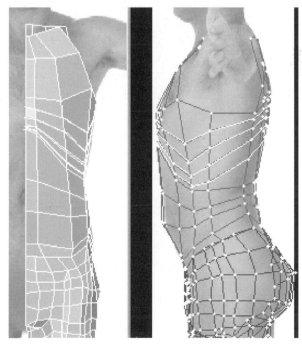

FIGURE 7.3   Make four more splits across the upper torso.

Look at the torso now with a rib cage inserted inside. The splits are set up to mimic the angle of the ribs. While our live model in these images doesn't have prominent ribs, you may be creating a character that does, and if the geometry is already set up in the right direction, it will be easy to model in the ribs. See Figure 7.4.

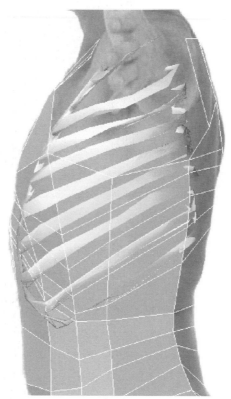

FIGURE 7.4   Set up the flow of the geometry to mimic the underlying anatomy of the ribs.

This is just one example of how you should consider and understand the underlying anatomy of what you are attempting to re-create.

We will now add another split across the chest, but we will connect up this split with the arm geometry, as in Figure 7.5. This will help us define the chest muscles.

We can now add some vertical geometry. Make two long vertical splits that connect from under the arms to the hip area. These should match up easily with the extra geometry that we created when we did the arms and legs. See Figure 7.6.

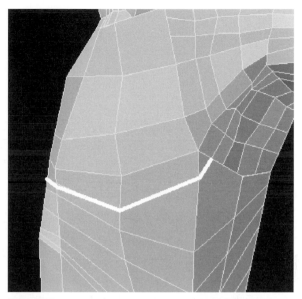

FIGURE 7.5   Make a split and connect up the chest with the arm geometry.

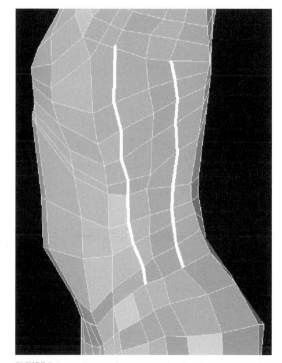

FIGURE 7.6   Make two long vertical splits that connect from under the arms to the hip area.

Perform another vertical split from the hip to the deltoid, as in Figure 7.7. This will neatly clean up the four-sided faces we had there.

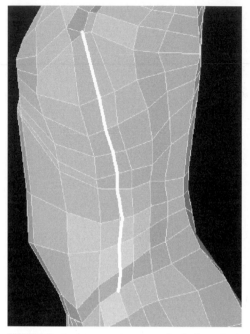

FIGURE 7.7   Perform another vertical split from the hip to the deltoid.

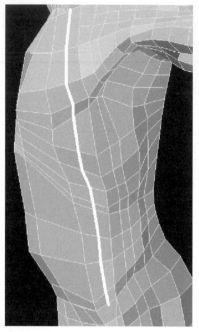

FIGURE 7.8   Create another long split down the length of the torso.

Let's continue creating our vertical geometry. Towards the front make another long split down the length of the torso from the neck to the hip, as in Figure 7.8.

While we are here, this is a good example of an area where we can clean up the geometry. You will see many such examples while building a model. Take a look at where our splits ended at the hip. See Figure 7.9.

If we make a small split connection, we will have two triangles next to each other, as in Figure 7.10.

Then, all we need to do is dissolve the edge between the triangles, or combine the faces to get a desirable quad. See Figure 7.11.

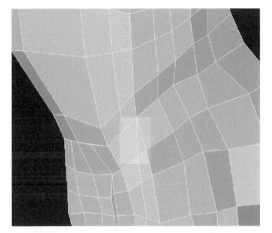

FIGURE 7.9   An area of geometry to clean up.

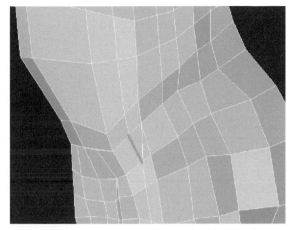

FIGURE 7.10   Make a small split to connect the geometry.

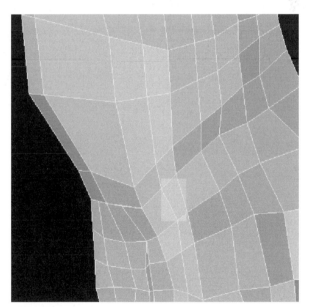

FIGURE 7.11   Dissolve the edge between the triangles to form a quad.

Next, make a long vertical split of the faces in the front of the torso, as in Figure 7.12.

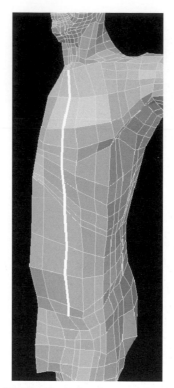

FIGURE 7.12   Make a long vertical split.

Throughout this portion of the modeling, we will be connecting up other portions of the finished geometry to the torso. In Figure 7.13, we make two horizontal splits across the upper chest to connect to the arm geometry.

Now make a long vertical split from the neck to the crotch. This neatly ties up the geometry from the different parts and gives us a decent amount of geometry to work with. See Figure 7.14.

Back at the midsection, make two splits across the body around to the back, as in Figure 7.15.

We are building a good amount of geometry on this torso, but what are we going to do with it? It is time to analyze the human body and make some decisions based on that. For instance, we will want to define the stomach region. The muscle that comes to mind there is the rectus abdominis. Modelers often initially tend to bring out the six individual "bricks" (or the "six-pack") that are visible on well-developed individuals; this is jumping the gun. We should define the broadest form of the rectus abdominis first. Once that is done, we can split in the individual muscles to the level we desire.

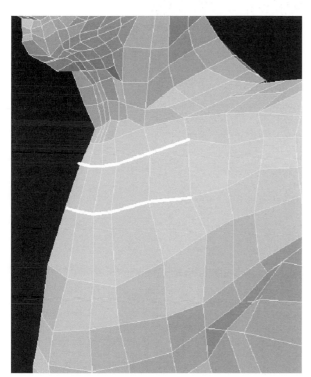

FIGURE 7.13 Make horizontal splits across the upper chest to connect to the arm geometry.

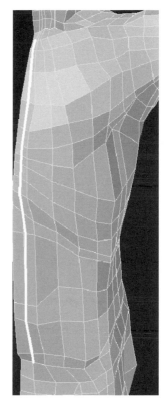

FIGURE 7.14 Make a long vertical split from the neck to the crotch.

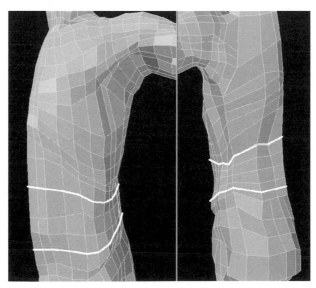

FIGURE 7.15 Make two splits across the body.

The major muscle forms we will define in the midsection are the rectus abdominis and the external oblique. Figure 7.16 shows these muscles drawn over our live model. A subtle and often neglected detail is that the rectus abdominis extends over the ribs slightly.

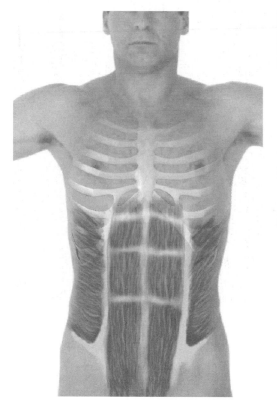

FIGURE 7.16 The midsection muscles.

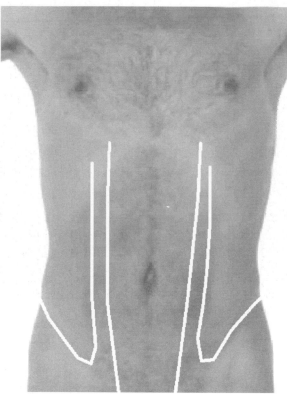

FIGURE 7.17 The simple lines to define the forms.

If we break the abdominal area down into simple lines to define the forms, it will look like Figure 7.17.

This is what we want to concentrate on. We will make an L-shaped split from the lower portion of the sternum around the top edge of the pelvis. Terminate both ends in triangles. You will have a three-/five-sided face combination at the corner of the split, so split those faces to make quads. See Figure 7.18.

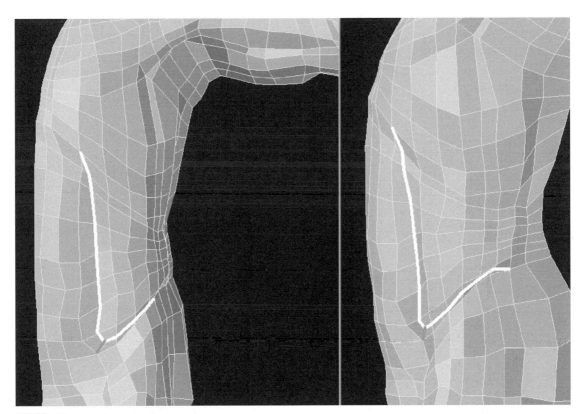

FIGURE 7.18   Form the abdominal muscles.

 You may wonder why some details we added by splitting faces are terminated in a triangle or abruptly in the middle of another face. Why not just continue with the split all around the model? The danger of that way of working is that you may end up with sections that have faces tightly packed together. These are difficult to edit and may cause unwanted hard edges. Working this way may also make the model too dense too fast. By terminating the splits, you do have the option of going back later and continuing with the split if the section is not too dense. It is best to keep your options open.

You will now want to use the newly created geometry to add definition to the abdominal form as well as to create the ridge of the oblique that runs along the pelvis. Check these forms by adjusting the lighting around the model, as in Figure 7.19.

Now we can go in and define those specific abdominal muscles that everybody wants. This is simply a matter of creating some splits across the geometry, as in Figure 7.20.

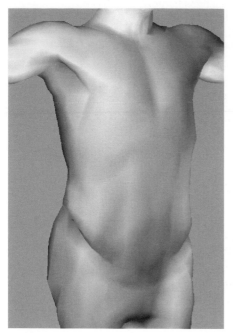

FIGURE 7.19   Check the forms by adjusting the lighting around the model.

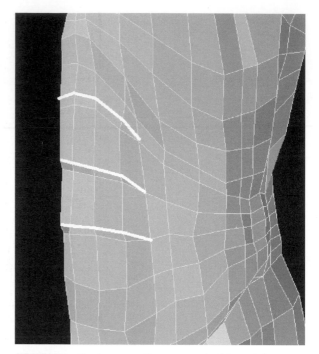

FIGURE 7.20   Create some splits to create the "six-pack."

Adjust the vertices to add the amount of definition you desire; or, to create an even more defined edge, split down the middle of those splits, as in Figure 7.21.

Our abdominal area is now finished.

Since most of us were not hatched out of eggs, we should now give some indication of where the umbilical cord was attached. This is in the form of the bellybutton and is simple to create. It is easiest to make the navel using the whole model, so if you are working on half the model, mirror the other side back. We will perform an extrusion of the two faces seen in Figure 7.22.

Extrude them as a group a small amount back into the stomach. Also, you may need to stretch them vertically, as in Figure 7.23.

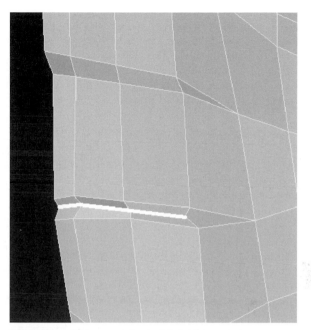

FIGURE 7.21   Add more abdominal definition.

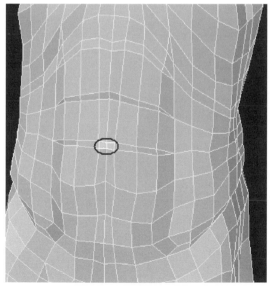

FIGURE 7.22   Select these two faces for extrusion when creating the bellybutton.

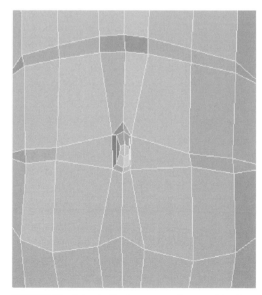

FIGURE 7.23   Extrude the faces a small amount back into the stomach.

If you performed the extrusion on a half model, or an unmirrored one, you may need to delete the faces that have formed in the midline. See Figure 7.24.

Let's leave the stomach and work back up the chest. We have an area underneath the pectoral muscle that has a large expanse between faces. See Figure 7.25.

FIGURE 7.24   Delete the faces that have formed in the midline.

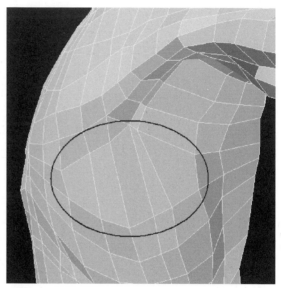

FIGURE 7.25   A large expanse between faces.

While there is nothing technically wrong here, the arrangement means it will be difficult to make subtle changes in the geometry since there are not enough faces to do so. To remedy this, make two splits: one that travels around the body and a smaller one, as seen in Figure 7.26.

We can clean up this geometry a bit more by deleting or collapsing the triangle face, as seen in Figure 7.27.

We can also add a little more by making the split seen in Figure 7.28.

You may have noticed that we have not done any work on the back yet. Well, it is time to take a trip around there. For starters, we will connect up the geometry from the other parts of the body. Make two long,

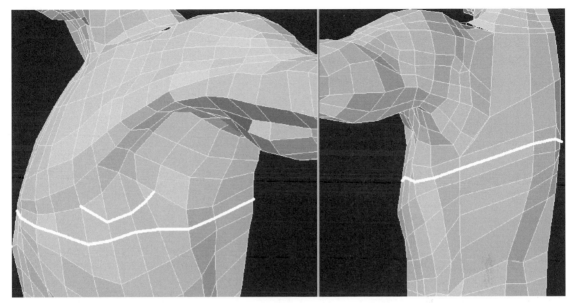

FIGURE 7.26   Add more geometry underneath the pectoral muscle.

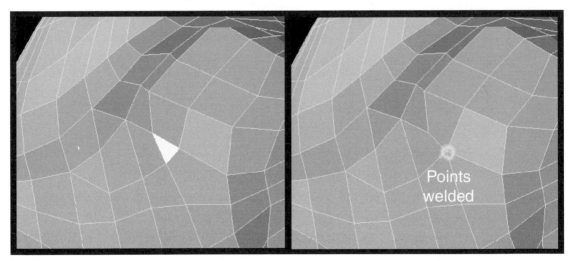

FIGURE 7.27   Clean up the geometry.

vertical splits that travel from the base of the rear end, up the back, and to the top of the head. You can connect up these splits with the two triangle faces on the top of the head, and then merge the two adjacent triangle faces into quads. See Figure 7.29.

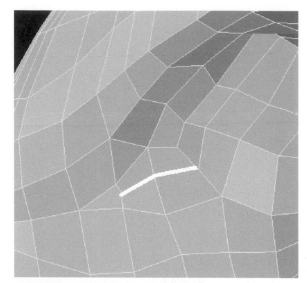

FIGURE 7.28 Split faces.

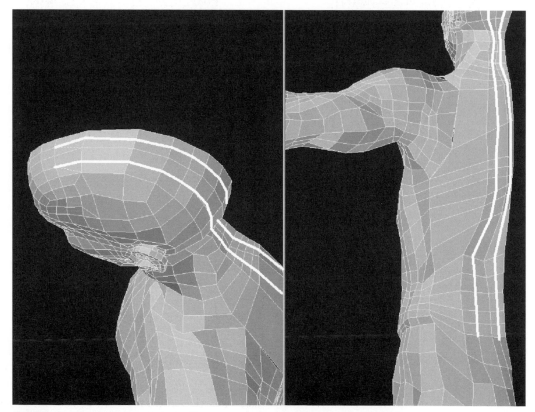

FIGURE 7.29 Make two long, vertical splits.

Now it's time for some horizontal splits. Up in the shoulder area, make three of them that connect to the arm geometry, and one that travels from the back to the front around the hip area, as in Figure 7.30.

Even out some of the faces on the back if they are very close together. You can do this manually or with a Smooth command that averages the distance between the vertices. See Figure 7.31.

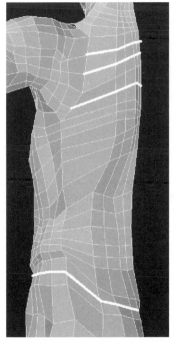

FIGURE 7.30   Connect the geometry by making horizontal splits.

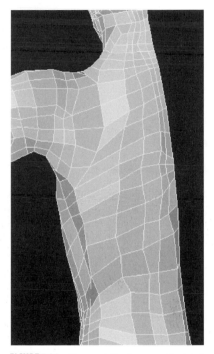

FIGURE 7.31   Even out the faces on the back.

We can still use some more geometry down the back, so make a long vertical split that travels from the hip to the side of the head, as in Figure 7.32.

Next, create a horizontal split across the upper back that connects with the triangle that was left on the shoulder. We can then merge the two triangles that form into a quad. See Figure 7.33.

If you are finding that the geometry in your model is getting a little messy, use a Smooth, Average, or Tighten tool to calm down the activity and allow you to see the broader forms again.

Once again, we find ourselves with a good amount of geometry, and the time has arrived to make some sense of it and push it into definite

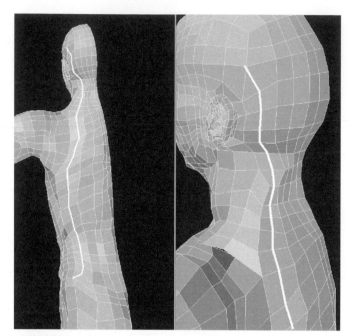

FIGURE 7.32 Make a long vertical split that travels from the hip to the side of the head.

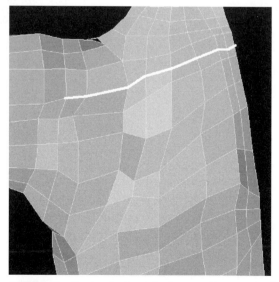

FIGURE 7.33 Create a horizontal split across the upper back.

anatomy. Again, we need to take a look at the anatomy of what we are attempting to create. Figure 7.34 shows a diagram of some of the muscles of the upper back.

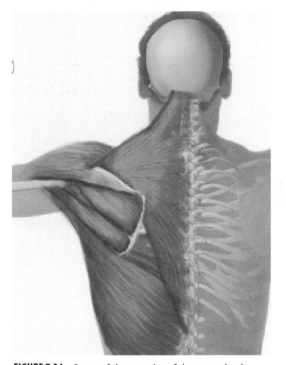

FIGURE 7.34   Some of the muscles of the upper back.

Quite a bit is going on underneath the surface of the back. We should look to the live model to see what registers on the surface to help us decide what to model in; we don't need to attempt to re-create every muscle there.

For this model, we will mainly give an indication of the scapula, and the muscles that extend off it: the teres major and the infraspinatus. We will also work on the trapezius. Figure 7.35 shows the basic lines we will be creating.

Starting with the scapula, split the faces as indicated in Figure 7.36.

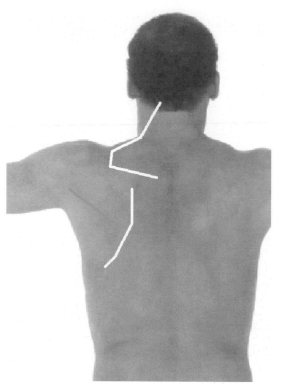

FIGURE 7.35 The basic lines of the upper back anatomy.

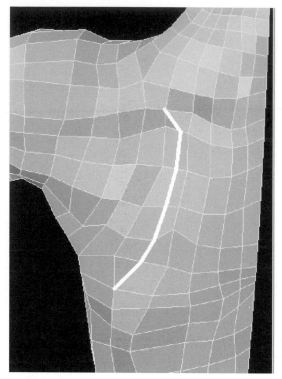

FIGURE 7.36 Add faces to indicate the scapula.

Now we need to pay attention to the muscles that emanate from the scapula. Create a split across the faces, as indicated in Figure 7.37.

We can sharpen the scapula definition by adding another split down its faces, as in Figure 7.38.

Since so much is going on here, be sure and check your geometry with lighting changes. See Figure 7.39.

Next, to give the lastissimus dorsi more definition, add another split that travels from the waist to under the arm, as in Figure 7.40. This is another popular muscle to accentuate when you are creating very strong-type characters.

As you can see, we are sharpening and refining our details. We can go around the model and continue to split faces as we see fit.

Figure 7.41 shows a tighter edge that is created where the thigh meets the buttocks.

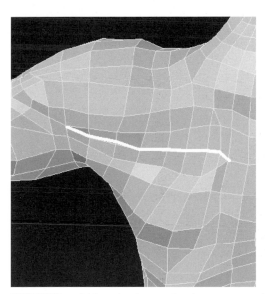

FIGURE 7.37   Add faces for the muscles that connect to the scapula.

FIGURE 7.38   Sharpen the scapula definition.

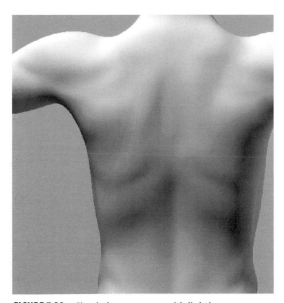

FIGURE 7.39   Check the geometry with lighting.

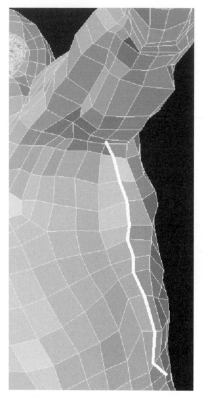

FIGURE 7.40 Give the lastissimus dorsi more definition.

FIGURE 7.41 Create a tighter edge along the buttocks.

Figure 7.42 shows the subdivided results of creating that edge.

Looking at the model, we could also use a bit more definition in the inner thigh area. Make two splits to help sharpen the definition there, as in Figure 7.43.

We will not be adding any genitalia to this model, but if you desire to, it shouldn't be too hard to figure out how and where to add this geometry. Unless your model is going to seen naked and you want it anatomically accurate, it is not necessary to include it.

Another bony landmark that we have not added yet is the clavicle, or collarbone. Due to the pose of our live model, this feature is largely hidden by the shifting of the muscles. However, if you plan to pose the model in an arms-down position, the collarbones should be visible on the surface. This is an example of modeling in details that aren't visible in the live model for some reason. Figure 7.44 shows the position of the collarbone in the live model.

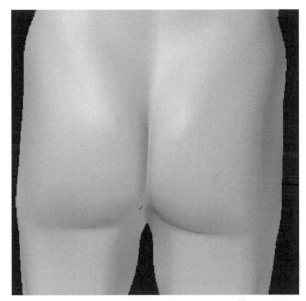

FIGURE 7.42   The results of creating that tighter edge.

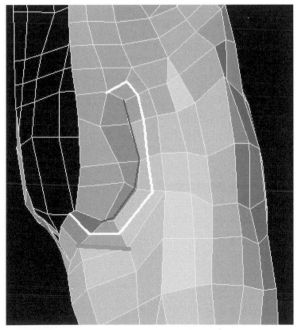

FIGURE 7.43   Add definition to the inner thigh area.

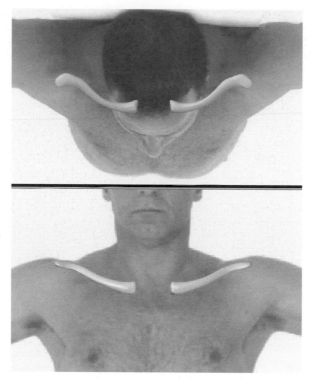

FIGURE 7.44   The position of the collarbone.

Adding the collarbone to our model involves splitting the faces along the edge to indicate the basic shape. We can then pull edges or vertices out a little to indicate the bone. See Figure 7.45.

If you find you would like more geometry to help form detail or to "hold" shapes as they subdivide, simply knife it in. Try to keep it flowing with the current geometry. Figure 7.46 shows more detail added to the neck for a little more definition. The split ended under the ear.

If you have not already been doing so, it is time to step back and take in the model as a whole. If you have been working on half the model, mirror it to be whole. View it from many angles and under different lighting conditions. Smooth any rough areas. Adjust and tweak it where you see fit. When you are happy with the results, pat yourself on the back—the geometry for the digital human is complete. See Figure 7.47.

Or is it? There is still room to add even more detail. For instance, you can slice in more faces to define the ribs. We also have not added any nipples. You can model these in by some simple extrusions, or you can take care of them with image maps. For the purposes of this tutorial, the amount of detail here is suitable and we are going to move on.

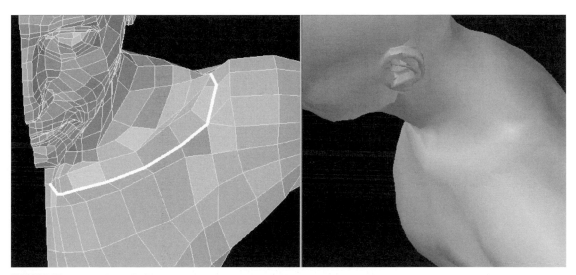

FIGURE 7.45   Create the collarbone.

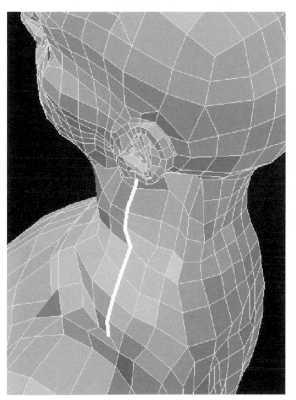

FIGURE 7.46   Add more geometry where needed.

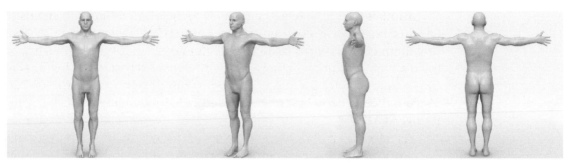

FIGURE 7.47   The completed geometry for the digital human.

REDUCING DETAIL

The process described in this book is one of working from low detail to high. The low-polygon model is gradually sliced up with more and more detail. The end result would be a medium- to high-resolution character. But what if you required a low-polygon model, such as for games? One solution would be to stop adding detail (such as the stomach and specific muscle detail) much earlier in the process. Figure 7.48 shows a low-resolution character.

In game characters, texture maps create the bulk of the illusion of detail. They supply the details and even baked-in lighting and shading.

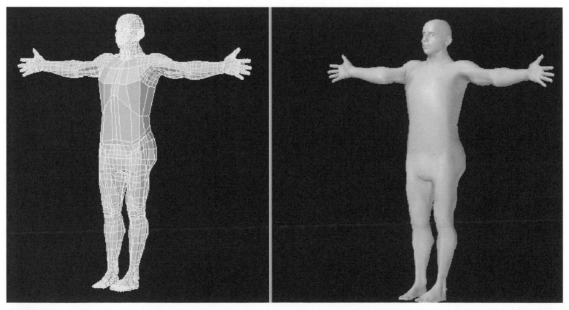

FIGURE 7.48   Making a low-resolution character.

Another way to reduce the detail is to dissolve out loops or chains of edges or faces. Some programs allow you to select geometry and remove it without creating holes in the model. It may seem counterproductive to build a high-resolution model and then remove all that work, but having the complex model does give you the option of returning to it. You can also use the high-resolution model as a guide for building the low-resolution version.

Yet another way to lower the polygon number is with a polygon reduction routine. Some 3D software comes with a built-in feature that does this; you can also find stand-alone programs that do this. These features and programs use a surface-simplification algorithm to reduce the number of polygons in the object while maintaining the forms. Using this method, you can reduce the number of polygons in your model a great deal without sacrificing much of the overall look. However, the resulting face layout can be rather "messy"; it doesn't lend itself well to animation. However, these models do make good stand-in versions for setting up a scene or for characters seen at a distance.

If you are going to use this method, it is probably best to start with a subdivided high-resolution version of your model (as opposed to the lower-resolution control cage, or pre-subdivided mode) before you use a polygon-reduction function. If you do that, more of the subtler details will be taken into account. Figure 7.49 shows several iterations of polygon reduction starting with the high-resolution head on the left.

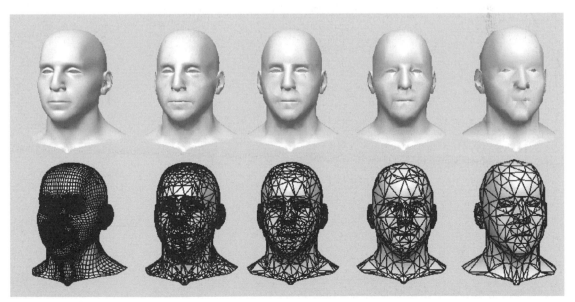

FIGURE 7.49   Several iterations of polygon reduction.

SUMMARY

It was quite the challenge, but we have finished the body—in form anyway. As you can see, our digital human still has a rather monotone color and is bald. Chances are, you will probably want your model to have a healthy tint to his cheeks. Turn the page, because we will get into texturing.

TEXTURING THE HEAD

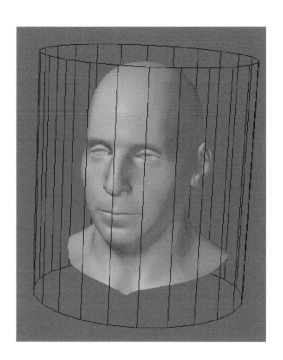

SETTING UP THE UV COORDINATES

This chapter will deal with texturing the head. This stage of construction can surely make or break a model. After we have put all this work into the geometry, we do not want to undermine it by skimping on the texture. Now that you feel the pressure, we will dive into it.

You can wreck a perfectly good texture map if you don't properly set up the UV coordinates for the model. We do not want our texture maps to stretch in an unseemly manner when we apply them to the model.

When you assign UV coordinates, the key is to examine the shape of the model and then determine the best initial mapping type to apply to it. Here, your choices are: spherical, planar, or cylindrical. We will not be using the box, automatic, or cubic mapping types. For these types, you need to have a decent 3D paint program to work effectively with them (this is because they break the UV coordinates into so many areas that it makes it almost impossible to paint over a 2D template).

Once you have picked a basic mapping type, you can always break the model down further with different mapping types. The more you break up the model into different maps, the more seams you will have to deal with.

For heads, cylindrical or spherical maps are obviously the best types of map to start with. In the case of this head and neck, a cylindrical map fits the shape the best. To help pick the mapping type to use, envision the shape around the model. See Figure 8.1.

So, if we apply a cylindrical map using the Y axis, we should end up with a UV layout something similar to Figure 8.2.

It looks pretty good, and in a perfect world we would be done. But it would serve us well to check how a test texture works before we start painting the real texture.

ON THE CD

The best way to test for texture UV issues is with a simple texture such as a checker pattern or grid. It's easy to make such a grid in any paint package, or you can load the Checker.png image from the reference folder on this book's CD-ROM. Apply the checker image, and observe the results. See Figure 8.3.

The bulk of the model looks good, but there are a few trouble spots: the edge of the neck where it flares out, the nose, and the top of the head. The problem with the top of the head is due to the poles of the map, the top, and the bottom. This occurs with cylindrical and spherical mapping. The good news is that this pinching occurs in a place that will be covered by hair (for this character), so we will not worry about it.

If we can't get the cylindrical map to completely conform to the model, we can conform the model to the cylindrical map. This will help

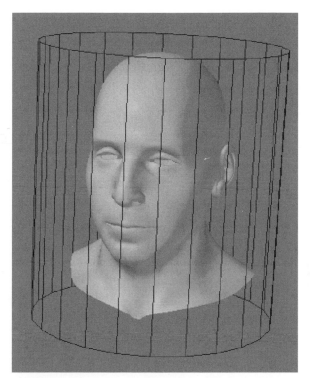

FIGURE 8.1   Envision the mapping shape around the model.

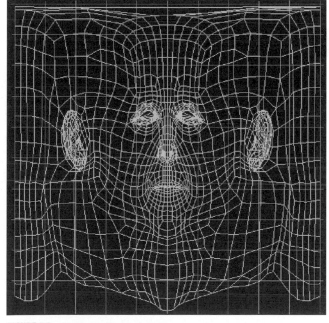

FIGURE 8.2   Apply a cylindrical map.

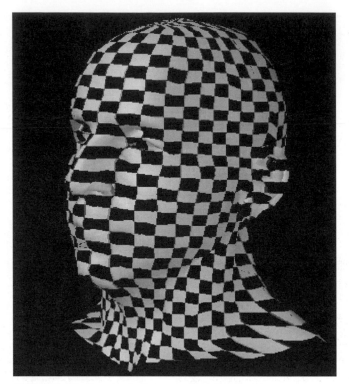

FIGURE 8.3 Apply a checker image to check for stretching.

alleviate some of the texture stretching. This trick is done through morphing. We will make an altered version that is slightly remodeled to eliminate face overlap and align some of the faces better for the mapping type. We will apply the UVs to this model and then morph it back into the original.

The challenge in altering the model in this way is to make sure the polygons retain their original proportions. If you stretch or compress faces too much while making the morph model, there will be texture stretching or squishing when you apply and morph back the UV.

We will start by rotating the corners of the neck down a bit. Make a copy of your original model to work on. This type of face movement is best done with some falloff, so that the surrounding faces move softly. Figure 8.4 shows the corners of the neck turned down.

You should also adjust the neck in profile. Pull out the front and back so that they are more tubular or cylindrical. Soften the line under the jaw as well. Also use a Smooth, Tighten, or Average function on the faces to help create a smoother surface. See Figure 8.5.

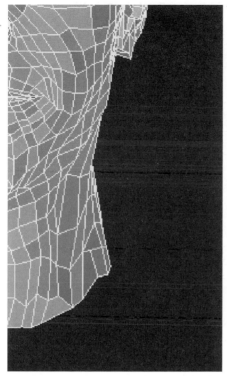

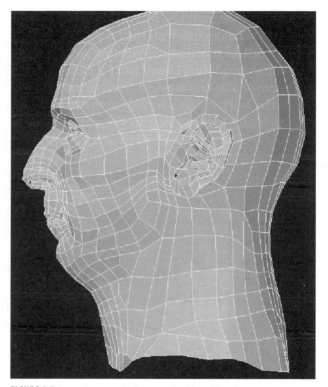

FIGURE 8.4   The corners of the neck turned down for the morph shape.

FIGURE 8.5   Continue with the morphed head for the UV map.

This will take care of the neck. Next, we will work on the nose. This is a tough piece since it sticks out far from the desired cylinder shape. We will not be flattening the nose, since that will alter the faces too much. We will concentrate on the outside nostril area since that has overlapping faces. Use a Smooth, Tighten, or Average function in this case. Do not be concerned with the inside of the nostrils. See Figure 8.6.

It is time to test the texture. Apply a cylindrical map to this head, and then morph it back to the original. Another option would be to transfer the UV coordinates to the original model, if your 3D program supports that. Check the mapping with the checker pattern. The problem areas should be much better. See Figure 8.7.

On certain areas such as the nose, the checker pattern isn't fine enough to judge texture distortion. In this case, you can make a smaller checker pattern, or you can use a noise or fractal noise pattern map. Fractal noise is a random, adjustable pattern that some 2D programs, such as Painter, can generate. At times, the size and randomness of the patterns

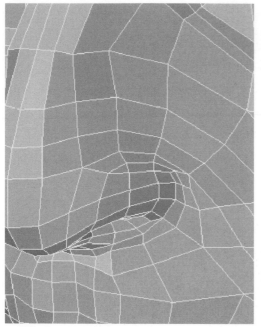

FIGURE 8.6   Smooth the outside of the nose to eliminate overlapping faces.

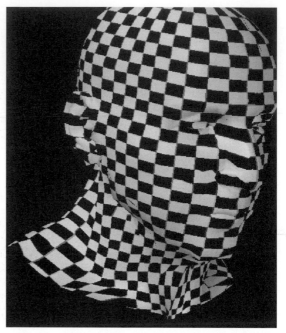

FIGURE 8.7   Recheck the UV mapping after the morph.

ON THE CD

can reveal more than the checker pattern. (There is a fractal noise pattern map (Fractal.bmp) on the CD-ROM in the reference folder.) Make sure that this is an image map, and not a procedural texture applied to the model, since procedural maps won't take into account the UV coordinates. See Figure 8.8.

There is still a little texture stretching along the side of the nose, but we can adjust our painting later to compensate for this. You may need to make several trips back and forth from the morph UV head to the original to check for unwanted texture distortion.

For this tutorial, we will not be making a morph for the ear. It does have some overlapping faces, and areas of some stretching. But since the ears do not have too much texture on them and the distortion should appear minimal, we will not make the UV map too complicated at this point. If you find this is a problem on a model, you can fix it by making separate planar maps for the front and back of the ears.

With the UV coordinates set up, we are ready to jump into the actual texture painting.

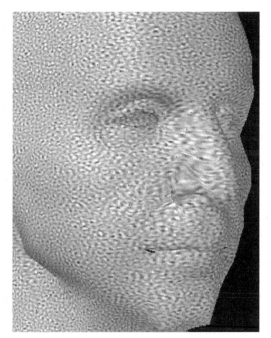

FIGURE 8.8   Check fine texture distortion with a fractal noise pattern.

USING COLOR MAPS

The first image map for this head that we will create is the color. Since we have a good reference from the live model (if you are using the one from this book), it will be a solid starting point around which to base all the other textures. We will actually use the photos of the live model in our texture map. Is this "cheating"? No, not really, because when you attempt to recreate in 3D something that exists in real life, it is important to use reality as much as possible.

We still need to do a good deal of work to the photo images of the live model before we can use them as textures. After that, we will still need to do some hand painting as well. All of you who like to paint textures by hand will get your chance to flex those muscles too.

The first step in painting a texture is to have a painting template to work over. This is the UV layout in wire frame, and it allows us to paint accurately over the details so that they line up on the model.

Some 3D programs allow you to export the UV map layout as a standard 2D file format at any resolution. The maps shown in this book are at

2,048 × 2,048 resolution. If you do not have the UV Layout Export feature, you can perform a standard screen capture and carefully crop the image. In any case, you should end up with an image similar to Figure 8.9.

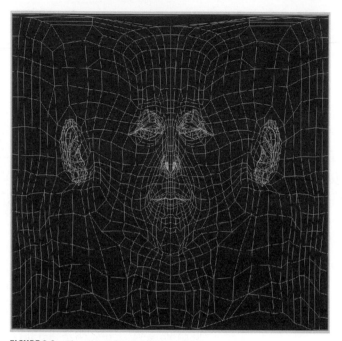

FIGURE 8.9   The painting template.

ON THE CD

Here is where we use the images of the live model in this texture map. Load into your paint package "HeadFnt" from this book's CD-ROM (in the reference folder). Or, load the close-up head shot of the model you have chosen to create. This is where having decent reference images will serve us well. If your reference images have too many shadows, or poor color quality, this way of working will be difficult or impossible. Even if your model doesn't resemble Frank, you can still work the reference images from this book.

Copy the head front images and paste them into a new layer on the painting template. Name this layer "Head Front." Obviously, you will need to resize it so that it fits the template. We are going to use only the color information from the very front of the head image. The goal is to align the eyes, nose, and mouth to the UV layout. To make this easier, you can work with the opacity of the head image layer turned down, or you can make a new layer, copy and paste the UV template over that, and then set the layer blend type to "Screen." Then, name it "Template" or "UV." If the template layer is black and white, as it is in this example, you should have a nice overlay of the UV template while you paint on the color layer in full opacity.

You will need to squeeze the head front image a bit to get it to fit the painting template. Use a Translate or Scale feature; you should end up with something similar to Figure 8.10.

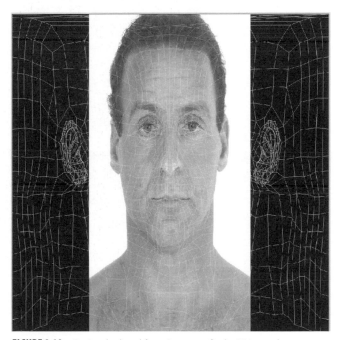

FIGURE 8.10   Resize the head front image to fit the UV template.

ON THE CD

Next, load "HeadSid.jpg" from the CD-ROM (in the reference folder), or load your live model's side head shot. Then, copy and paste it into new layer in the painting template image. Name this layer "Head Side." Naming layers is just a good habit to get into, no matter how simple the image. Next, resize the head side image using the ear and head front image as a guide. See Figure 8.11.

Now, here is the real work. The first step in making this a usable texture map is to paint out major landmarks of anatomy such as the eyes and nostrils. The eyes will be 3D objects in our model, so we don't want the image map projected over the entire face. The nose has shading that we do not want on the image map either. Good tools to use here are

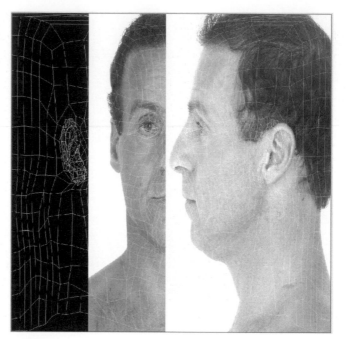

FIGURE 8.11   Add and resize the head side image.

Stamp or Clone. Sample areas from around the spots you want to paint out. Pay attention to any repeating patterns, and sample often while working. Retain certain shading such as the coloring on the upper eyelids. We will eventually get rid of all signs of shading, but for now, your image should look like Figure 8.12.

While we are at it, paint out the ear from the head side image. See Figure 8.13.

Next, we will blend the head side image onto the front so that the two appear to be part of a continuous surface. We will lose much of the information that shows the front of the face. You can either erase the unwanted information or use a layer mask to block it out. The layer mask technique allows you to show and hide the layer safely without actually losing it permanently. See Figure 8.14.

We also will not be using any of the hair color information in these images. We have not yet covered hair, as you know; we will give Frank some hair in Chapter 9. For now, we will shave Frank's head. To paint out the hair from the original image maps, use the Stamp or Clone tool to sample skin areas over it. You can also copy and paste large pieces of skin

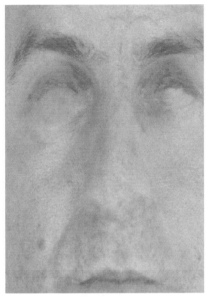

FIGURE 8.12   Paint out major landmarks such as the eyes and nose.

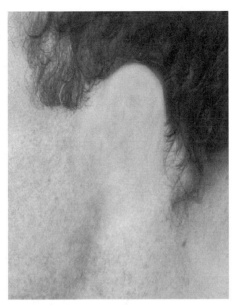

FIGURE 8.13   Paint out the ear.

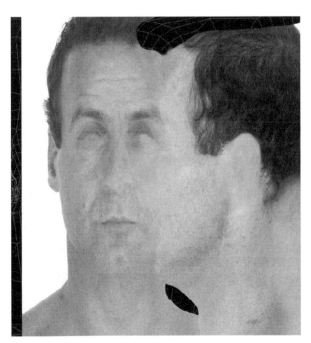

FIGURE 8.14   Blend the side of the head.

color to cover larger areas. We will, however, leave the eyebrows as part of the image map. See Figure 8.15.

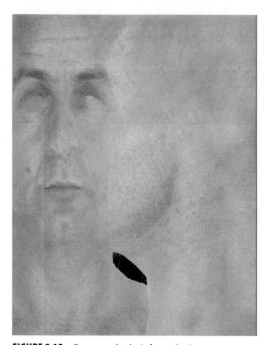

FIGURE 8.15   Remove the hair from the image.

While we are at the side of the head, we'll use the Airbrush tool to add some reddish tones around the ear. We'll use the UV template as a guide so that we stay within the geometry. See Figure 8.16.

To cover the other side of the head, copy the head side layer into a new layer, flip it horizontally, and move it over. Fill in any holes that lack color. See Figure 8.17.

We created some symmetry with that last maneuver, and perfect symmetry is the last thing you want in an organic creation. However, we can easily remedy this later with a few brush strokes.

This would be a good point to check how the texture is working on the 3D model. Apply the texture, and view the model from every angle. Check to see how certain landmarks, such as the eyebrows and the mouth, fit. See Figure 8.18.

If some areas are off, you can fix them back in the paint program. For example, if the eyebrows are too high, one method to fix them is to select that region, cut and paste it into a new layer, and then move that layer

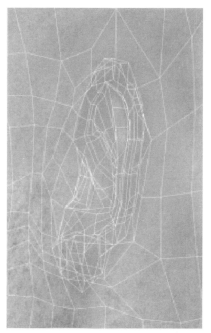

FIGURE 8.16 Add color to the ear.

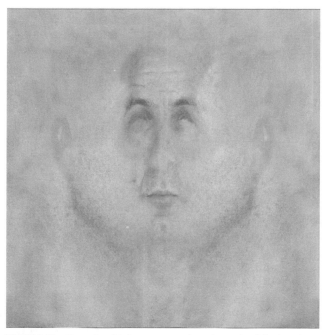

FIGURE 8.17 Copy the side layer over to the other side of the head.

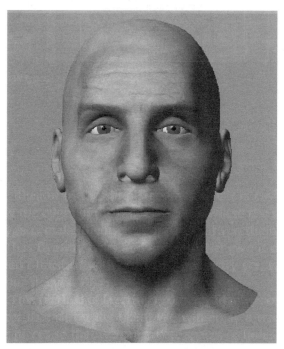

FIGURE 8.18 Check the texture on the model to see how it registers.

down a bit. Another useful tool (found in Photoshop 7) is the Liquefy brush. This allows you to push the image around smoothly. Lastly, you can move some of the vertices in the UV map to make adjustments.

The head may look pretty good at this point, but we need to take care of a few more aspects, notably the sheen or highlight that is prominent on the forehead and other areas. This is due to skin oils and can be minimized during photography with powder, but it's impossible to completely eliminate these highlights at that stage. While these highlights look natural, they dictate a fixed lighting arrangement that conforms to the lighting on the texture map. If we want more flexibility during lighting, we will have to make the map more neutral.

Return to the paint program and use tools such as Photoshop's Replace Color command. A magic wand tool that selects colors of a similar nature would work too. The idea is to select all the shiny tones on the skin. The next step is to reduce the lightness or tone so that you make it closer in value to the rest of the skin. Use tools such as Hue/Saturation or brightness/contrast adjustments. It may take you several attempts to get the entire selection. See Figure 8.19.

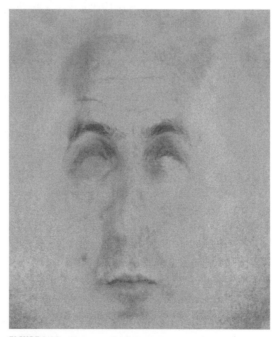

FIGURE 8.19   Remove the hot spots.

If you would like to experiment without being afraid of messing up the original image, copy it to a new layer for these changes.

Another way to knock out the highlights is to make a new layer above the originals and set it to Darken Blend mode. Reduce the layer opacity to about 80%. Then, paint on the bright areas with a skin tone. See Figure 8.20.

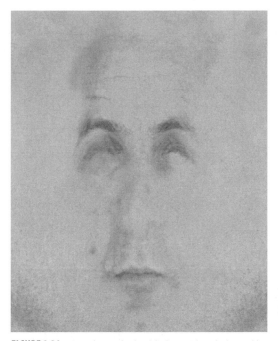

FIGURE 8.20   Knock out the highlights with a darkened layer.

Now it is time to put a little life back into this map. The color adjustments we've made have caused the skin tones to be a little flat. Also, we still have some uneven skin tones, such as on the side of the forehead. We are going to do some hand painting to punch this back up and add details.

Make a new layer and name it "Details." You can add as many detail layers as you need for experimentation purposes. Also, keep the original live model images handy as a reference. We will be painting in skin tones, but it is important not to spray them in even tones as with an airbrush. If you look closely, skin is made up of many spots of color. The variation will be different from person to person. Even when attempting to create a young and smooth skin tone, you should break it up with a speckling of tones to make it realistic. When viewed from a few steps back (or due to the limitations of output properties such as video resolution or film grain), the spots of color will blend together nicely and will appear natural.

You can painstakingly paint these tonal variations by hand by using a small brush size. However, most software has settings that will make this go much faster. One simple technique is to make a custom brush shape that consists of numerous random spots of color. You can then stamp this brush shape around the canvas. Use several custom brush shapes so that you avoid any repeating patterns.

To make a custom brush shape, create a new document at a small resolution such as 128 × 128. Paint some random spots in the canvas. Most paint software will allow you to capture this image and use it as a brush shape, as shown in Figure 8.21. You can quickly build up a library of these brushes.

FIGURE 8.21   Create a custom brush shape.

Some programs also have a setting in the brush control that allows you to scatter dots as you draw across the image. You can vary and change the spacing and randomness of the dots based on numerous factors—from pen pressure (for those using drawing tablets) to speed or tilt. This feature is a great way to paint small, or large, spots of color. In the case of the human face, we do not want anything too big. This will all be done subtly.

Figure 8.22 shows a comparison of the image before (left) and after (right) we used this method of spot painting.

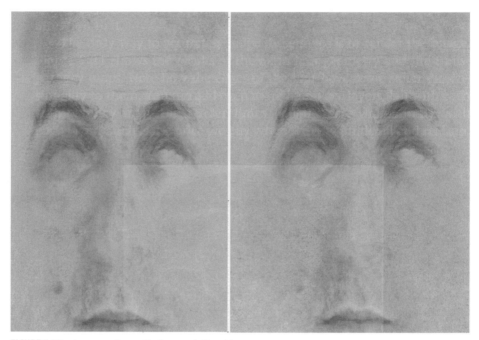

FIGURE 8.22   A comparison of before and after skin tone.

The skin now appears more even and alive. Although the amount of reddish tones around the nose, cheeks, and forehead varies in people and ethnicities, you will find noticeably more in Caucasians than in people of other backgrounds.

In areas such as the nose, there was some texture stretching due to the UV map layout. It helps to make the details you paint smaller—use smaller dots or brush sizes—so that when the texture stretches when it's applied to the model, it will not be as noticeable.

You can use "Details" layers to paint other details such as pores, moles, and other blemishes. For added flexibility, you can use separate layers when you want to experiment with or adjust any details.

Figure 8.23 shows the completed color map for the head. A pink tone was painted to match up with the UV details of the lower eyelid. Also, using a Clone or Stamp tool—or just by hand-painting details—change any areas that are too symmetrical. You should use these few tools to alter any place where you will easily see repeating or symmetrical patterns. When you are done, save this image as "HeadC," the "C" meaning color. (You can come up with your own naming conventions and abbreviations; just make sure that they are consistent and clear.)

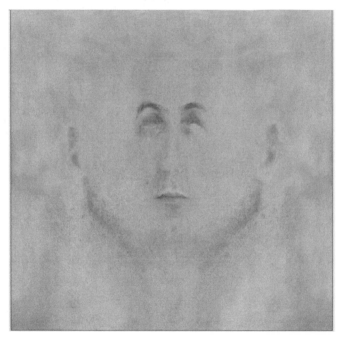

FIGURE 8.23   The finished color map for the head.

Of course, test the color map frequently on the model. See Figure 8.24.

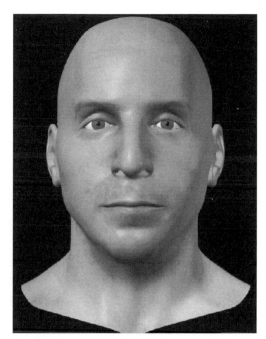

FIGURE 8.24   The color map applied to the model.

Using Bump Maps

A couple of other maps will greatly affect the look of our head model. The first up is the bump map. This map will give the illusion of 3D texture on a model, although it will not actually change or add any geometry. If you look at the edge of the surface, this illusion will be clear. Therefore, bump maps are good for creating subtle texturing such as light wrinkles and pores. See Figure 8.25.

Bump maps are usually painted in shades of gray, with lighter tones representing the raised portions and darker tones the deeper ones. This makes it easy to visualize what you are doing, but you need to render the bump map in your 3D software to accurately check how it will affect the model. Be prepared to do many tests. 3D paint software aids greatly in this area since it allows you to see how the bumps will render as you paint. For this tutorial, we will use the more common 2D painting software.

We will use the color map as a basis for making the bump map. To begin, copy and paste your color map into a new document. Change the object to a grayscale image. You can also remove all color saturation from

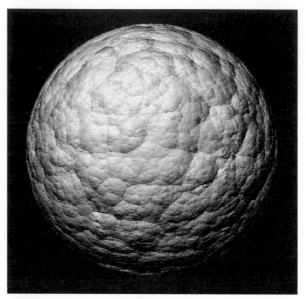

FIGURE 8.25   Bump maps affect the shading on the surface but do not change the geometry.

the image. Save this as "HeadB," the "B" standing for bump. This naming convention will make it easy for you to identify the image map when going through your directories. See Figure 8.26.

This is a decent start, but as with the color map, we need to do some work on it. Always keep in mind what the tones of gray will do to the texture when the bump map is rendered. As mentioned, lighter shades represent raised areas, and darker shades the recesses. The map as it stands now has some areas that work for this and some that do not. For example, the forehead works, but the eyebrows do not. We want the brows to appear to be raised, yet the map is dark there. You could trace over the brows with a light color, but there is an easier way.

With a Lasso Select tool, trace around the eyebrows, and then copy and paste them into a new layer. Label this "Brows." Now, invert or make a negative of that layer. You should end up with something similar to Figure 8.27.

This doesn't look so great either, but if we carefully erase the darker gray around the brows, we can blend this brow layer into the layer below. You can also use a layer mask. The results should be similar to Figure 8.28.

The next area we want to apply this trick to is the lower half of the face and neck. This is because, on a male character, there will most likely

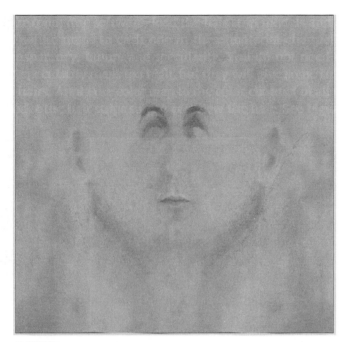

FIGURE 8.26   The bump map starts with a grayscale of the color map.

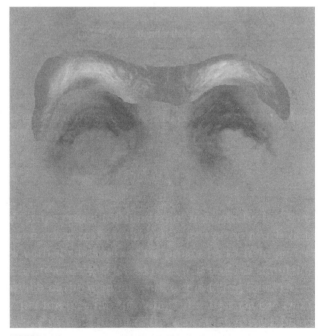

FIGURE 8.27   Make a new brow layer and invert it or make a negative of it.

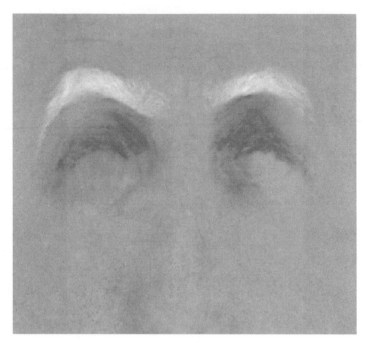

FIGURE 8.28 Blend the brow layer to the one below.

be beard stubble that will show up dark in the grayscale. We want to invert that so that the stubble on the bump map is light. Use the Lasso Select tool to select the whole lower face from under the nose down to the neck, and then copy and paste it into a new layer. Then, make that layer negative or invert it. See Figure 8.29.

The first thing you will notice is that the tones do not match up well between layers. You can remedy this by adjusting the brightness/contrast for that lower face layer. You should be able to get the tones to match; then you can blend the rest with soft erase action. See Figure 8.30.

We will now need to go in and fix the lips after this last operation. Either on the lower face layer, or by making a new copy of the lip area in a new layer, create a negative of the lips' tones. Also paint some darker lines to represent any cracks or lines you see in the lips. You can do this with airbrushed tones, or with the Burn and Dodge tools to lighten and darken. Lip cracks, like many details, will vary person to person. There is a tendency to want to overdo this detail, so take a close look at your live model for reference. There may be few lip cracks to paint (sorry to disappoint). See Figure 8.31.

FIGURE 8.29   Make a negative of the lower face area.

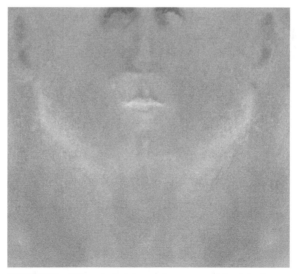

FIGURE 8.30   Adjust the brightness/contrast to blend the layers.

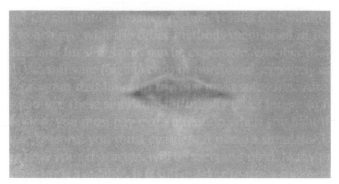

FIGURE 8.31 Correct the lip area.

Now we should go back in to punch up and define detail that may have gotten lost when we initially made these maps. It is good to have the reference images of the live model handy. Making texture maps such as these are not just a matter of pasting the photographic reference images over the model. You will need to use your observant eye and paint back in what should be there—or what you think should be there.

Make a new layer. Here, we will paint in some of the fine wrinkles that appear around the eyes. You can use the UV template to help you paint more accurately here if you need. Try to stay away from pure white or black when you paint the details. It is easier to darken or lighten a more neutral tone than it is to try to adjust the maximum tones of the scale. You can paint these details with shades of gray, or there is another technique. Fill the new layer with 50 percent gray, and then set the Layer Blend mode to Overlay. Now you can use the Burn and Dodge tools to create your tones. Figure 8.32 shows the finer details painted around the eyes.

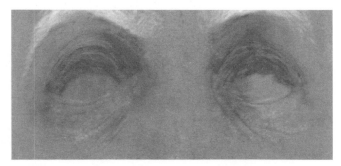

FIGURE 8.32 The finer details painted around the eyes.

On yet another layer, we will punch up some of the fine forehead wrinkles. Use the faint remnants from the previous maps and the reference images as a guide. See Figure 8.33.

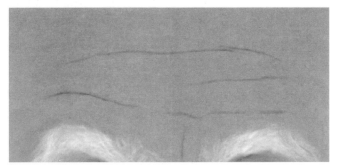

FIGURE 8.33   Add the forehead wrinkles.

 It is a good idea to put all these details on separate layers. This will allow you to change, delete, and otherwise adjust them in many ways. Using many layers will just give you that much more flexibility.

The skin on our foreheads isn't usually completely smooth and flat with thin groves in it. There are subtle variations on the surface. To create this variation, we will add some lighter tones. Make a new layer and fill it with 50 percent gray. With the Dodge tool or an airbrush that is a lighter shade of gray, add some broad, raised areas around the wrinkles. See Figure 8.34.

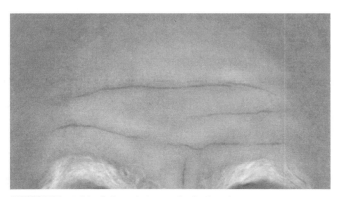

FIGURE 8.34   Add subtle variation to the forehead.

We can now get into even finer detail. The last stop on this train is the skin pores. Some remnants of the original image map are left over from the original maps, but most have been obliterated. While pores are essentially dots all over our face, if you look more closely, you will see variations in their shape and pattern. For example, on the forehead, they will be slightly stretched out rather than perfectly circular. You can modify the brush shape to reflect this if the paint software has this control. If it doesn't, you can paint them in with your own custom brush tip, as described earlier. A scatter-type brush will save you great amounts of work, and you won't have to individually paint each pore by hand. You can also create a custom brush shape with a number of pores that you can stamp around. Be sure to make several variations on these. Figure 8.35 shows a close-up of the forehead and cheek areas with added pores.

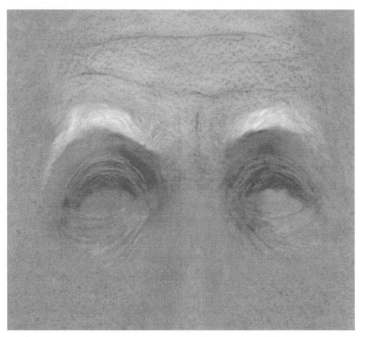

FIGURE 8.35   A close-up of the forehead bump map.

Do plenty of test renderings before you become too content with the 2D bump map. What may look good in 2D might not translate well when rendered. Figure 8.36 shows a rendering of the head with the color and bump maps applied.

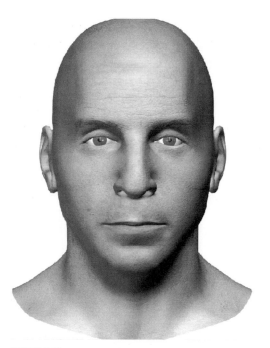

FIGURE 8.36   A test rendering of the head with the color and bump maps applied.

Keep adjusting your bump map until it "feels" right. This doesn't mean that every pore has to be perfect. It means that the overall effect of all this detail should produce a natural impression. If a detail jumps out at you in any way, re-examine it and rework it if necessary. Even if a detail of the map doesn't look wrong but still draws your eye to it in a distracting way, consider changing it. The goal of this tutorial is to create a natural-looking head, and unless there is a feature that is prominent, then you do not want to draw the viewer's attention to it with over-wrought image maps. Your desired outcome, how close the character will be to the camera, and the output medium should determine how much you will work the detail. Many times, the individual maps will not be too impressive when viewed on their own, but they will work great on the model. This should be the canvas where you judge your maps. Remember, these image maps are not meant to be hung on museum walls (but if you get one displayed there, congratulations!).

Using Specularity Maps

You may have noticed that the head has a dry, matte finish. Skin has a varying amount of oils on it, which results in a sheen. The best way to achieve this look with our tools is with the specularity settings. Adjusting the specularity can make an object appear to be made of plastic, metal, or glass. Of course, this is exactly what we don't want for a human head. In fact, it is the toughest aspect to fight when you are creating computer-generated organic forms. But with some controlled mapping, we can use the specularity to our advantage.

You will most likely be able to globally adjust the specularity on the surface of your model through a slider or numeric input. This will cover the whole model but might not be appropriate for the entire surface. See Figure 8.37.

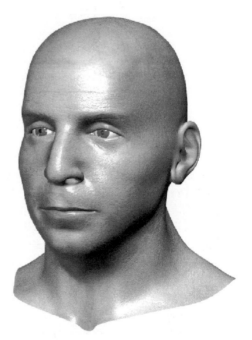

FIGURE 8.37   Adjust the specularity globally, but it might not be appropriate for the entire surface.

You may need to adjust additional parameters for the specularity. Glossiness or spread will control how tight a highlight is. In general, skin highlights will not be tight; rather, they will spread out broadly over the surface and not be too sharp.

Additionally, your software may offer different shading types or algorithms to assign to the object surface or material. The two most likely to be used for our purposes are Phong or Blinn. The difference between the two is in how they render the highlights. Phong produces harder specular highlights than Blinn. The latter may be better suited for skin. See Figure 8.38.

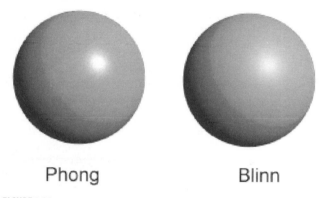

Phong   Blinn

FIGURE 8.38   The Phong and Blinn shading types.

Your software may also allow you to layer different shading types. For simplicity's sake, this tutorial will focus on one layer of textures for each mapping type. When you feel more confident with the process, you can experiment with building more complex textures.

Various parts of our faces are oilier than others. The nose and forehead have a tendency to be shinier than the neck, for example. This is where we will control the specularity with a map to put more or less shininess in areas where we want it.

Go back into your paint program. This time around, we will be using the bump map as a basis for the specularity map. Make a copy of the bump map and save it as "Frank_Head_S," the "S" standing for specularity.

As it stands now, the image will be way too light for a specularity map. It takes very few white areas for realistic specularity. The first thing we will do is reduce the brightness. The easiest way to do this is by using the brightness/contrast settings. You may need to adjust the settings a couple of times to get the desired results, which should look something like Figure 8.39.

You do not want the darks to be completely black. A good way to check the dark value is with the Eyedropper tool. This tool gives you

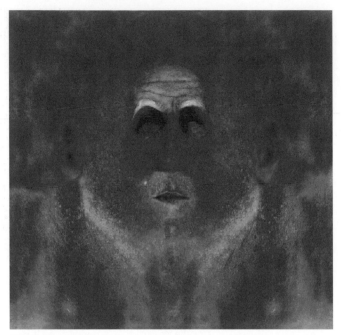

FIGURE 8.39 Reduce the brightness/contrast settings of the specularity map.

numeric feedback on the area it is placed over. In Red Green Blue (RGB) mode, the values 10-20 are a good standard to start with. In your 3D software, you can always adjust this further if the values are too high. It's better, however, to err on the side of too bright rather than too dark.

We now have a decent starting point for the specularity map, but we need to adjust some areas of this map. First, the eyebrows are too white. You can easily adjust this by painting over them with a darker shade, preferably a tone sampled from the surrounding colors. Performing these adjustments on another layer will allow you to go back to the original. Also, the forehead is a little bright, so we want to tone it down. We do want to retain some brightness as compared to the surrounding areas since most people's foreheads do tend to be shinier than the rest of their face. See Figure 8.40.

Other areas that are still too bright are under the jaw and neck. Darken these in the same way as you did the forehead. In addition, some spots, such as the lips, are not bright enough. The lips are an obvious place for specularity, but do not overdo it unless you are making a char-

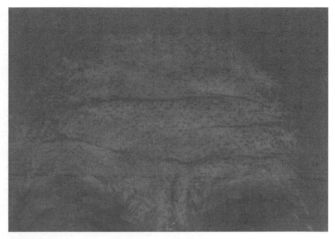

FIGURE 8.40   Adjust the forehead specularity.

acter with lipstick or one who licks his lips a lot. Apply a light shade around the lips, smudging or blurring it to the surrounding area. Use the UV painting template to help guide you here. See Figure 8.41.

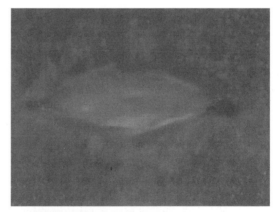

FIGURE 8.41   Lighten the lips' specularity.

The ears also have a tendency to be shiny, so paint some lighter shades over them, using the template as a guide. See Figure 8.42.

This would be a good time to test the specularity map on the model. Render several angles of the head with a simple lighting setup. Also,

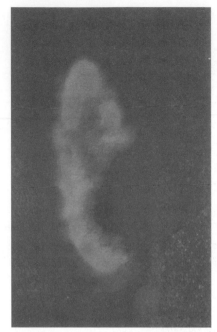

FIGURE 8.42 Adjust the specularity on the ears.

move the lights around to check how all the maps react with each other and the lights. Go back to any map to make adjustments if necessary. See Figure 8.43.

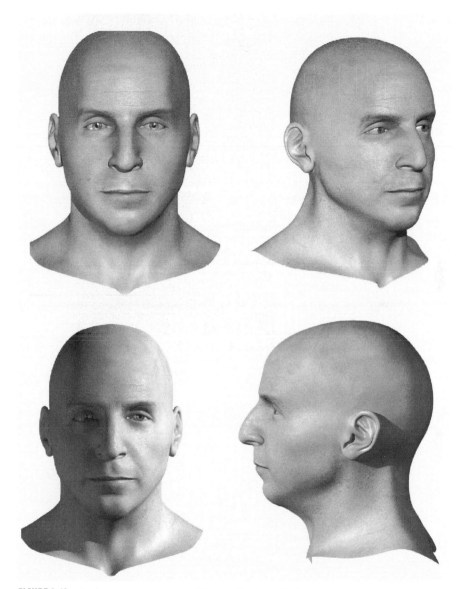

FIGURE 8.43   Perform test renderings of the head to check the textures.

SUMMARY

We have reached the end of another challenging subject. Texturing a human head is a demanding aspect of building the model. It can easily bring it to life or it can send it to the grave. Making special morph shapes will help alleviate the textures when you assign the UV maps. Using real photos for texture maps can be a good starting point for the final texture. You can apply the techniques you learned for texturing the head to the rest of the body.

HAIR

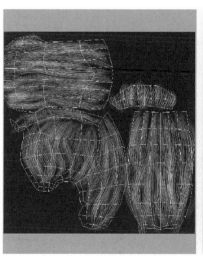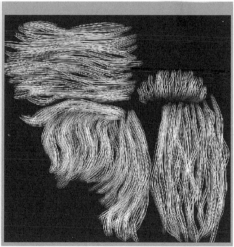

CREATING HAIR ON THE MODEL

We would all agree that bald characters look cool and rough. There is certainly a time and place for these types. But most of the time you will need or want to put hair on your characters. This is, yet again, another challenging aspect of modeling humans.

Hair is perhaps the trickiest part of a digital human. This is a product of the familiarity we all have with hair (since we see it every day) coupled with the complexity of it as a unit. Thousands of hair follicles sprout from our heads, in dozens of combinations of color, texture, and styles. Hair can look controlled or messy or any combination of the two. It reacts to light and wind. All of these factors add up to making it a very intimidating thing to tackle in 3D.

Before you gear yourself up for modeling each hair fiber, you should think about how your model will be seen and used. Determining this can make the job of creating hair much easier. Once again, knowing the output and your needs will help you plan how to construct your models.

SIMPLE HAIR

We will start with one of the easiest methods of creating hair. This involves modeling the overall form of the hair with geometry, then letting texture maps do the rest of the work. This technique is most effective on short hair styles. You can get a surprising amount of mileage out of this method.

When you model hair in this manner, it is important to observe and replicate the whole mass of hair on the head as opposed to trying to capture the smaller clumps or shapes. Study the hair style of your model, or reference images, by looking at the basic silhouettes. This will indicate the volumes you need to model.

Within this method, you may choose to model the hair geometry right out of the existing geometry on the head, or you may decide to create a separate piece of geometry that sits on the head. The advantages of modeling the hair geometry as a part of the head is that it allows you to consolidate geometry and textures into one model. Another advantage of this method is that it renders quickly. However, modeling the hair geometry as a part of the head can make it tough to get more complex hair styles.

On the other hand, the advantage of modeling the hair as a separate model to be placed on the head is that you can easily adjust or change the hair model independently of the head. You can even share "hair pieces" with other models, with some adjustments. In addition, the geometry of the hair can be at a different resolution than the head model.

Let us explore an example of growing the hair out of the existing head geometry on our Frank model. Load your Frank head model into your modeling package; in addition, have the front and side views of the live model present. We will use them to select the geometry of where the hair will be. Give these faces a grouping or part name of "Hair" so that you can easily select the faces later if need be. See Figure 9.1.

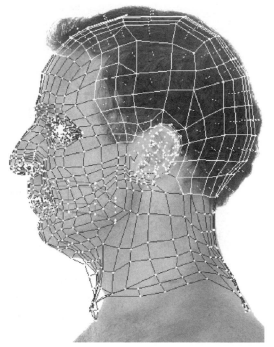

FIGURE 9.1   Select the geometry for the hair using the live model image as a guide.

From here, we will extrude all of the faces to bring them out from the head. This is the main geometry we will be focusing on to form the hair. See Figure 9.2.

From here, shape this geometry to capture the broad forms of the actual hair. Eliminate sharp edges in areas such as the sides of the head, where the hair gradually tapers into the head. Unless your subject has overhanging bangs, there shouldn't be too many harsh edges in the transition from the hair to the head. See Figure 9.3.

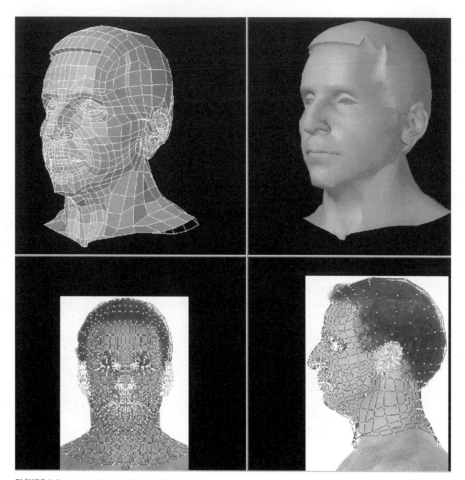

FIGURE 9.2   Extrude out the hair form.

We are now ready to add the textures. This example builds on the textures we created in Chapter 8, in which we textured the head bald.

You may need to adjust the UV map slightly since the new extruded hair faces were created right over the head geometry. Pull these points up a little in the UV map window to create some space for the texture. Try not to change the face UV layout. See Figure 9.4.

Export this UV map layout as a painting template and load it into a paint package. Load the color map for the head that we created in Chap-

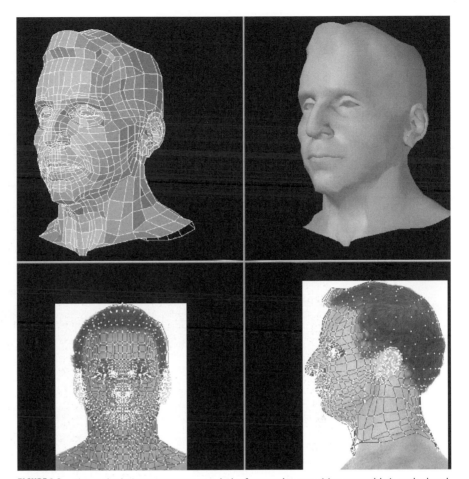

FIGURE 9.3   Shape the hair geometry to match the form and to transition smoothly into the head.

ter 8 and paste the UV template over it again to act as a guide. Now, load in the front and side reference images of the live model. First, copy and paste the side view into the color map image in a new layer; then, transform it so that it roughly fits in the area where the hair is on the model. Save this image with a different name, such as "CHair." See Figure 9.5.

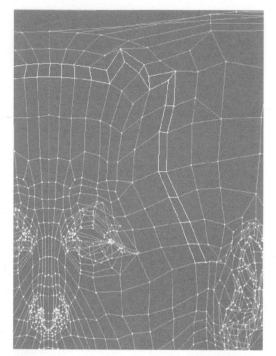

FIGURE 9.4 Adjust the UV map for the edge of the hair.

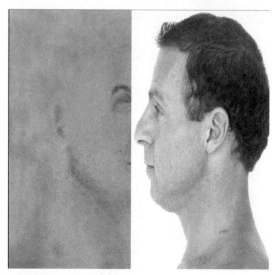

FIGURE 9.5 Align the side head image on a new layer.

Erase most of the side head image so that you can fit it to the texture easier. See Figure 9.6.

From here, do a little creative cloning to fill out areas that do not have hair. See Figure 9.7.

For the very front of the head, we will use the Frank front image. Creating the hair here is the same as with the side, except in this case we will use much less of the original image. See Figure 9.8.

FIGURE 9.6   Erase most of the side head image.

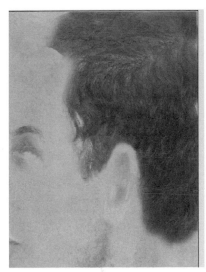

FIGURE 9.7   Clone to fill out areas that do not have hair.

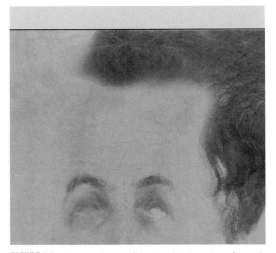

FIGURE 9.8   Use the front of the head hair texture from the front shot of the live model.

Replicate the other side by duplicating the hair layer, flipping it horizontally, and then moving it over. Do some cloning of different areas to get rid of any symmetry if necessary. See Figure 9.9.

FIGURE 9.9   Replicate the other side.

You can replicate these steps to make the new bump and specularity maps. You do not need to copy and stretch the original live model image over the other maps; simply copy the hair layer and paste it into a new layer on the subsequent map.

For example, Figure 9.10 shows the hair image inverted with some contrast adjustments and placed on a new layer in the bump map.

Figure 9.11 shows the same technique applied to the specularity map. In this case, we greatly turned down the hair layer's brightness.

When applied to the model, these extra maps give a decent impression of hair that you can use in many situations (such as game models or productions where there isn't time to make more advanced hair models). See Figure 9.12.

Figure 9.13 shows another example of hair grown out of the head geometry.

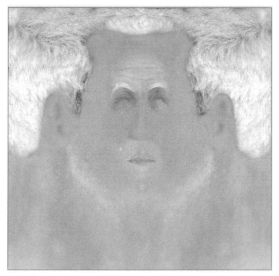

FIGURE 9.10   The hair image placed in the bump map.

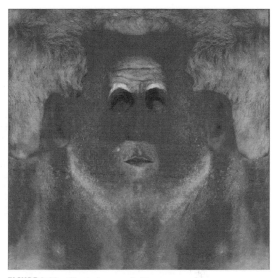

FIGURE 9.11   The hair specularity map.

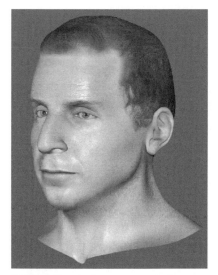

FIGURE 9.12   The hair maps applied to the model.

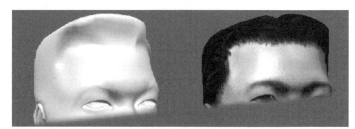

FIGURE 9.13   Hair grown out of the head geometry.

You can get a bit more elaborate and creative with hair geometry. Figure 9.14 shows a character with a ponytail. We accomplished this simply by extruding selected faces and then shaping and tapering them. The hair texture was hand-painted instead of grabbed from a photo reference.

Figure 9.15 illustrates how you can keep a woman's hairstyle simple by having it pulled back in a bun. We achieved this hand-painted texture by using a high-contrast color scheme to give the illusion of depth.

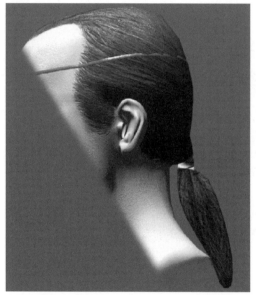

FIGURE 9.14   A character with a ponytail modeled out of the head geometry.

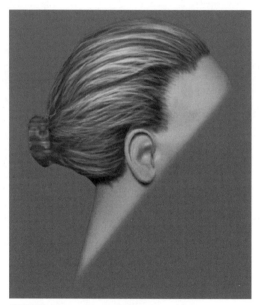

FIGURE 9.15   A simple woman's hairstyle.

A good visual library of hair types can always come in handy; if you don't use the library for reference, then it will be useful for actual texture maps. Whenever you can, ask friends or coworkers if you can photograph their heads. If they claim they are having a bad hair day, say, "That is perfect for my needs." Many fashion magazines also have good photos of hair styles. As with everything else when you are creating a digital human, it is crucial to always remain observant. See Figure 9.16.

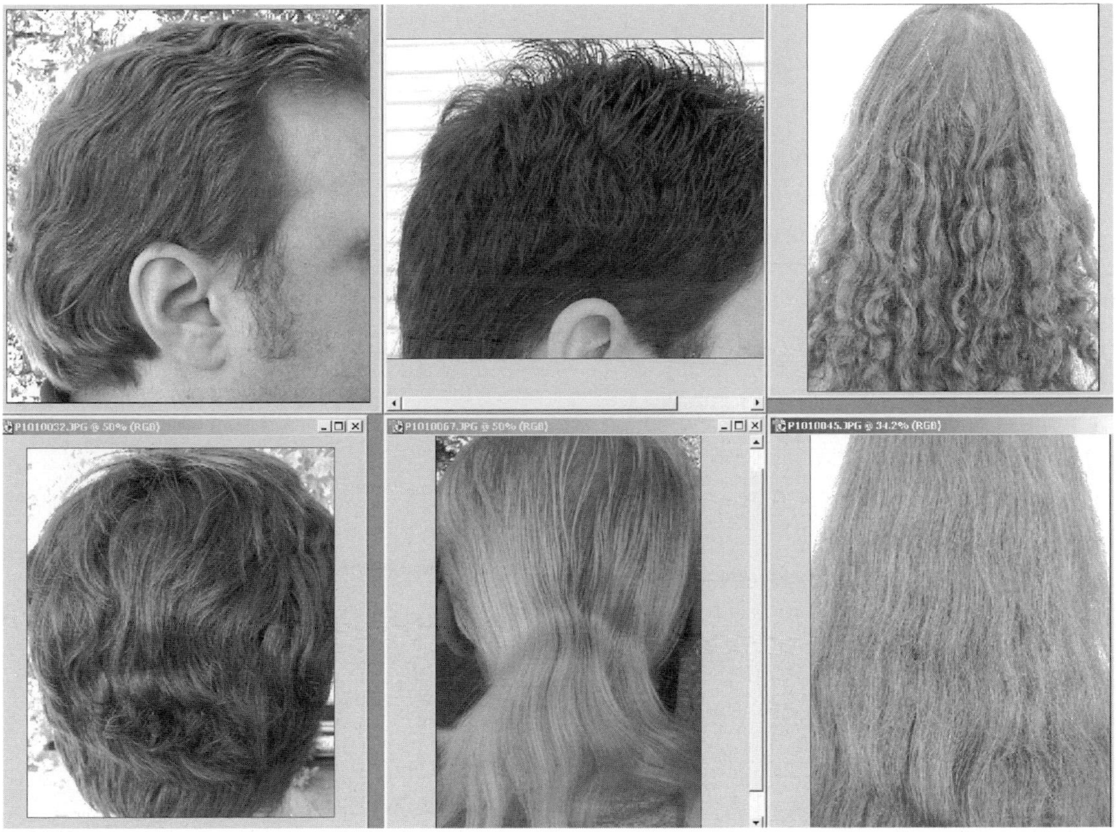

FIGURE 9.16   A visual library of hair types.

LAYERED GEOMETRY

The illusion of the simple-geometry hair is easily destroyed when you view the edges of the model. Here is where the sharp, clean edges of the polygons make themselves apparent. Even the most well-kept hair style still has flyaway hairs and a depth that give it extra dimension. So, we haven't finished with our hair's geometry yet; we still have a few tricks up our sleeves.

This method of layering geometry involves creating one or more hair pieces that sit on the head. We will apply a transparency map to these hair pieces so that we can create spaces or holes between the hairs. This in turn will create some depth and will soften the edge of the hair.

To create a hair piece, select all the geometry that makes up the hair portion of the head model (if you named this geometry earlier, this will be easy), copy it, and make a new object out of it. If your software supports layers, place it on another layer. Now, size this geometry up a very small amount, such as 1mm. This will create a small space between it and the head geometry. See Figure 9.17.

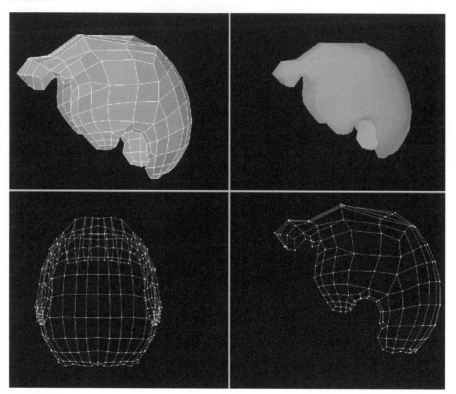

FIGURE 9.17   Make a new object out of the hair geometry.

Since we will be using transparency on this object, make the faces double sided.

It would be best to apply new UV coordinates, different than those we had on the head. Since we are going to paint some fine lines on these maps, we want to avoid some of the potential stretching at the poles that can occur with a cylindrical map. Since this is a pretty simple shape, a few planar maps will cover this form nicely. When you break down the maps, you will have) sides, top, back, and front. First, select the geometry that roughly makes up the sides of the head, and apply a planar UV map on the X axis. A planar map on the Z axis will make up the back and front of the hair. Lastly, one planar map on the Y axis will comprise the top. In your UV editor, arrange these separate pieces so that they don't overlap, similar to what's shown in Figure 9.18. Name this "HairUV."

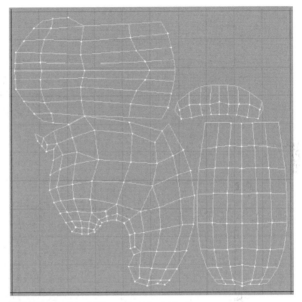

FIGURE 9.18   The UV layout of the hair piece.

Give this geometry a name of "HairLayer1." Next, copy and paste the geometry into yet another layer, and size up it again. Name this geometry "HairLayer2." We now have two extra pieces of geometry to work on for the hair. Save a painting template of the hair UV and load the template into your favorite paint program.

Here, we will paint black and white maps for the transparency. We will be painting lines that represent hair. Be sure and leave some space between these lines so that the underlying layers show through. You can use a small-diameter brush, but you can do all this faster if you create a custom brush of several dots so that you draw more than one hair at a time. Paint two separate maps, one for each hair piece. Be sure to paint each map by hand, and not just copy one to the other. By hand painting, you will ensure that the maps have some variety since you cannot paint each line exactly. Figure 9.19 shows the two hair transparency maps, with the UV painting template viewable under one.

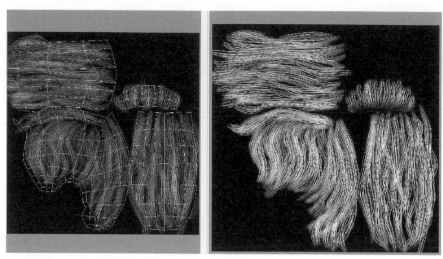

FIGURE 9.19 The two hair transparency maps.

Figure 9.20 shows the hair piece geometry on the model. It does look odd, but once the transparency kicks in during rendering, having this geometry here will make a huge difference.

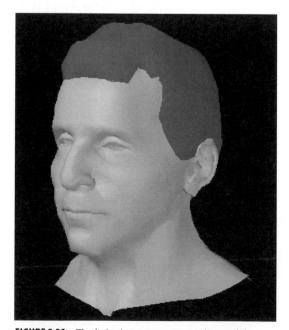

FIGURE 9.20 The hair piece geometry on the model.

When you are done painting the maps, apply them to the transparency channel of the two hair pieces. You can vary the color of the two pieces a bit, or you can apply a simple color map to them. However, since very little of their geometry will be seen, it will not matter all that much. Play with the specularity settings too. Different hair types have varying specularity. A little bit helps, but too much will appear odd and will call attention to it.

The only way to accurately judge these maps is to render the image. Figure 9.21 shows the results of the extra hair geometry and the transparency maps. Note how the edges of the hair have some softer dimensionality to them. You can add even more hair piece layers, but with each transparency map, the render times will increase dramatically with each layer. Such is the price we pay when striving for detail and realism.

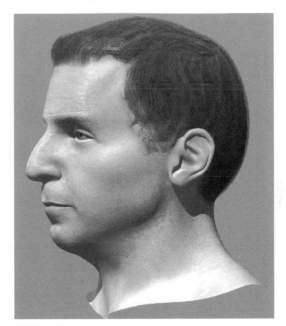

FIGURE 9.21   The extra hair geometry rendered to show the transparency.

You can use this layering technique to create long hair as well. To illustrate this, follow along with this simple tutorial.

We will be creating hair strips. These are simple rectangular strips of geometry that will have the transparency, color, specularity, and bump maps applied to them. As in the previous example, they will be layered to create depth.

To begin, make a flat box with 3 × 6 divisions, although the actual number isn't that crucial. Surface this as "HairLayer1." Make a planar UV map to cover this form. See Figure 9.22.

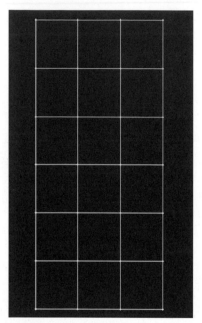

FIGURE 9.22   Make a hair strip.

Duplicate this object twice and put the copies on separate layers. Now, we will model each piece slightly differently, giving them the bends and curves of a strip of hair. Separate each layer by a small amount so that the strips are not intersecting. See Figure 9.23.

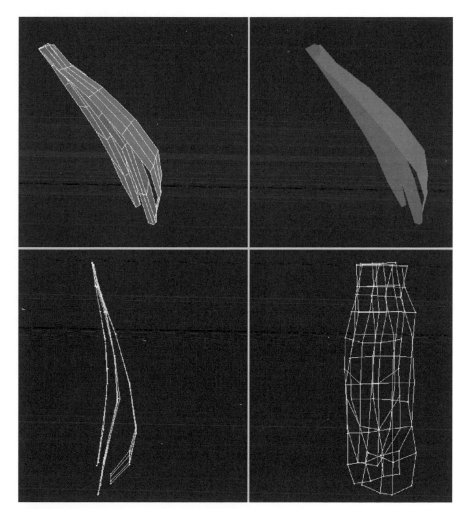

FIGURE 9.23   Model the hair strips.

Again, you need to generate a UV painting template. Bring this into the paint program, paint three separate black and white hair maps, and then save them as individual files. See Figure 9.24. These will be used in various capacities, as you will see.

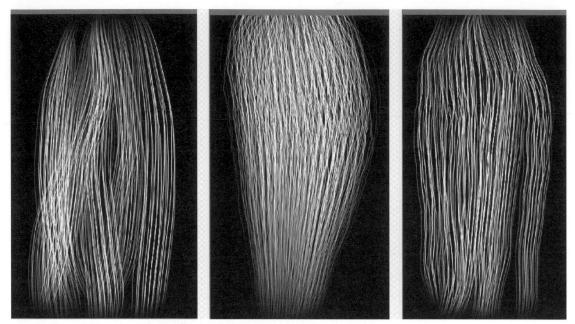

FIGURE 9.24 Paint three separate black and white hair maps.

Also, paint a simple hair color map, as seen in Figure 9.25. We've used one for this example, but you can use more for variety if you like.

FIGURE 9.25 Paint a simple hair color map.

In your rendering software, load the hair strip models and apply the black and white maps to each one in these material channels, respectively: transparency, bump, and specularity. You do not need to set the bump and specularity maps too high, but they will give some subtle shading to the hairs. Apply the color map to the color channel of all three hair strips. Render the hair strips so you can view the hair. See Figure 9.26.

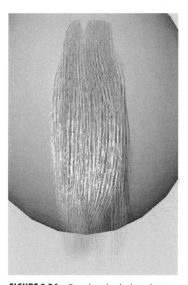

FIGURE 9.26   Render the hair strips.

You can create numerous strips to cover a head and then model the strips into different styles.

HAIR GENERATORS

Layered hair strips create the illusion of hair nicely, but sometimes you may need even more realism than they can offer. Much of today's software comes with, or has access to, programs to help generate hair on models. These are usually referred to as hair and fur simulators, and they take away much of the manual work of modeling hair. These simulators offer many parameters for "growing" the hair or fur right off of the model, and they include many of the aspects that we have created with maps, such as color and specularity. There are also features to help "comb" the hair in different directions. See Figure 9.27.

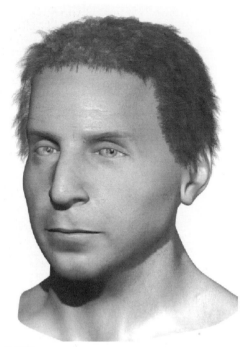

FIGURE 9.27   An example of hair grown off the surface of the model using a hair generator.

If you adjust the settings, you can get different looks for the hair, as in Figure 9.28.

With hair simulators, you can get natural, random effects such as fly-away hairs. You can also grow or place guide hairs on the model to help style the hair. These are usually splines of some sort, simple geometry that doesn't render. Each guide hair can represent hundreds or thousands of rendered hairs. As a result, you do not need to place one guide hair for every hair on the head. Figure 9.29 shows an example of long hair guides placed on the head.

Figure 9.30 shows the resulting rendering from the hair guides. This is probably what Frank looked like in his younger years.

You can also apply motion to these guides to allow movement either by adding bones in them or by applying some motion simulation. The latter makes the process more automated but also more complicated, taking more computational power during rendering.

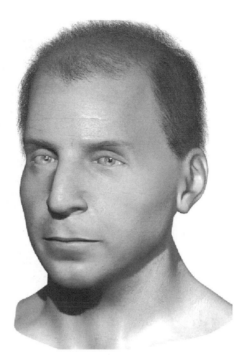

FIGURE 9.28   Adjust the settings to get different looks for the hair.

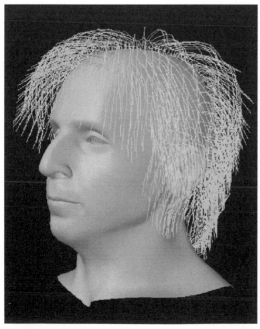

FIGURE 9.29   Long hair guides placed on the head.

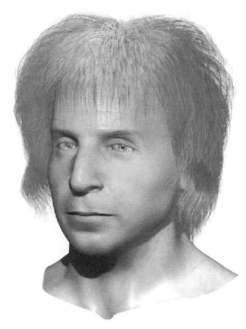

FIGURE 9.30   The resulting rendering from the hair guides.

Hair and fur simulators produce realistic results that would be hard or impossible to achieve with the other methods mentioned in this chapter. However, hair and fur simulators can be expensive, whether they come included with the software (higher-end) or purchased separately as a plug-in (a separate program that links up to your main software). Also be aware that when you use these simulators, it usually takes longer to render images. In addition, you must pay extra attention when you light the hair.

For these reasons, you must evaluate if using a simulator is worth it, considering how your characters will be seen and used. Many times, even if a hair simulator is available, it is still quicker to use a cheaper hair trick, as described earlier.

LASHES

One last bit of hair detail we will deal with is the lashes. These are easy to make and will add more subtle detail to your character's eyes. We have lashes on the top and bottom of our eyelids, the upper being the largest and most prominent. We usually associate eye lashes with women wearing mascara, but everybody has them.

The first method of creating lashes involves very simple geometry. We will achieve the illusion of the actual lashes by using image maps. To begin, have the head model loaded and zoom into the eye area. Create a flat rectangle divided in three segments. We will then bend this to hug the contour of the upper eyelid. See Figure 9.31.

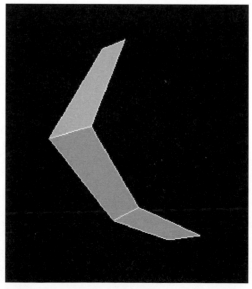

FIGURE 9.31　Start the upper eyelash.

Figure 9.32 shows the lash placed against the upper lid.

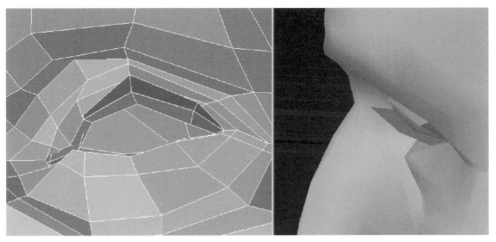

FIGURE 9.32   The lash placed against the upper lid.

Since we will be subdividing the lash along with the head, we will want some extra geometry to help it hold its shape. Split the faces, as shown in Figure 9.33. This new geometry will also allow us to give the lashes some curl. You can make the lower lash in the same way or by duplicating the upper lash and rotating it. Remember to make the lower lashes smaller than the upper ones.

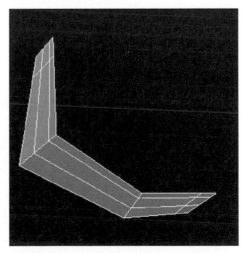

FIGURE 9.33   Add extra geometry to the lashes.

Next, position the lashes against the lids. See Figure 9.34.

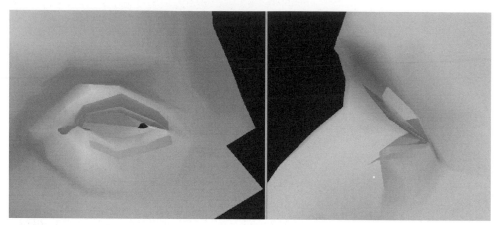

FIGURE 9.34   Position the lashes against the lids.

Now we need to assign some UV coordinates to the lashes so we can texture them. The obvious choice here is planar mapping. If the lash geometry is angled a little too much, rotate it so that it lies flatter. After the UV map is assigned, you can rotate it back. Make a planar UV map along the *Y* axis for the lashes. You will probably need to move or rotate the lash geometry in the UV editing window so that the lashes do not overlap and to take advantage of the space. Figure 9.35 shows the UV layout of the lashes. Export this as a painting template.

Load the template into your paint program. We will be painting transparency maps again, so we need just a grayscale color scheme. Carefully paint the lashes, tapering them at the tips. The best way to do this is to use a drawing tablet, which will allow the color and width of the brush to lessen as the pressure is released. Observe real lashes and notice the variations in them. Do not make each one equal. Draw some close or stuck together. See Figure 9.36.

Save this with an appropriate filename. In your rendering program, load the head model with the lashes and assign the lash image map to the transparency channel. When the lashes are rendered, most of the geometry will disappear due to the transparency, leaving the illusion of the lash. For a subtle bit of dimension, also assign the lash image to the bump channel. Adjust the lash image until you are happy with the results. See Figure 9.37.

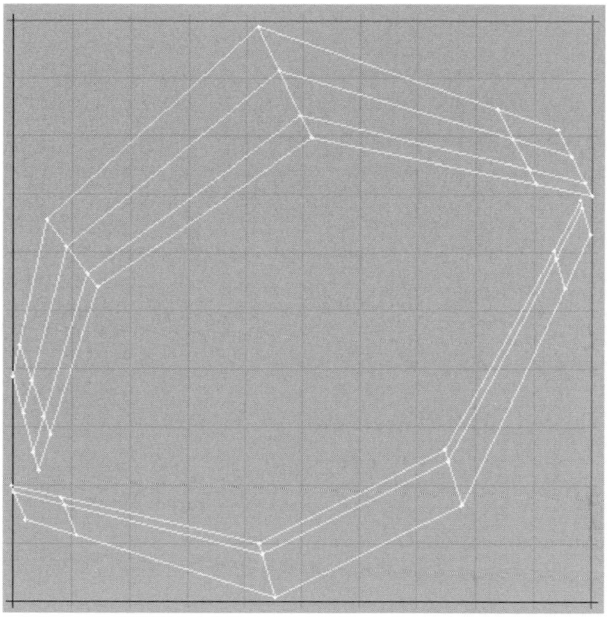

FIGURE 9.35   The UV layout of the lashes.

FIGURE 9.36   Paint the lashes over the template.

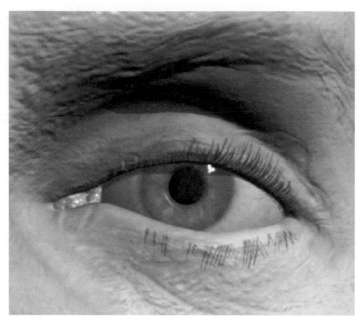

FIGURE 9.37   The transparency mapped lash geometry.

This technique will work well in many cases, but sometimes you might have to get really close and will want more from the lashes. In this case, we will make them individually out of geometry. Again, we will just model one and will let the computer do much of the work in duplicating the lashes.

A lash is a simple shape. Begin by creating a segmented rectangle, as seen in Figure 9.38.

Then, taper it towards its tip, as seen in Figure 9.39.

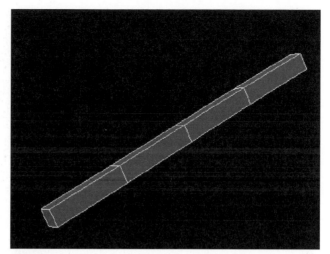

FIGURE 9.38   For an individual lash, begin by creating a segmented rectangle.

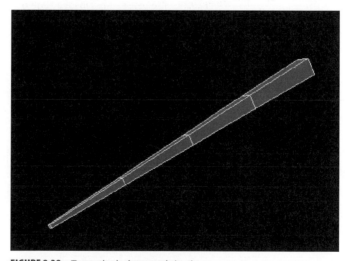

FIGURE 9.39   Taper the lash towards its tip.

Lastly, give the whole form a bend, as seen in Figure 9.40.

You now have an eyelash. There are various ways to duplicate this lash along the eyelids. You can manually make new copies and position them. As you make a few copies, copy that group and move it to duplicate a number at a time instead of just one. If your software allows, you

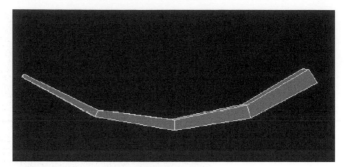

FIGURE 9.40   Give the whole form a bend.

can clone copies of the lash along the geometry of the eyelids. You can also clone copies along a spline path that conforms to the lids. Whichever method you choose, remember that it's important to add variety and randomness to your lashes. See Figure 9.41.

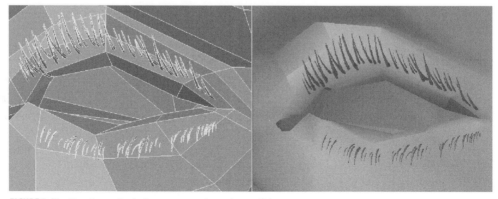

FIGURE 9.41   Duplicate the lash geometry along the eyelids.

Figure 9.42 shows the rendering of the geometry to create the eyelashes.

The geometry to create the eyelashes has the advantage of being true geometry that you can shade. However, the extra geometry does push up the complexity of the model. This complexity can take longer to render and may require more memory to display.

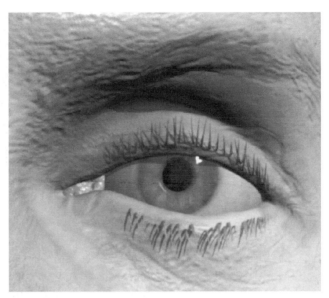

FIGURE 9.42　The geometry to create the eyelashes.

SUMMARY

This wraps up the challenge of creating hair on our digital human. It is, no doubt, one of the toughest aspects of the model. We now have a number of techniques up our sleeves to produce convincing hair in just about any software. We learned how to use simple hair geometry as well as the hair simulation features in more advanced software. As with most facets of this process, the most valuable tools are good observation, attention to detail, and patience. Turn the page to find out how we can bring our human to life.

10

SIGNS OF LIFE

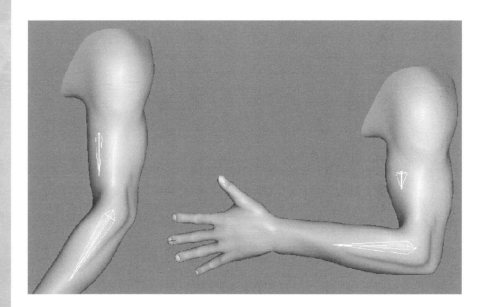

POSITIONING THE MODEL FOR BONES

Chances are, you will want your digital human to come to life in some way beyond the splayed position it was modeled in. The obvious choice for creating the illusion of life is to animate your person, but even if your desired final output is still images, a character will usually be posed in some action or natural gesture.

If you are just looking to put your character in a static pose, a straightforward method of doing this is to select faces or vertices of the joints or body parts and then just bend or rotate them. You can do this technique in even the simplest 3D programs. This is an easy concept to get your mind around, but in reality it does involve quite a bit of clean-up work and remodeling to get the anatomy to look good again. Each new pose requires you to create a separate sculpture.

Luckily, most 3D animation programs have features called "Bones." They act in much the same way as the bones in our body; they allow you to position whatever model they are placed inside. Bones are usually represented in all programs in a similar tetrahedral shape and do not show up in final renderings. See Figure 10.1.

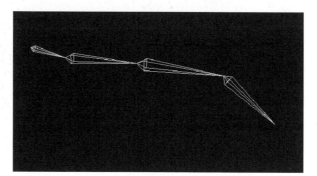

FIGURE 10.1   Animation bones.

Even if you want to create still images of a character, inserting bones is good idea because doing so allows you to easily create a variety of poses.

Rigging a character for animation is an art in itself. The process can become quite complex, and a full exploration of this deep subject is beyond the scope of the book. This chapter offers a basic overview of bringing a human model to life that can be applied in most 3D packages.

The Neutral Pose

Right now, we have our digital human modeled in a T shape. This is also called the DaVinci or Christ pose. This is a typical neutral pose since the arms are outstretched halfway between the fully up and the down-by-the-sides position. It is easy to model and texture in this shape since the geometry lies on straight planes. It also may seem the most logical position to have a model in before you insert bones. See Figure 10.2.

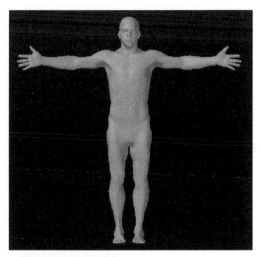

FIGURE 10.2   The typical neutral pose for modeling, texturing, and setting up bones.

However, you can get some undesirable deformations when the model starts in this neutral position. Specifically, there will be problems around the arm, shoulder, and chest areas. We take for granted how much shifting of anatomy goes on when we do something as simple as raise our arms. Muscles change shape in several spots. A simple bone setup in a 3D package doesn't take into account what the shoulder muscles would do when the arm is lowered. Usually, you can make the shoulder area look only so good, even using some complex tricks. Figure 10.3 shows the model from this book posed with one arm bent downwards using bones. Apparent problem areas are the shoulder, under the arm, and the chest. Our pectoral muscles fan out when our arms are outstretched, and compact when they are down. Since the pectorals extend from the rib cage into the upper arm, it is very difficult to control all aspects of this muscle with bones.

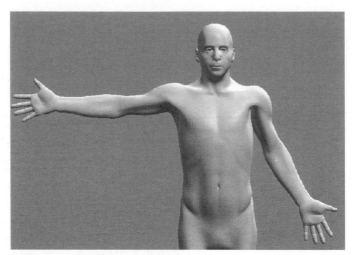

FIGURE 10.3 Problems arise in the chest and shoulders when you rotate the arm down.

What do we do about this issue? The T pose may be good for modeling, but it does not represent the most natural position a human will be in. Most of the time, our arms are down by our sides. However, modeling and texturing a model with his arms in that position makes it difficult to work in between the arm and the body. It will also cause problems when we raise the arms with bones.

A good middle-ground neutral pose for adding bones would be having the arms partially down, at a 30- to 45-degree angle, and slightly forward. This position creates minimal distortion when the model lowers his arms. Using this position could create problems if the model raises his arm straight up, but you must assess how often your character will be doing that. Later in this chapter, we will cover some tricks to help with this. Another way to handle it would be to make a separate model for scenes when the arms are in those extremes.

For this example, we will make a new neutral pose—arms partially down and forward. Therefore, we will have to remodel our digital human somewhat. Why didn't we just model it this way to begin with? As mentioned, it is easier to model and texture with the arms on level planes. Don't worry, though; the work we have already done is not lost or wasted.

Make sure you save this new pose as a separate model so you can return to it if you desire.

We will first focus on the forearm and hand area. The forearm is a tricky bit of anatomy since its two bones, the ulna and radius, interact in a unique way; the radius twists over the ulna when the arm rotates. See Figure 10.4.

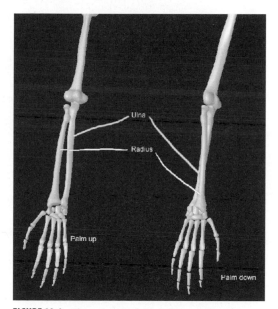

FIGURE 10.4   The twisting of the radius over the ulna.

This, in turn, causes a complex twisting of the forearm muscles. It's difficult to visualize how to model the forearm in the rotated position, so we will need to construct our model with the bones and muscles in a more linear position.

However, the rotated position is a pretty common one for the arm. Rather than trying to achieve this with bones, we will alter our neutral-pose model.

Begin by selecting the vertices or faces of the hand and wrist and give them a slight rotation. We will not be rotating the whole forearm in one motion; rather, it will be a series of twists, and each time we will select a little more geometry. See Figure 10.5.

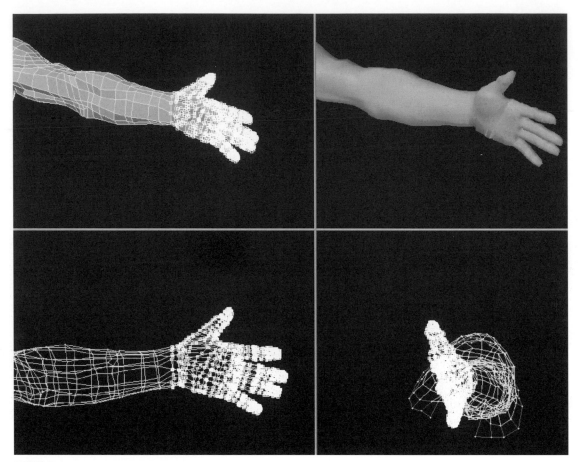

FIGURE 10.5 Start rotating the forearm.

Expand the selection by one or two rows down the forearm, and continue the rotation. See Figure 10.6.

Perform this a few more times, stopping before the elbow. When you are done, the palm of the hand should be facing downward. You may need to do some clean-up sculpting to get the arm to look natural. Be sure to use a reference to get the shape right. See Figure 10.7.

Once you're done with that, give the whole lower arm (forearm and hand) a little bend at the elbow, as seen in Figure 10.8.

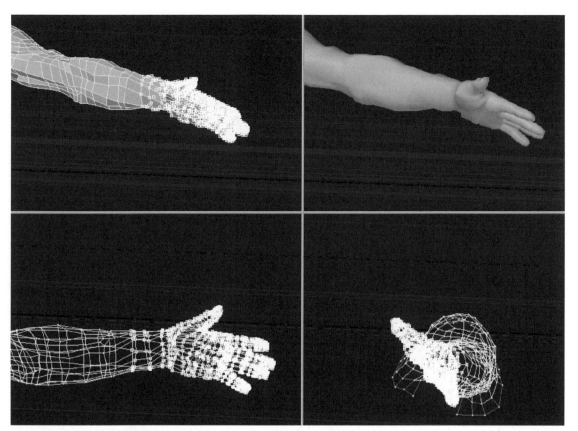

FIGURE 10.6   Continue the rotation.

We will now bend the whole arm down and forward. This will take some remodeling of the shoulder and chest, but just take it slow and it will come together. For instance, select all the vertices of the arm well into the shoulder and give it a small rotation down. Then decrease your selection and do another rotation, and then another. We're using the same method as when we rotated the forearm. You do not want to try to move too much at once. If you do, you'll just need to do more cleanup. Figure 10.9 shows the rotation of the whole arm.

That is not so say that we don't have any cleanup to do already. Areas such as under the arm and the chest will need a little work, as you can

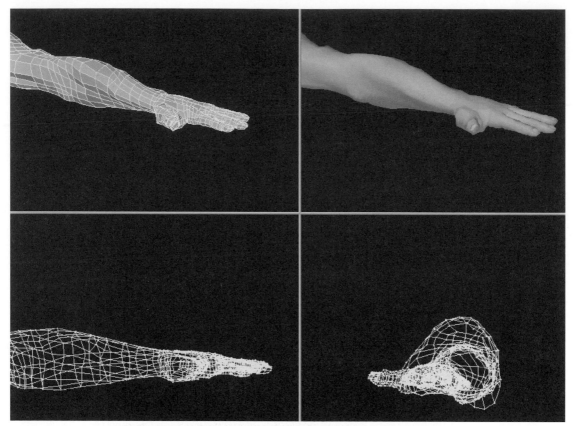

FIGURE 10.7 The completed forearm rotation.

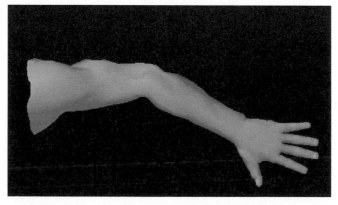

FIGURE 10.8 Give the whole lower arm a little bend at the elbow.

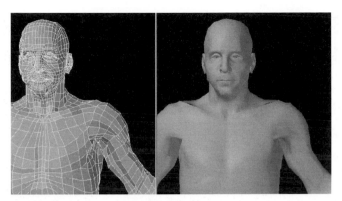

FIGURE 10.9   Begin the rotation of the arm.

see in Figure 10.9. Tools such as Smooth or Average Vertices will help make those spots visually easier to deal with. See Figure 10.10.

The shoulder area also needs some major attention. The shoulders will most likely bulge out a bit unnaturally from the rotation. This bulge looked fine when the arms were up, but it doesn't reflect how the muscle would flatten a little when they are lowered. You should drop the shoulders a little, since the live model will often raise or hunch the

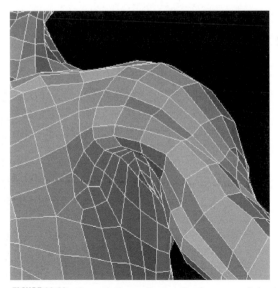

FIGURE 10.10   Smooth the vertices under the arm and chest.

shoulders in the arms-up position. A Magnet or Soft Selection tool will help shape the shoulders without obliterating the form. See Figure 10.11.

From here, it is a matter of working on the chest muscles and how they attach to the arm. Bring this geometry down a little, as in Figure 10.12.

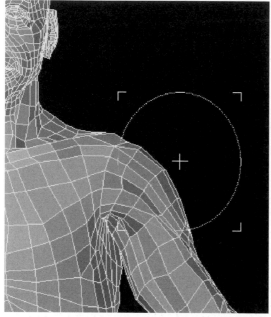

FIGURE 10.11 Reduce the shoulder bulge with a Magnet or Soft Selection tool.

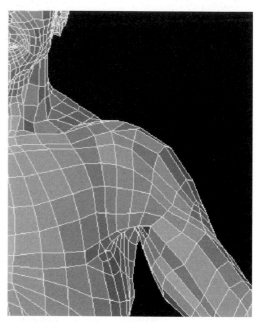

FIGURE 10.12 Adjust the chest geometry.

That about does it for our new neutral pose. Your results should look something like Figure 10.13. This small bit of work we just did will do wonders for when the model is posed with bones.

BUILDING A HUMAN ANIMATION SKELETON

When we talk about building a human animation skeleton, we are not referring to the bones in our physical body, but the ones in our digital body. It's beneficial to understand our real skeletons, but we will not replicate a skeleton exactly in 3D. Instead, we will build a 3D version that functions the same but will not look the same in every aspect.

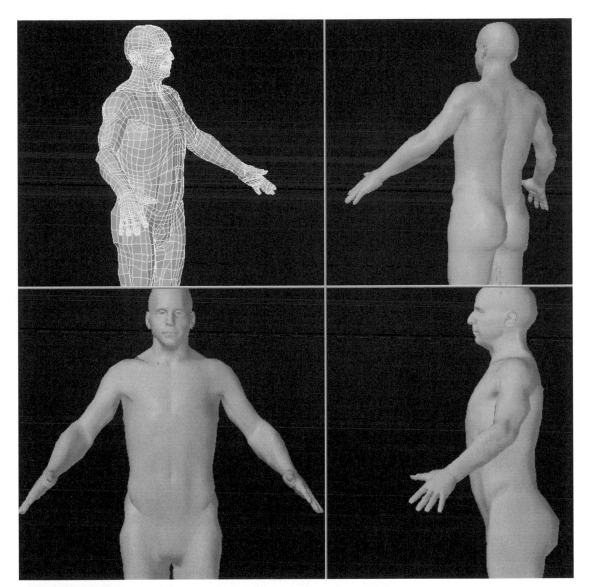

FIGURE 10.13   The finished new neutral pose.

Most 3D packages allow you to easily create joints by simply drawing them on the screen. When you draw one joint after another, the new joint becomes the child of the previous one. This sets up a hierarchy so that the child inherits the rotations and movements of the parent. You should make sure that the arms are parented to a bone on the spine so that when the body bends, the arms will follow.

First, we will look at a basic skeleton and see how we can improve it for our purposes. Most programs that support bones allow you to draw the joints on the screen with the mouse. This is how this skeleton was created. See Figure 10.14.

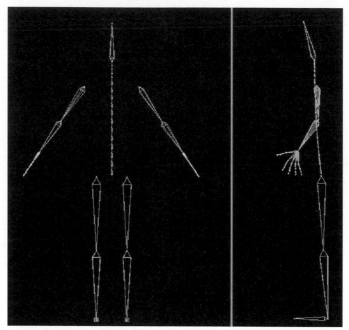

FIGURE 10.14 A basic skeleton.

We will work our way from top to bottom, and will discuss a few simple changes that will help with animation. Our first stop is the upper arm/shoulder area. While most of our arm movement does come from the arm bones, a bone or two from the spine to the upper arm does help in more natural movement. Having a shoulder joint will allow for shoulder movement that will affect areas of the upper torso as well. See Figure 10.15.

Next, you can break up the forearm into two, or even three, joints. This may look odd but will allow us to simulate the twisting of the ulna and radius. It may prove unnecessarily complicated to try and rig two bones that twist over each other the way the real counterparts do. See Figure 10.16.

While the human spine has 24 vertebrae, it may prove overkill to include that many in the animation skeleton. In fact, depending on the

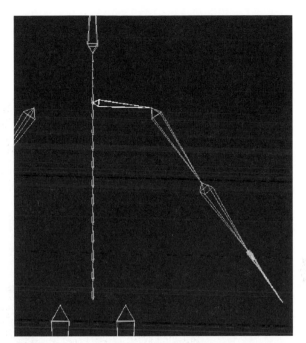

FIGURE 10.15   Add a shoulder joint.

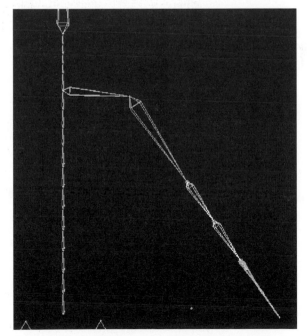

FIGURE 10.16   Split the forearm bone to allow for twisting.

character, you may need only a small fraction of that—as few as five. Additionally, the chest area with the rib cage doesn't bend a great deal, so we can place fewer joints there in our digital human. In addition, we should also connect, or parent, the upper leg joint to the spine. See Figure 10.17.

Now jump down to the foot. The ankle joint here is in the wrong place. You need to move it up to where the joint actually bends. This may look odd but is more accurate. While we are here, we can break the foot bone up into two joints; this will allow the character to stand on the ball of his foot. We can also add toe joints, depending on the animation needs, but for this example they are not necessary. See Figure 10.18.

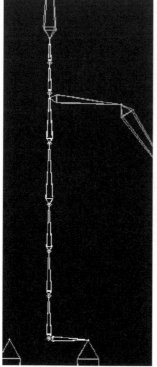

FIGURE 10.17 Reduce the number of spine joints.

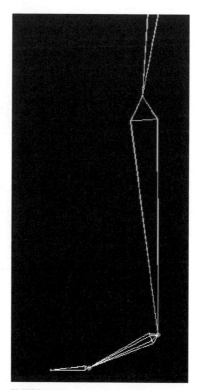

FIGURE 10.18 Adjust the ankle joint position and break the foot up into two joints.

Joint Types

Now that we have set up a skeleton, it is important to understand the different joint types and how they will bend. When bones are initially created, they will move freely on every axis.

In the knee and elbow you will find a hinge-type joint. These joints move in only one direction, much like a lid on a box or a single-shaft pivot. Limiting these areas to this type of movement will prevent unnatural and painful-looking poses. See Figure 10.19.

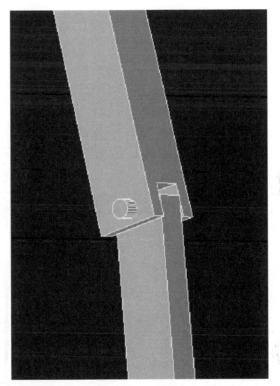

FIGURE 10.19   The hinge pivot.

A ball-and-socket joint is found in the shoulder and hip areas. This allows the greatest range of movement as the joint can rotate freely in most directions in a cup-like cavity. See Figure 10.20.

Limited moveable joints are found in the spine. This type of joint allows rotation in all directions but to a much lesser degree than the ball-and-socket. The spine bends more as a whole unit than at individual joints. The spongy cartilage between the vertebrae allows for this. See Figure 10.21.

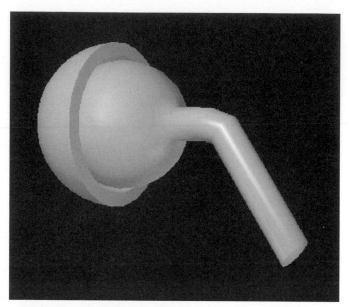

FIGURE 10.20   The ball-and-socket joint.

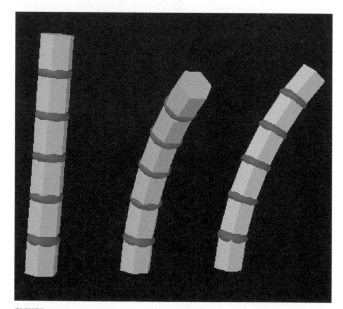

FIGURE 10.21   The limited movement joints found in the spine.

Areas such as the interaction between the ulna and radius represent a pivot-type joint. This is where a cylindrical form rotates around a shaft. See Figure 10.22.

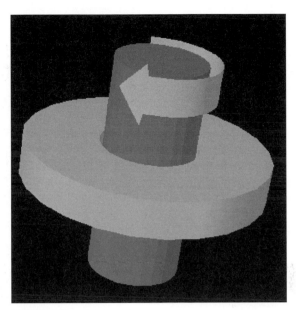

FIGURE 10.22   The pivot joint.

Determining the correct joint type is the first step of making a good skeleton. The next is to set the joint rotation limits so that the joint will not go past a certain number of degrees. Figure 10.23 shows a limited joint. This is helpful for areas such as the knees, which you do not want to bend backwards. Most programs allow you to turn off axis channels that you do not want to rotate as well as to set numeric values for the amount of rotation on desired channels.

Controlling Vertices

Once you have created the skeleton, it is time to attach the mesh to it. You can usually do this with a simple click or two. Once the skeleton is attached to the mesh, however, there are a few ways of determining how the bones affect the mesh. You want the individual bones to grab the appropriate vertices of the mesh. This is usually referred to as *influence* or *envelop*.

The simplest method offered by some programs requires you just to attach the skeleton to the mesh, and then leave it up to the algorithm of the bones to grab the correct vertices. But we all should know that when you leave things up to chance, they might not work as expected. Often, unwanted vertices become attached to the wrong bones. Figure 10.24 shows a portion of the chest being affected by the upper arm bone.

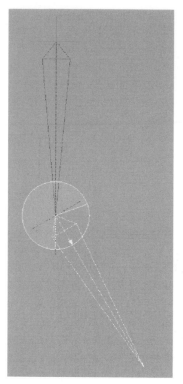

FIGURE 10.23 Limit the joint movement.

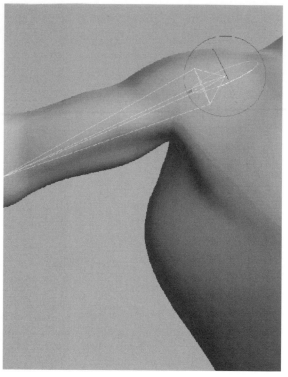

FIGURE 10.24 A portion of the chest being affected by the upper arm bone.

You can remedy this by inserting hold bones. These bones (such as a limb bone) will not be animated; rather, they are put in place to hold certain geometry from being affected by other bones. Figure 10.25 shows hold bones put in the chest to keep it in place as the arm is raised.

Your model and movement will determine how many hold bones your digital human will need. The hold bones usually work well; however, they do add more items to a scene and increase the model's complexity. Another way you can use hold bones is in other functions such as making the character breathe. You can size chest hold bones up and down, thus pushing out the mesh and creating the illusion of breathing.

Another method of controlling the bones involves setting up a capsule-shaped force field or range of influence around the bone. All vertices within will be affected by that particular bone. This is easy to set up, but it gets somewhat difficult to grab the correct vertices in some areas. These spheres of influence can have a maximum and minimum value, enabling

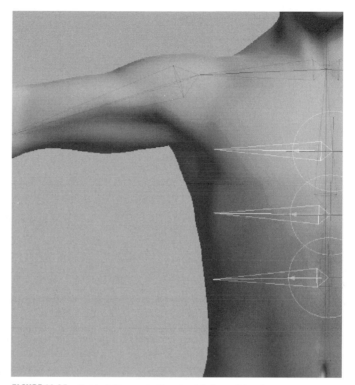

FIGURE 10.25   Put hold bones in the chest to keep it in place.

a soft edge effect. Again, you can use extra bones to hold certain areas. See Figure 10.26.

The most precise method of assigning specific vertices to bones is using point weighting. Here, you can have the ultimate control over every vertex on the model. Typically, most programs allow you to paint the weight influence over the mesh. Then you can assign a bone or bones to that weight map, which can be named so that it's easy for you to identify it later. Weight values can taper and soften over an area, giving a more natural deformation as a bone moves. See Figure 10.27.

Because you can be so specific when assigning vertices with this method, you don't need to use hold bones. As a result, the skeleton can be more efficient. But with more control comes more set-up time and more aspects to keep track of. For this reason, using weights for bones may be overkill on simple models or projects. The best way to see what method suits you is to try the simplest approach first and see if its

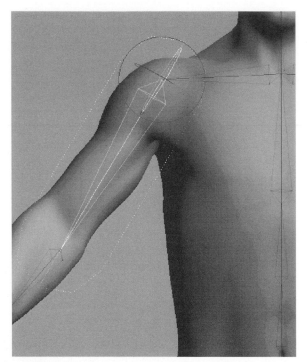

FIGURE 10.26 Bones can have a sphere of influence to affect geometry.

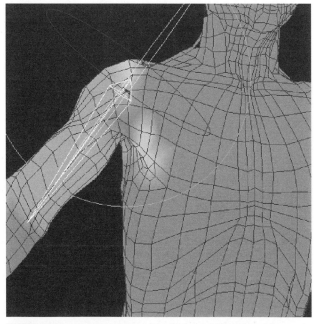

FIGURE 10.27 Assign weight values for bone influence on the mesh.

limitations hamper the project. If they do, then bump up the control level with added bones, or go to weighting, if your software offers it.

MUSCLES

Once you have your skeleton in place and moving in a correct manner, you will want to fine-tune how the mesh deforms. In the case of a human, we will want some simulated muscle movement.

When you first bend the joints of a mesh, certain areas might not look too pretty. For example, an arm can crimp much like a bent garden hose. See Figure 10.28.

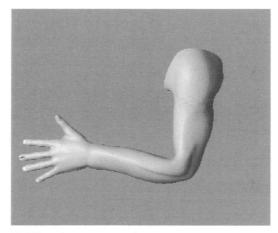

FIGURE 10.28   Bones can crimp an arm like a garden hose.

Therefore, we need to use some tricks to simulate muscles. Again, your options will depend on the program you use. The solutions range from simple to complex.

The easiest solution comes in the form of skin deformers. These are settings or control lattices that will affect a specific joint on the skeleton and the surrounding vertices on the mesh. See Figure 10.29. You can gain a decent amount of control over how the mesh deforms, and this may be good enough in many cases.

Extra bones can help you create muscle bulges and other natural-looking deformations. "Muscle bones" are specifically created to deform an area of the mesh so that you can simulate muscle contraction and re-laxation. These special bones can be key framed (whereby you record a

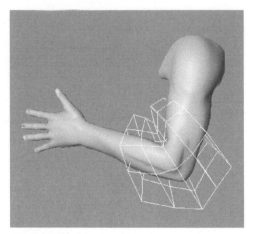

FIGURE 10.29   A lattice helps when you want to deform an arm.

marker for the place, rotation, and size on the timeline during animation) at the appropriate moments during the animation.

You can automate this process by setting up an expression or a set driven key feature. Expressions are mathematical formulas that modify the values of an item based on many parameters of others. For instance, an expression can change the size of a muscle bone based on the rotation of a forearm bone. Your software may have preset expressions for many common formulas so that you do not have to know the math to plug it in. Figure 10.30 illustrates how a set driven key was used on a biceps muscle bone to change its size to simulate the contraction and bulge of that muscle based on the rotation of the forearm bone.

The next level of muscle control is to actually model the changed muscle shape as a morph target or shape displacement. These displacements are normally associated with facial expression shapes but can occur anywhere on the model. In this case, again, the rotation of a bone will trigger the displacement.

Some programs allow you to model the morph shape on a mesh while it is being deformed by the bones; others do not. If your program doesn't allow you to do this, just make the best guesses you can and perform tests.

Figure 10.31 shows a biceps contraction shape created through a modeled displacement shape and triggered when the forearm is rotated. Modeling a muscle shape gives you a great deal of control in the look of the final deformation as you are pulling and pushing every vertex into place yourself. Nothing is left to chance. You can sculpt the muscle ex-

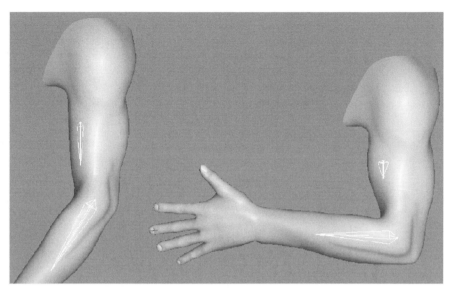

FIGURE 10.30   Use a set driven key to simulate the contraction and bulge of a muscle based on the rotation of the forearm bone.

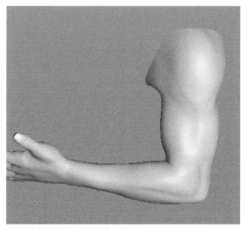

FIGURE 10.31   A biceps contraction shape created through a modeled displacement.

actly the way you want. The downside is that you may need to create many of these displacement shapes for an entire figure. To avoid unnecessary effort, decide on where to place these morph shapes based on your needs, storyboards, and tests. It may turn out that only a few spots would benefit from this work.

The current trend in many high-end productions that utilize computer graphics for character animation is simulating a character's muscles. This involves actually building muscle and bone geometry that flexes and moves realistically. This, in turn, deforms the outer "skin." The results are incredibly realistic as there really is a sense of anatomy moving beneath the skin.

As you might imagine, this simulation increases the model's complexity. Not only do you have to create the bones and muscles as geometry, but you also have to work out how they interact with the animation skeleton. You need a deep understanding of anatomy to determine where muscles attach and at which bones. These muscles have to be rigged to bulge, jiggle, and stretch appropriately, which may require more bones or simulations. Finally, all of this has to react properly with the skin.

If your software offers some sort of collision detection with rigid and soft bodies, such as a cloth simulator, you can adopt it for muscle simulation.

If you are taking this approach, you don't have to create every muscle and bone in the body. Muscles can be grouped for simplicity. Figure 10.32 shows a simple muscle simulation for an arm. As the animation skeleton changes, the various muscles do too, thus changing the outer skin.

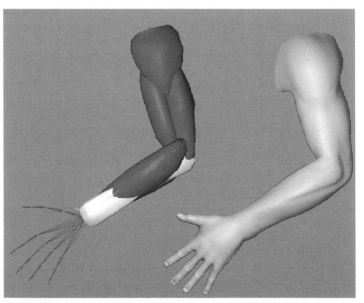

FIGURE 10.32   A muscle simulation for an arm.

Creating this type of set-up is not something you want to attempt lightly, but it can add a new level of realism to your animation should you feel up to the challenge.

FACIAL EXPRESSIONS

Facial expression is, of course, an important part of bringing a digital human to life. A face will truly look alive if you create a few well-done expressions. Humans are capable of a myriad of facial expressions that capture a wide range of emotions, and they all emanate from a very concentrated area.

Speech also creates facial expressions. When you animate your character's dialog, the mouth takes various shapes, depending on what phonemes are being spoken. You do not need to form every letter of the alphabet; oral shapes can be broken down into several basics. The following is a list of the minimum phoneme shapes; they can be combined to form many more:

1. O, as in toad
2. A, as in cake
3. F, V
4. W
5. T, D (these require the mouth to be open and the tongue to be visible)
6. E, as in beat
7. P, B
8. M
9. Oo, as in smooth
10. Th (the tongue would show between the teeth)

The best tool you can have for facial reference is a mirror. Practice forming the various phonemes in front of it and you will gain a great deal of insight into how to model these shapes.

Expressions come in six basic, universal categories that have many mixtures and variations: anger, sadness, joy, fear, disgust, and surprise. It is important to understand your character's personality and his motivations when you are determining a facial expression. An evil warlord's smile will have a different feel than that of a friendly wood elf.

If you want to accurately model facial expressions, it's important to understand the underlying anatomy of the face and the muscles that help form our expressions. See Figure 10.33.

Here is a list of the facial muscles along with their basic function:

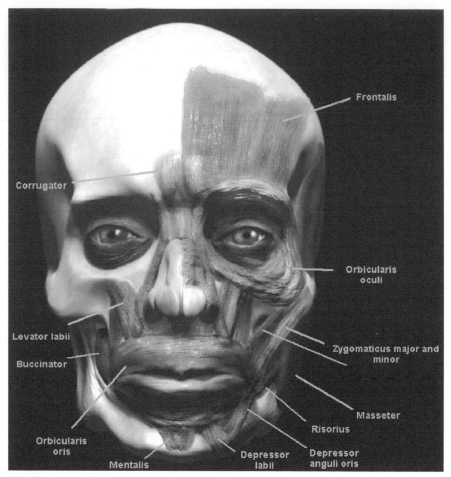

FIGURE 10.33 The facial muscles.

Frontalis. This pulls the eyebrows up (creates surprise).

Corrugator. This pulls the eyebrows down (creates a frown).

Orbicularis oculi. The contraction of this results in squinting and crow's feet (wrinkles around the eye).

Levator labii. This pulls up the top lip (creates a sneer).

Zygomaticus major. This pulls the mouth corners into a smile.

Risorius. This pulls the mouth muscles down and to the side (crying).

Orbicularis oris. This curls and tightens the lips.

Depressor labii. This pulls the bottom lip down, as when you are speaking.

Mentalis. This wrinkles the chin and pushes the lower lip up (pouting).

When you are ready to change the model's facial shape, one way is to add bones to the face. Figure 10.34 shows a head and facial expression created with numerous small bones placed in various locations. A ring of bones is placed around the mouth to simulate the Orbicularis oris muscle, which is the large muscle that surrounds the mouth. Two bones were placed above the eyebrows. The cheek area has two bones situated and angled to where the Zygomaticus major muscle would be. You can also use weight maps to control where the bones influence various sections of the face. Alternatively, you can place hold bones in areas of the face (such as the nose) where you do not want excess movement.

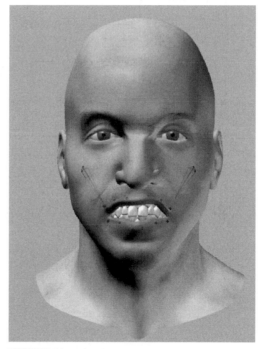

FIGURE 10.34   A facial expression created by placing numerous small bones in a head model.

When you are placing bones to create a facial expression, you can simply grab the bones and move them until you achieve the desired shape. This almost feels like you are manipulating a digital puppet, so this technique may be a bit cumbersome to attempt speech.

A more popular method of creating the facial expressions is to model them individually as morph targets or displacement shapes. This involves pulling and pushing the vertices until you achieve the expression, and then recalling it later when needed during animation. To model the face, you can use any deformation tools your software offers, including the aforementioned bone method or wire deformers. Once you have shaped the face into an expression, you can save the file.

You can create modeled facial expressions in a couple ways. One is to model the whole face into the desired shape. The other is to model sections of the face and then blend them later during animation. For instance, you can model expressions for the mouth, brows, and eyes separately. This allows you to take a mix and match approach when creating the desired expression. Most software offers a mixing panel with sliders for ramping up or down and mixing the different modeled shapes. See Figure 10.35.

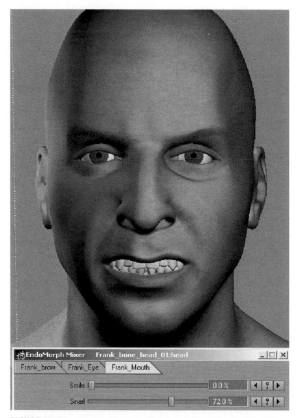

FIGURE 10.35 Most software offers a mixing panel with sliders that allow you to mix the different modeled shapes.

Creating an Expression: The Smile

The following tutorial will show you how to create a smile. The smile is a deceptively simple image to create on a 3D model, but it does require a balance of many factors to get it to look correct.

When someone smiles, much of the action happens on the lower half of the face. There will also be some subtle changes to the eyes.

We all know how to draw a smile. See Figure 10.36. A simple curved line is all it takes to convey one.

FIGURE 10.36   The drawn smile.

However, if we attempt to replicate this on our 3D model, it will look decidedly odd. See Figure 10.37.

A smile doesn't happen just on one plane of the face. The major underlying force behind the smile is the Zygomaticus major muscle (also known as the smiling muscle). This attaches to the side of the head and to the corner of the mouth. When it contracts, it will raise and pull it back. See Figure 10.38.

Therefore, we should pull the vertices in that direction while creating this expression. This muscular action is also going to affect other parts of the face, not just the corners of the mouth. As the corners pull back, the flesh around it will be affected. In this case, our nasallabial fold intensifies. See Figure 10.39.

Continuing this chain reaction, the cheeks will rise and push out. See Figure 10.40.

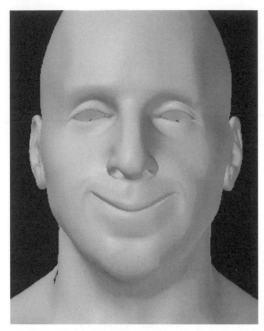

FIGURE 10.37 A smile looks odd when just you just curl the mouth.

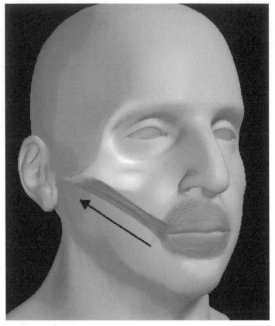

FIGURE 10.38 The Zygomaticus major muscle's line of contraction for a smile.

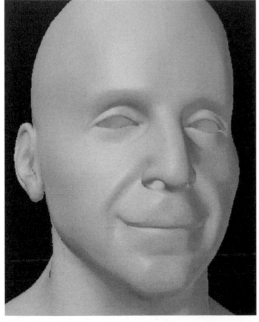

FIGURE 10.39 As you smile, the nasallabial fold intensifies.

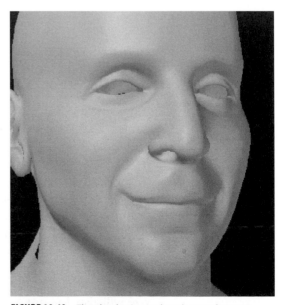

FIGURE 10.40 The cheeks rise and push out when you smile.

The eyes will also be affected. The lower lid will certainly rise and will appear straighter across the eye. See Figure 10.41.

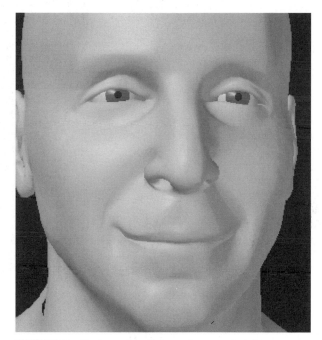

FIGURE 10.41   The lower lid will rise and appear straighter.

Depending on the intensity of the smile, the upper lids may close as well, making the eyes squinty.

We are not quite done. Jump back down to the lips. As the smile broadens, the volume of the lips becomes thinner. If the lips are kept together, it will appear as if the person is stifling a smile, for at some point the lips will part and reveal the teeth. When you model this, it is important to have the teeth geometry present. Make sure the lips do not pass through the teeth. See Figure 10.42.

On the polygonal end, it is important that the faces retain roughly the same volume as they started with in the neutral face.

This means that when you model the changes for facial shapes, you should try to maintain the polygons' size ratio; don't stretch or compress them too much. If you don't maintain their size, the results will reflect the most in the texture maps as areas will stretch or compress noticeably; you will also find unnatural movement on the face during animation. See Figure 10.43.

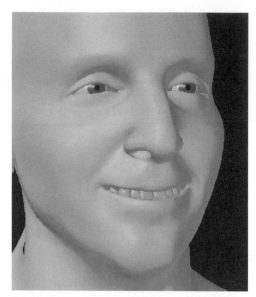

FIGURE 10.42 As the smile broadens, the lips thin and part.

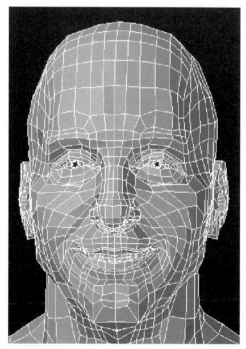

FIGURE 10.43 When you create a facial shape, it is important that the faces retain roughly the same volume as before.

SUMMARY

Bringing the digital human to life demands much from the artist—from the technical to the aesthetic. If you have never attempted any of this before, start simple and work up to more complex techniques. Determine your needs and build accordingly. You may find that a basic skeletal set-up works just fine. But before you have your character recite all of *Hamlet*, try to create a few effective facial shapes, and understand what is happening under the surface of the skin.

We now have now brought one digital human to life. This is exciting, but the following two chapters will show how we can utilize all this work to create even more characters.

REFERENCE MATERIAL

The Artist's Complete Guide to Facial Expression by Gary Faigin.
ISBN 0-8230-1628-5

This book thoroughly examines human facial expressions and will give you further information about the topics covered in this chapter.

11

CREATING NEW CHARACTERS

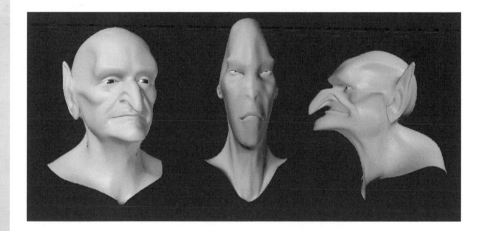

CREATING NEW CHARACTERS FROM THE HUMAN MODEL

It has been an intense and demanding journey to create our digital human model. One of the rewards for taking the time to build a quality model is that you can adapt and rework it into many other characters.

In this chapter, instead of illustrating how to rework the Frank model into another human, we are going to cut loose and really have fun by showing a range of fantasy characters that we can build from his mesh.

TOOLS FOR 3D SCULPTURE

Chapter 2 touched upon some polygonal modeling tools. Here, we will put a few select ones to use. We already have a mesh to work with, so we will not be creating any more polygons; rather, we'll just be moving them around.

One way to alter a group of faces would be to select the vertices and simply move them. See Figure 11.1.

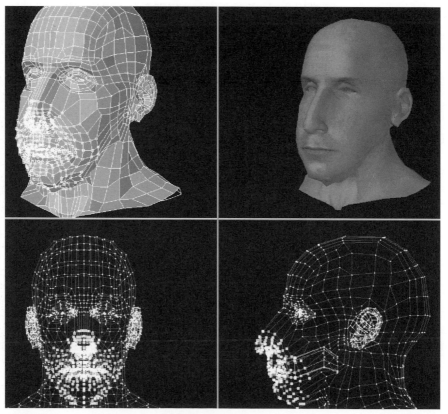

FIGURE 11.1 Grab and move a group of vertices.

This is okay, but in the process you are stretching some faces a good deal. This will be reflected in the textures when the image is rendered. If you wanted, you could go in and manually adjust the vertices to fix this, but that can be tedious.

It would be best to use some sort of soft deformation tools instead. Such a tool allows you to alter the geometry with a falloff of the tool's effect—that is, a radius is defined around the center of the tool. The further from the center the tool is, the less effect the tool has on the geometry. Soft deformation tools may go by such names as Soft Selection, Proportional, Magnet, Cage, or Lattice. We will now show some examples of using these soft deformation tools.

Figure 11.2 shows a Magnet operation that we will use to alter the lower half of the face. The center of the ring will have the strongest effect, with a gradual falloff towards the edges. Notice how the faces retain their proportions in comparison to the hard move illustrated with Figure 11.1.

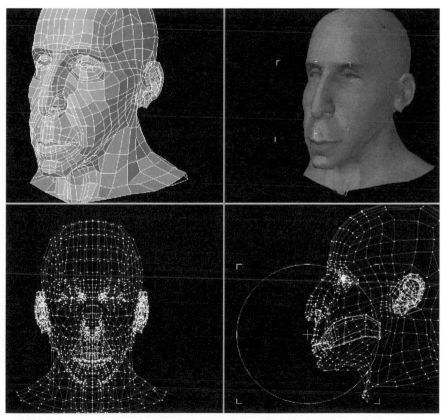

FIGURE 11.2   A Magnet operation with falloff along the model.

You can usually control the type of falloff algorithm in most programs. The algorithm will affect the shape of the falloff and how it moves the faces. Figure 11.3 shows several different falloff shapes.

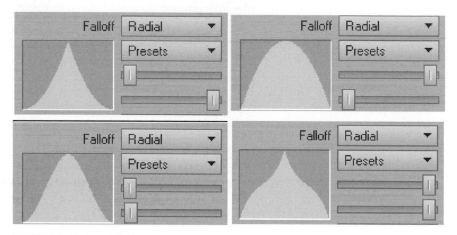

FIGURE 11.3   Various falloff shapes.

Lattice or cage deformers are another way to make large, smooth changes. This involves setting up a simple box-like cage around the object. As the vertices of the cage are moved, the whole model that it surrounds deforms smoothly. The more subdivisions the cage has, the more control you have over area changes. See Figure 11.4.

Other programs offer you still more tools. One of them allows you to deform the model based on a curve or spline. Basically, a curve is created and the model will conform to its shape in a number of ways. It, too, can make for quick, broad changes. Figure 11.5 shows how LightWave's Spline Guide tool deforms poor Frank.

Another type of 3D sculpture tool that works in a very natural manner is a brush that you drag over the model to get smooth changes. This feels similar to 2D painting, but in this case you are changing geometry instead of applying color to a canvas. You can alter the brush's diameter, or sphere of influence, and size as well as the falloff type and opacity. You can pull out or push in geometry along its normal axis (or on any given axis) as well as smooth it. Doing this, as well as working on a pressure-sensitive drawing tablet, is a very intuitive and easy way to model. Alias/Wavefront's Maya has a Sculpt Polygon tool that allows you to work this way. Figure 11.6 shows Maya's Sculpt Polygon

Pixologic's ZBrush and Electric Image's Amorphium are standalone software that specialize in natural 3D sculpture. Both of these programs

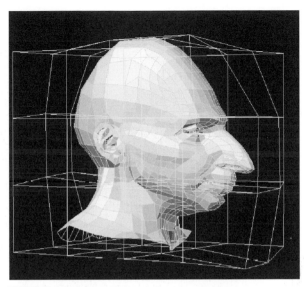

FIGURE 11.4   A lattice or cage deformer on an object.

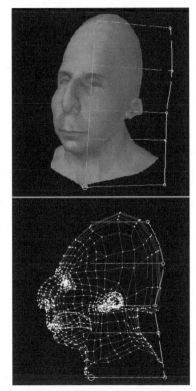

FIGURE 11.5   Use the Spline Guide tool
to deform a model.

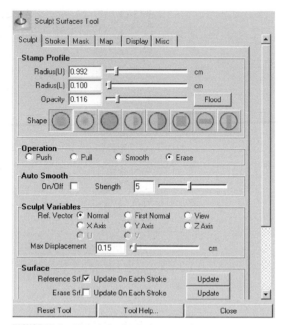

FIGURE 11.6 Maya's Sculpt Polygon tool.

allow you to import models, but ZBrush has the advantage of retaining any UV coordinates you may have set up elsewhere. This allows you to easily go back and forth between programs and lets you remodel without worrying about re-assigning UV coordinates. Figure 11.7 shows Frank's head geometry ready for 3D sculpting, in this case in ZBrush. *X*-axis symmetry is turned on and the brush size is set.

When you're beginning to model, use larger brushes to pull the model into a basic shape; then work your way down to the detail. See Figure 11.8.

Figure 11.9 shows the results of the 3D sculpting changes. We now have a nasty troll in the place of friendly Frank.

With the freedom that 3D sculpting tools afford us, it is tempting to use them without regard to the layout of the original mesh. You can work this way, but you'll have to do a lot of cleanup later. We still want to pay attention to the flow of the polygons that we took such pains to set up earlier. If we do, we'll be easily able to edit the mesh should we need to go back into the model—and chances are we will. Be sure to work in an un-subdivided mode to see the faces and to keep from creating a gnarled mess of polygons. See Figure 11.10.

A few other perks are awaiting us for working in this manner. Our image maps should fit right back onto the mesh, nicely conforming to the

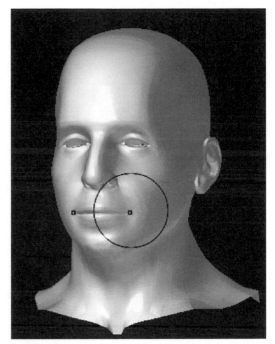

FIGURE 11.7   The head model imported into ZBrush to take advantage of the 3D sculpting tools.

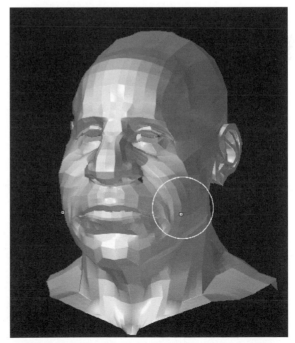

FIGURE 11.8   Begin to alter the model with 3D brush strokes.

FIGURE 11.9   The results of the 3D sculpting changes.

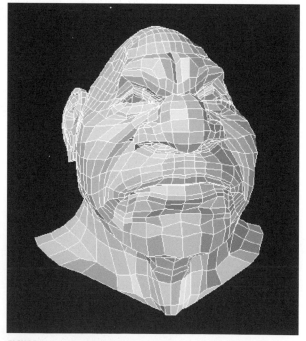

FIGURE 11.10   Be sure to maintain the quality of the underlying mesh while 3D sculpting.

new model shape. This is because it still has the UV coordinates that were set up earlier. See Figure 11.11.

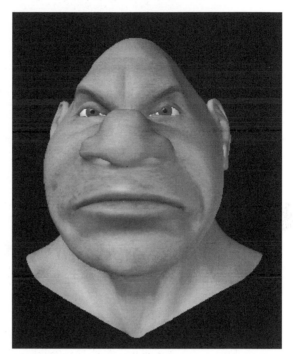

FIGURE 11.11   The texture maps will still conform to the altered head.

Another perk is that any facial morph shapes can be propagated to the new head. This works if your software stores the morphs in the same object file they were created on. It also requires that you didn't alter the point count of the different models; that is, add or remove geometry. In this example, the original Frank head was morphed into the troll head. The troll head retained the facial morphs that were created on the Frank head. Depending on your alterations to the geometry (the new character), some morphs may need additional adjustments, but the basic morph shapes are a good start. See Figure 11.12.

In just a short time, you can get a variety of characters using the various sculpting deformation tools. With their natural feel and speed, you can sketch in 3D. Figure 11.13 shows characters created from the original Frank head.

Similarly, applying a few color and tonal adjustments—such as hue/saturation and brightness/contrast—to the original texture maps can yield new ones for the appropriate characters. See Figure 11.14.

FIGURE 11.12 You can transfer facial morphs to the new model.

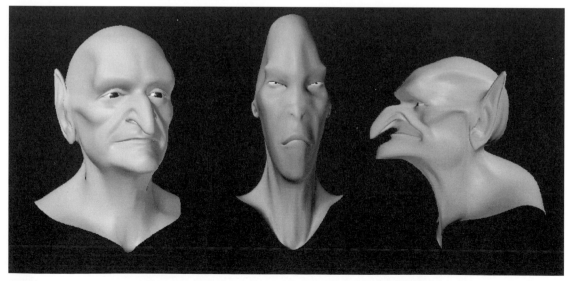

FIGURE 11.13 You can get a variety of characters using the various sculpting deformation tools.

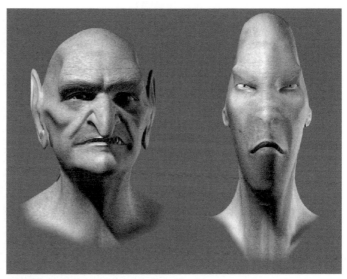

FIGURE 11.14   Adjust the color and tone when you create new characters.

You can, of course, continue to alter and add to these new color maps any way you see fit. They can be good starting points for creating new texture maps.

 When creating new character objects and textures, make sure to save them with different names than the originals.

You can also alter bodies easily with the sculpture deformation tools. Figure 11.15 shows a couple of examples.

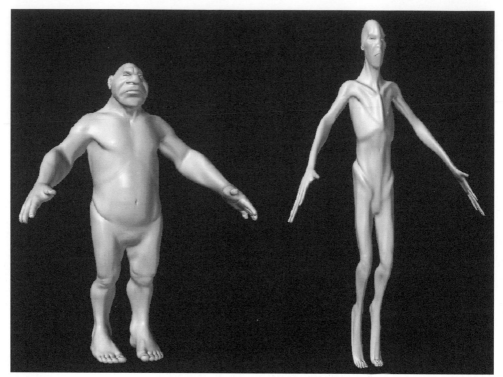

FIGURE 11.15   Use the sculpture deformation tools to alter bodies easily.

SUMMARY

This should give you a good taste of the mileage that you can get from the human model using the 3D sculpture and deformation tools. There is a limit to how much you can change the base human figure model into something else before it becomes more work that it is worth. But who knows? It is now up to you to see how far you can take it.

The changes we can make to the base male mesh do not stop here. We have neglected the female form until now. Turn the page and explore how we can turn the very masculine Frank into a female.

12

THE FEMALE

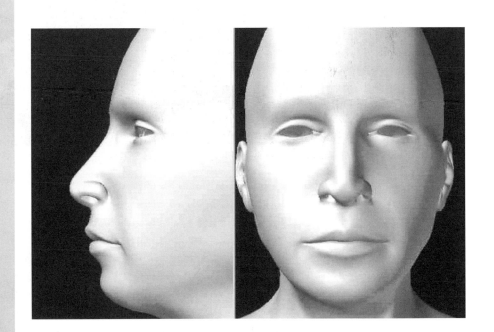

CHANGING THE MALE MODEL INTO A FEMALE

Turning a male model into a female one may seem like it is just a matter of making a few obvious changes, but there are plenty of subtle differences as well.

Although we won't be using any specific live reference here, you should certainly have reference material open when you model a female character. Anatomy books and even fashion magazines are useful in showing a variety of female faces and forms. This tutorial will create a generic, young female head and body. There are obviously many body types and shapes. You can make any additional changes to suit your needs. Please note that many of these changes are generalizations, as young females can share many structural qualities of males, especially in the face.

This chapter will again illustrate how much you can get out of a good base human model.

THE HEAD

Frank may be a handsome fellow, but it is questionable that he would make a proper woman if we just changed his body. Therefore, we will start by altering the head. This will involve making the features softer and altering some proportions.

Start by loading a finished male or the Frank model you have created by working through this book. This example uses the "arms down" version, as created in Chapter 10, but this detail is unimportant.

The main tools we will use in the transformation will be magnet operations, basic vertex moving, smoothing, and welding. During the modeling process, we will be working from broad changes down to the finer details.

The first changes we'll make to the head area are thinning the neck and making the jaw line not quite as wide. Frank has a masculine, thick neck, but this would look odd on a traditional female. Use a Magnet or equivalent tool to take in the sides of the neck, as in Figure 12.1.

Now we can work on some of the facial features. The first stop is the nose. We will make it smaller and change the profile. Select the nose geometry and scale it down slightly. Next, use a Magnet tool to make the profile straighter. Also, make the nose thinner by taking in the nostrils. These operations may require you to clean up some vertices afterwards—either manually or with a Smooth operation. See Figure 12.2.

The next facial feature to alter is the lips, certainly a main focus and definitive aspect of a classic female face. You can make the lips fuller by adjusting the vertices around the edges. The upper lip edges are raised,

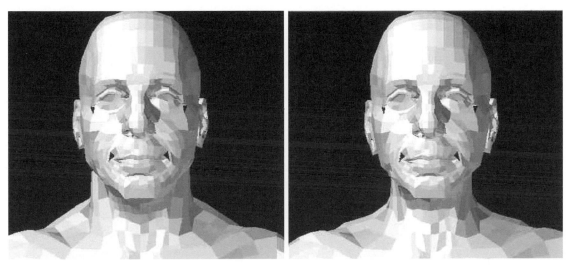

FIGURE 12.1   Make the neck and jaw thinner.

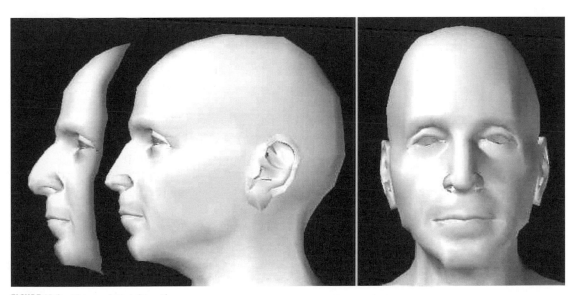

FIGURE 12.2   Thin and straighten the nose.

creating more of a peak towards the center, and the lower lip edge is pulled down. The indentation under the lip is also softened. Figure 12.3 shows these changes with the model viewed in subdivided mode.

While we are near the lips, let's soften the nasallabial folds to make her look younger. You can do this by selecting the faces and performing a Smooth or Average operation. See Figure 12.4.

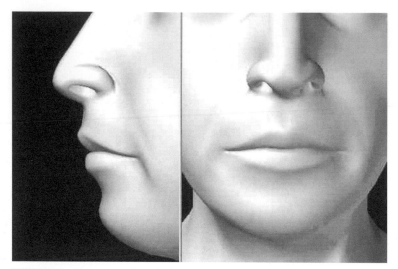

FIGURE 12.3 Changes made to the lips.

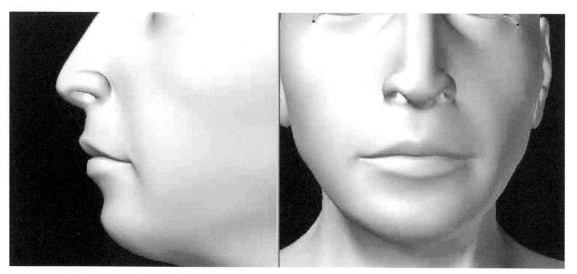

FIGURE 12.4 Soften the nasallabial folds.

You can make the cheeks look younger and fuller by raising the geometry a small amount and smoothing the area. See Figure 12.5.

To help give a more feminine appearance to the eyes, raise the outer corners a small amount. Do not overdo this or the eyes will appear too stylized. See Figure 12.6.

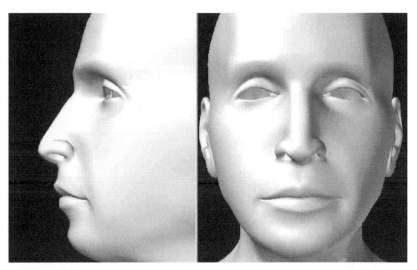

FIGURE 12.5   Make the cheeks fuller.

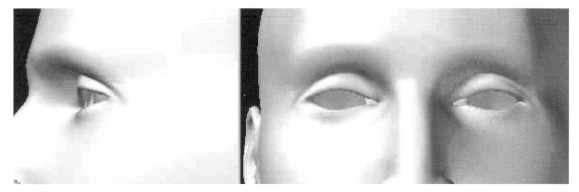

FIGURE 12.6   Raise the outer corners of the eyes.

When taking some of the maleness out of the face, you also need to make the eyes less deep-set. Instead of pulling the eyes forward, we can push the forehead back. See Figure 12.7.

Lastly, we will make the ears smaller. This is a simple scale operation. See Figure 12.8.

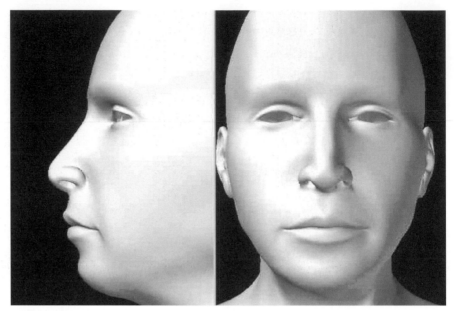

FIGURE 12.7 Make the eyes less deep-set by pushing the forehead back.

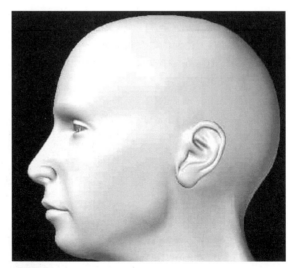

FIGURE 12.8 Make the ears smaller.

THE BODY

When we step back and view the head on the body, it appears decidedly out of place. See Figure 12.9.

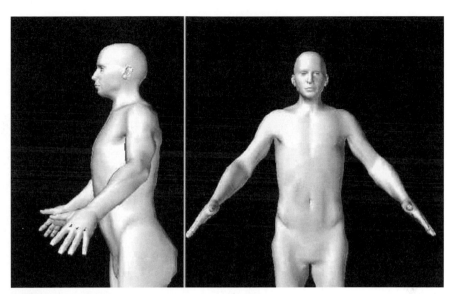

FIGURE 12.9   The head now is out of place on this body.

It is time to make some major adjustments to the body. First, we should adjust the shoulders and overall volume of the torso. Figure 12.10 shows the shoulders and width of the upper torso taken in. In addition, the profile shows how we made the chest less barrel-like by using a Magnet tool.

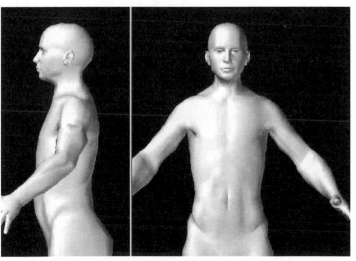

FIGURE 12.10   Adjust the shoulders and overall volume of the torso.

Next, reduce the bulk of the shoulders and arms using Smooth and Scale tools, making these areas thinner and slighter. See Figure 12.11.

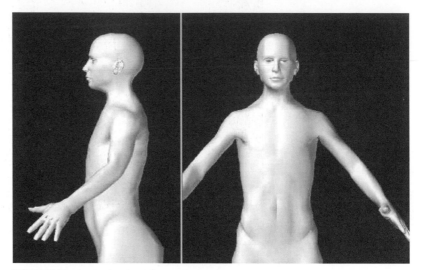

FIGURE 12.11 Make the shoulders and arms thinner and slighter.

One change affects another. The hands are now a little too large and manly for these arms. Scale them down to better fit with the arm proportions. See Figure 12.12.

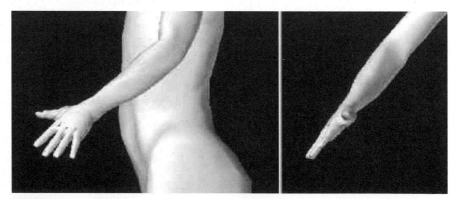

FIGURE 12.12 Scale the hands down.

The figure is now appearing more feminine. However, the rib cage is still too wide. Narrow it a little more and make it thinner at the waist with the Magnet tool. See Figure 12.13.

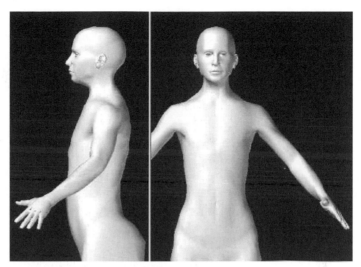

FIGURE 12.13   Narrow the ribs and the waist.

Next, the bulge of the stomach is reduced and made flatter. The hips are widened with the top edge (iliac crest) brought forward and down. The hip shape is one distinctive difference between males and females. See Figure 12.14.

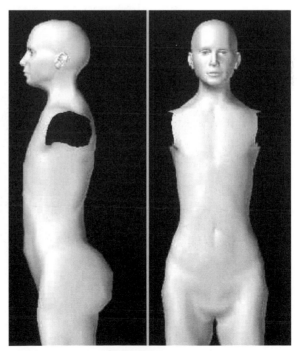

FIGURE 12.14   Alter the stomach and hips.

You may have wondered why we haven't yet built the breasts, surely a notable feature when you define a female body. While breasts may be obviously important, you should still pay attention to the body as a whole and make sure it appears feminine, even without the breasts. If the figure looks like a female without them, then you are on the right track. The other practical reason not to include the breasts yet is that you may still want to make alterations to the figure to get the proportions correct. The more geometry you pile on, the more difficult it will be to make changes, and the more reluctant you may be to do so.

Moving on down, we alter the rear end. Women tend to have more fat in this area and in the upper thighs than men. You can soften the look of the buttocks by lowering their center of gravity and widening them at the bottom edge. The work done on the hips earlier should already be helping with this region. See Figure 12.15.

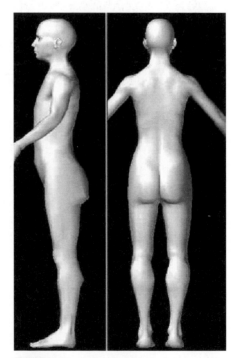

FIGURE 12.15   Adjust the rear end.

The last adjustment we will make for the lower body is to the legs. They can be softened with a Smooth operation. Reduce the size of the calves and the feet. See Figure 12.16.

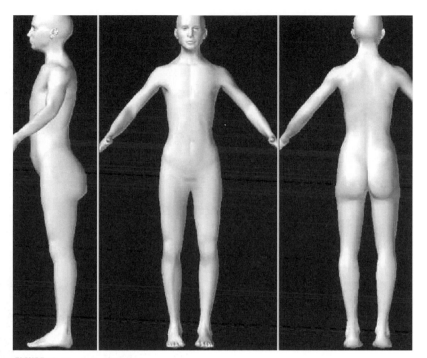

FIGURE 12.16   Adjust the legs.

Now we are ready to add the breasts. There are a couple of different approaches we could take, but for this example we will construct the breasts as separate geometry and then attach them to the body. The other option would be to extrude them out of the existing chest geometry, but this will leave a configuration of faces that can be difficult to shape easily since there will be a square configuration when you extrude them. It would take a fair amount of vertex pushing and cleanup to get them looking realistic. See Figure 12.17.

Therefore, we will start with a sphere to make a breast. Create an oval sphere with 14 sides and 12 segments, as seen in Figure 12.18.

The segments or subdivision number (which is how many polygons are along the height and width) for the sphere is a rough guess in terms of what it would need to be later welded to the chest geometry.

Next, cut the sphere in half, as seen in Figure 12.19.

Now the real shaping begins. Give the breast a sense of weight by putting a slope along the top portion, with the bulk of the faces biased towards the bottom. The poles of the sphere will be where the nipple is eventually built. See Figure 12.20.

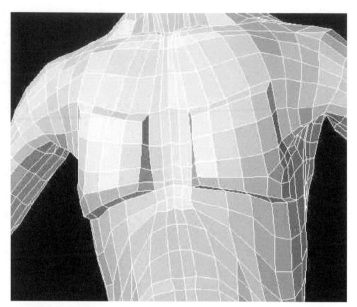

FIGURE 12.17 Breasts extruded out of existing chest geometry can be difficult to shape easily.

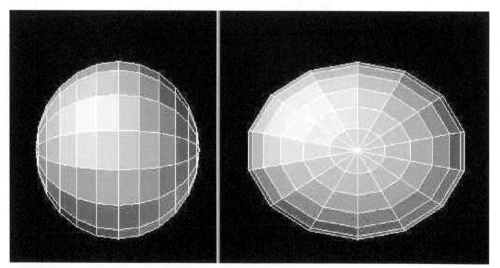

FIGURE 12.18 Start the breast as a sphere.

Now it is time to position the breast. It should be rotated outward slightly, with the nipple area pointing out from the body at an angle. Breasts do not point straight out from the chest. The best way to position the breast is in the top view and with both breasts visible; this allows you

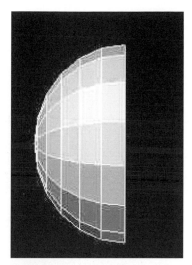

FIGURE 12.19   Cut the sphere in half.

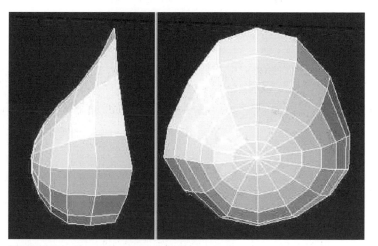

FIGURE 12.20   Put a slope along the top portion of the breast, with the bulk of the faces biased towards the bottom.

to get a good indication of what angle they are pointing at. Also make sure there is a smooth transition from the top of the breast into the chest. See Figure 12.21.

Now comes a bit of cutting and welding. This sounds harsh but is easy. First, we need to delete some geometry on the chest in order to attach the breasts. Figure 12.22 shows the faces that are deleted on the chest. The breast geometry was used as a guide to determine what faces

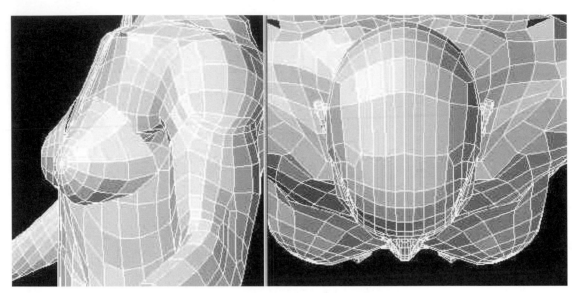

FIGURE 12.21   Position and angle the breast on the chest.

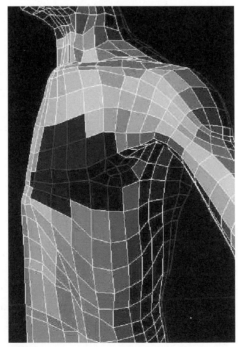

FIGURE 12.22   Delete faces on the chest in preparation
for attaching the breast.

to delete. It is not an exact operation. If you accidentally delete too many faces, you can always build them back in.

Position the breast geometry over the hole in the chest. You can attach it by welding and creating new faces, depending on the area. Figure 12.23 shows two points at the top welded to the chest.

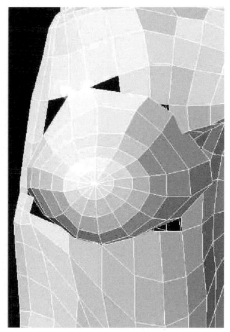

FIGURE 12.23　Position the breast geometry over the hole in the chest and begin welding the points.

Figure 12.24 illustrates how five new faces are created to fill the gap between the separate geometry.

Next, build another face along the underside and weld two vertices along the side. See Figure 12.25.

Some of the geometry will not line up neatly all around the breast. Instead of pulling faces into awkward positions to weld them, we can slice extra faces into the breasts to help out with a cleaner join. Figure 12.26 shows how we used a Split tool to add a new row of faces.

Now we can build a face to fill the hole as well as do two more welds. See Figure 12.27.

We are now faced with the most awkward area, toward the side near the underarm. The faces do not match up, so we should split some new faces in the breast geometry, as in Figure 12.28.

FIGURE 12.24   Create five new faces to fill the gap between the separate geometry.

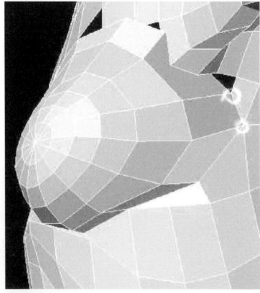

FIGURE 12.25   Continue to attach the breast geometry by welding and building faces.

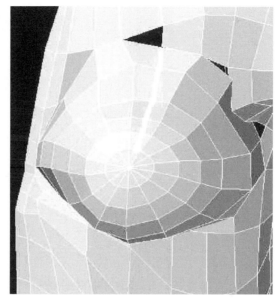

FIGURE 12.26   Slice extra faces into the breasts to help out with a cleaner join.

FIGURE 12.27   Add a face and weld points to fill the holes.

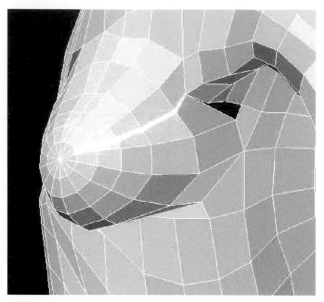

FIGURE 12.28 Add faces on the breast.

Now, split a triangle face at the edge of the breast geometry, as in Figure 12.29.

The last step of joining the geometry is to weld one point and create a new face, as seen in Figure 12.30.

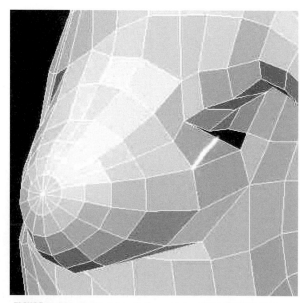

FIGURE 12.29 Split a triangle face at the edge of the breast.

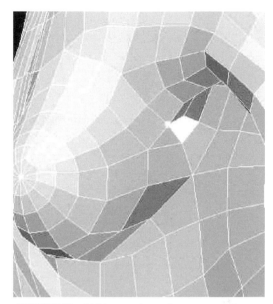

FIGURE 12.30   Weld one point and create a new face.

The breast is attached. Examine the geometry for areas to optimize or fix. We can clean up a spot at the top edge of the breast by splitting a new set of faces across to the triangle face, then merging the two triangles created into one quad. See Figure 12.31.

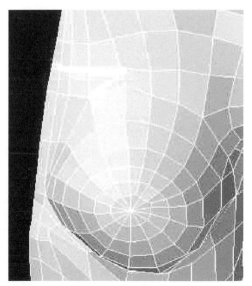

FIGURE 12.31   Split a new set of faces across to the triangle face.

Now we will work on the nipple. Merge all of the faces that formed at the pole of the breast sphere into one polygon. See Figure 12.32.

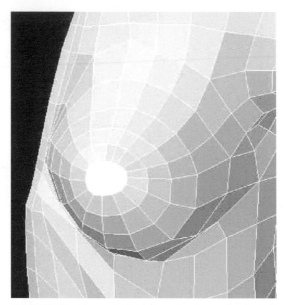

FIGURE 12.32   Merge all of the faces that formed at the pole.

We will be extruding out the nipple, but this operation will be cleaner and easier when we deal with one face rather than many.

Next, extrude this face a small amount, as in Figure 12.33.

Extrude and scale this new face again, as in Figure 12.34.

Next, make a couple more extrusions to finish off the nipple, as in Figure 12.35.

One last bit of cleanup is to turn the last extruded face into quads. This is not crucial but will make for a cleaner subdivision. Also some programs, such as LightWave, cannot subdivide faces larger than quads. See Figure 12.36.

If you have not done so, now is a good time to review your work on the chest in a subdivided mode. Mirror the missing half of the model if

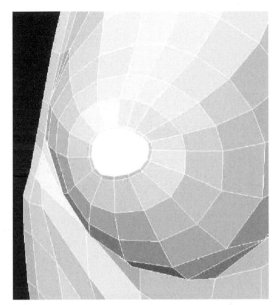

FIGURE 12.33   Extrude this face a little.

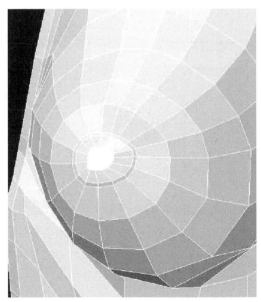

FIGURE 12.34   Extrude and scale this face.

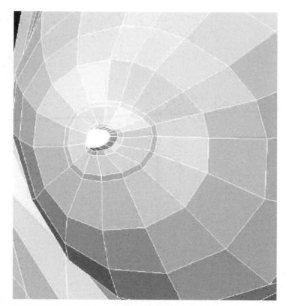

FIGURE 12.35   Make a couple more extrusions to finish off the nipple.

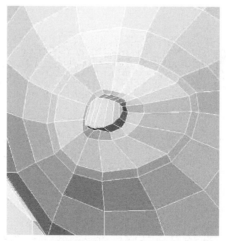

FIGURE 12.36   Turn the last extruded face into quads.

you were just working on one half. Do the breasts look like they naturally flow off of the body, or do they look stuck on? It is important that the underlying geometry and form of the chest not be distorted. Breasts reside on top of the muscles and ribs; they do not cut into the chest. See Figure 12.37.

Finally, step back and observe the whole figure. See Figure 12.38.

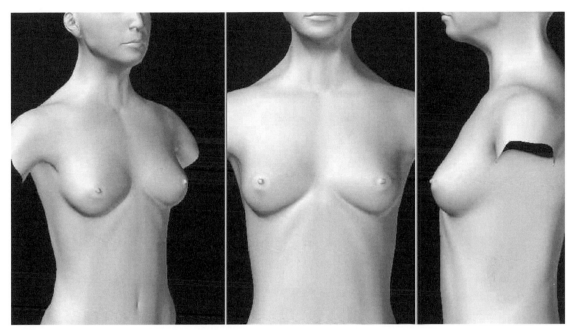

FIGURE 12.37   The finished breasts.

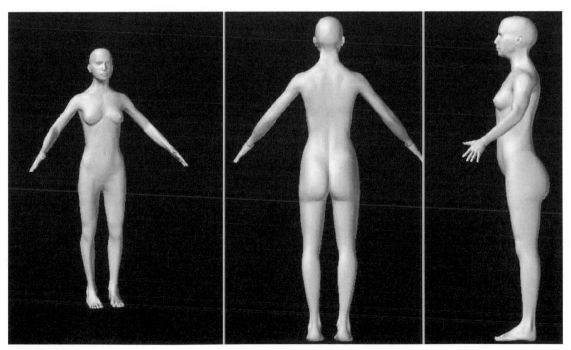

FIGURE 12.38   The finished female figure.

From here, you can texture the female figure and give her hair in the way we learned earlier, or you can explore other creative alternatives. See Figure 12.39.

FIGURE 12.39   Alternative forms for the female figure.

SUMMARY

In this chapter, we have created a woman from a man—not out of a single rib but out of a mass of polygons. The differences, both major and minor, all add up to what makes a convincing female figure. All it takes is a little work and a good deal of observation.

The last chapter will wrap up the digital human experience and will show you how digital humans do not have to go out into the world naked.

CLOTHING

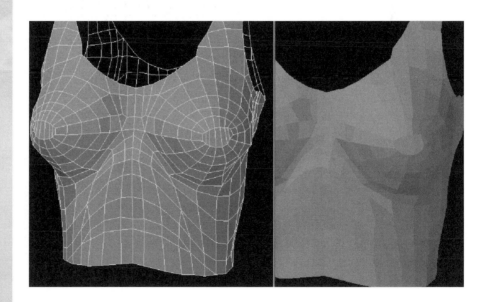

CLOTHING

Chances are you will want to give your digital human some garments to wear before sending him or her before the camera. Clothing can help define the personality of a character or a time period in history (or the future) in which the character existed.

This chapter will explore a couple of different methods for creating clothes. You may wonder whether you still need to do all the modeling on the body if a character is to be clothed. Technically, no. But having an accurate representation of the human form underneath is a good idea. Clothing can conceal the body quite a bit, obliterating forms and anatomy. If you attempted to model a clothed character without decently representing the body underneath, you would be in danger of losing the proper proportions. Once you complete a clothed character, you can delete the unseen geometry; doing so will save memory and rendering times.

As when you created the figure, it is important to have reference material handy. If you do not personally have on hand the clothes you want to model, you should look at a photo reference. The nice thing about clothing is that it sits still for long periods of time and does not need to take lunch breaks.

SIMPLE CLOTHING

Creating simple clothing utilizes the model's existing geometry. Simple clothing, such as stretch pants or tights, can be fairly skin tight.

We will now create some simple clothing for the female character we created in Chapter 12. We will give her an outfit she could exercise in—tights and a sports bra. To begin, load the female character into the modeling program, and zoom to her upper thigh and midsection. Select the geometry from around hip level to mid thigh. Copy and paste this geometry into a new layer, or make a new object out of the selection if your program does not support layers. See Figure 13.1.

Give this new geometry a separate color and surface name, such as "Tights" or "Pants." Next, we need to make a neater edge for the waist and thigh. Use the Split tool to draw a cleaner edge in these areas. See Figure 13.2.

You can delete the row of geometry above the new lines to clean up the edge, as in Figure 13.3.

Just as we did with the character's body, we will subdivide and render her clothes. Therefore, we need to ensure that certain areas, such as

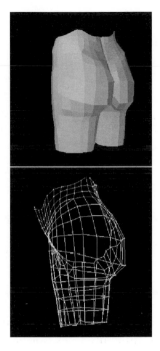

FIGURE 13.1   To make the tights, copy and paste the waist and upper thigh geometry into a new layer.

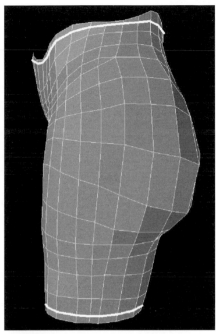

FIGURE 13.2   Create the straight edge of the tights with the Split tool.

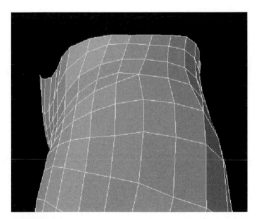

FIGURE 13.3   Delete the geometry above the split.

the edges of the garments, hold their shape. Add another row of faces with the Split tool to help maintain a crease during subdivision. See Figure 13.4.

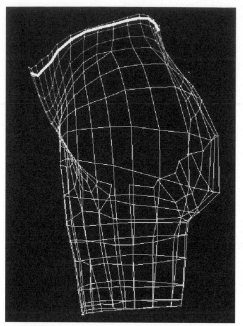

FIGURE 13.4   Add more geometry near the edges to help them maintain a sharp crease during subdivision.

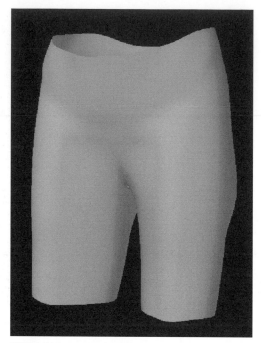

FIGURE 13.5   Make the tights 10mm thick.

Cloth is thin, but not as thin as a polygon. We need to give the tights a very small thickness, such as 10mm, using the Extrusion command. See Figure 13.5.

Be sure to test the clothes on the figure, and if geometry from the character pokes through, you can enlarge the clothing, pull the offending areas out, or delete the figure's geometry that isn't seen. Figure 13.6 shows the tights on the female character.

For the sports bra, we will utilize the same technique with an added step for control. This step involves using the Boolean tool. A Boolean operation is the computation of the intersection of two objects. Most 3D modeling software supports Booleans.

We will use this tool to create an object that represents the edges of the sports bra. A Boolean operation will be performed with this object on the female body, and the rest of the clothing-creation process will proceed much as with the tights.

To begin making the sports bra, create a 2D shape that represents the shape of the clothing. This can be made from splines or a polygonal form. It does not need to be detailed, but it's best to do this with the figure present as a guide. Your program's Layers feature will be helpful here. Make

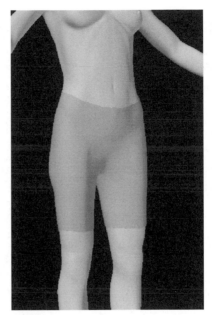

FIGURE 13.6   The finished tights on the
character.

sure the edges of the garment extend beyond the boundaries of the figure, as in Figure 13.7.

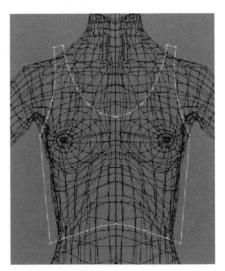

FIGURE 13.7   Create a 2D shape in preparation
for the Boolean operation.

Perform the Boolean operation to have the clothing intersect and combine with the figure's geometry. It is always a good idea to make an extra copy of any geometry before performing any major operations. Depending on your software's features, you can have the geometry inherit the surface attributes of the cutting geometry. Doing so allows you to get an automatic and easy surfacing of the clothing. Be sure to consult your software manual for what options are available for the Boolean feature. See Figure 13.8.

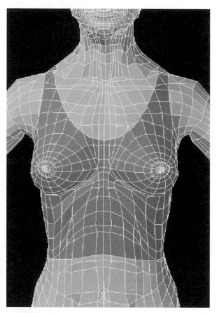

FIGURE 13.8 Use a Boolean operation to cut the clothing geometry into the figure.

Separate the new clothing geometry for more modeling work. Most likely, we will need to clean up some faces. These faces might be N-sided polygons or small clusters of awkward faces. This will most likely occur at the edges, so go through and weld or delete points until the edge is straight and clean. See Figure 13.9.

We now have a decent shape for the sports bra, but it is a little too sheer. We will need to soften some of the underlying anatomical detail that shows through. For example, the nipples should be toned down or eliminated. To do this, either use the Smooth feature, or delete, combine, and rebuild the area so that it is smoother. See Figure 13.10.

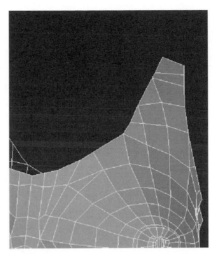

FIGURE 13.9   Clean up the edge faces after the Boolean operation.

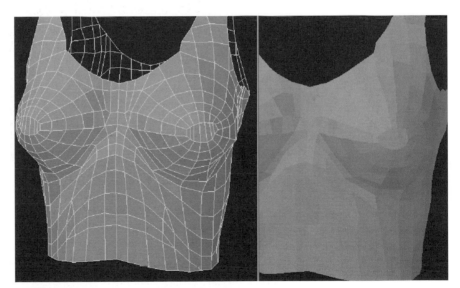

FIGURE 13.10   Smooth the nipple geometry.

The other areas that should be softened are under and in between the breasts. Since fabric is spanning between the breasts, the definition will not be as strong. Use the Smooth tool, or pull geometry out a bit to soften these spaces. See Figure 13.11.

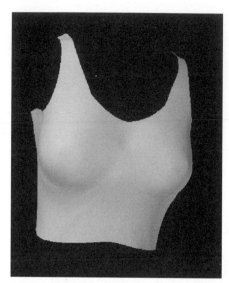

FIGURE 13.11   Soften the spaces around the breasts due to the fabric.

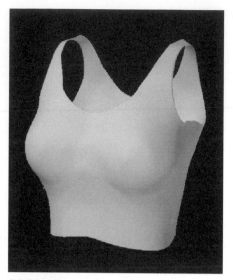

FIGURE 13.12   Use the Extrusion command to give the sports bra some thickness.

As with the tights, give the sports bra some thickness with an extrusion. See Figure 13.12.

View the clothes on the figure. See Figure 13.13.

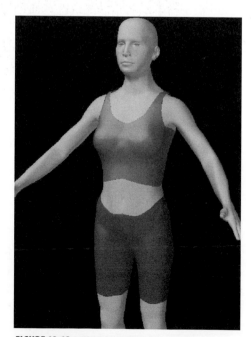

FIGURE 13.13   The clothes on the figure.

COMPLEX CLOTHING

The clothing example on the female is simple to create and can work for a number of situations. But sometimes we will want clothes that do not hug the body so closely. In these cases, we will need to delve into more complex clothing-creation techniques.

Unlike the modeling we have done so far, creating complex clothing lends itself well to spline modeling. A spline is a curve that is defined by two or more points placed in the 3D space. It does not have any volume and therefore is not rendered. Figure 13.14 shows four splines laid out in 3D space. They connect at the corners.

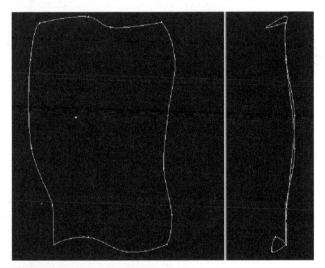

FIGURE 13.14   Four splines placed in 3D space.

Several splines can be assembled together to form a surface (sometimes called a *patch*) that will render. Figure 13.15 shows a polygonal surface that was generated from the four splines.

Each program varies as far as how it works with splines and their derived surfaces, but the basic principles are the same; three or four splines are connected to form a patch or surface.

The rubber band-like splines are an easy way to create the contours of clothing. You can adjust them so that they fit over the figure, and then generate your surfaces. If the surfaces aren't satisfactory, you can adjust the splines to re-generate a new surface.

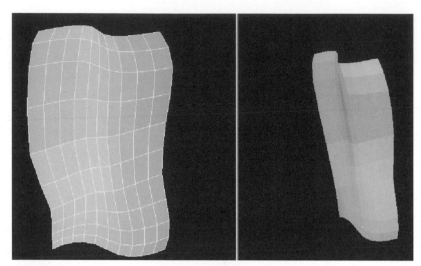

FIGURE 13.15 A polygonal surface is generated from four splines.

The following is an example of creating clothes for Frank, starting with pants or jeans. Using splines, we lay out the contours of one half of the jeans. See Figure 13.16.

FIGURE 13.16 Splines are created for the contours of one half of a pair of jeans.

The next step is to create the surfaces from the splines. Do not make it too dense, as the polygons generated will be subdivided, as with the body. The example here used approximately six to eight perpendicular and parallel segments per patch. Figure 13.17 shows the spline-generated surfaces for one half of the jeans.

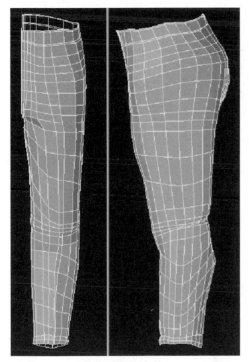

FIGURE 13.17   The spline-generated surfaces for the jeans.

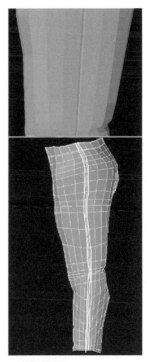

FIGURE 13.18   Add a crease on the side of the jeans.

From here, detail is added. Add two vertical splits close together down the side of the jeans to create a seam. See Figure 13.18.

Jeans usually have pockets. To add some side pockets, use the Split tool to define the edge of the pocket, as in Figure 13.19.

If there are any *N*-sided polygons, clean them up by welding points or using the Split tool, as in Figure 13.20.

Pockets would be useless without some depth to store things in them. Select faces and extrude them in and down slightly. To create the illusion of depth, the pockets do not usually need to be deeper or more complex than this. See Figure 13.21.

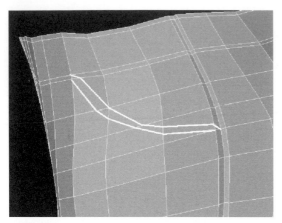

FIGURE 13.19   Define the edge of the side pockets with the Split tool.

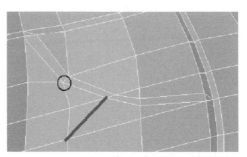

FIGURE 13.20   Get rid of any *N*-sided polygons in the pocket area.

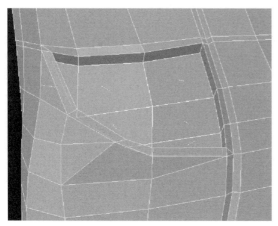

FIGURE 13.21   Extrude faces in for the pockets.

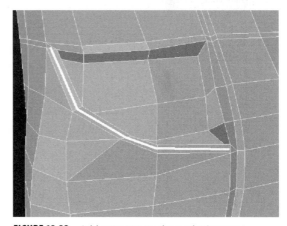

FIGURE 13.22   Add geometry to the pocket's seam.

To help maintain the pocket's sharp edge, split more geometry into the seam of the pocket, as in Figure 13.22.

The waistline seaming will also need some polygonal reinforcements for subdividing. In Figure 13.23, two extra rows of faces are split into the waistband.

Other details, such as the belt loops, can be modeled separately from a simple segmented box, as in Figure 13.24.

This belt loop can then be duplicated and placed around the waistline, as in Figure 13.25.

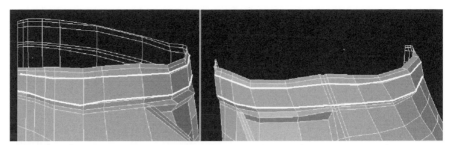

FIGURE 13.23   Add two rows of faces to the waistband to help it maintain a crease during subdivision.

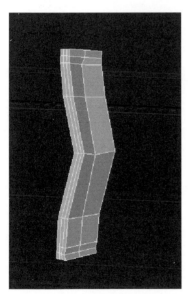

FIGURE 13.24   Model the belt loops from a segmented box.

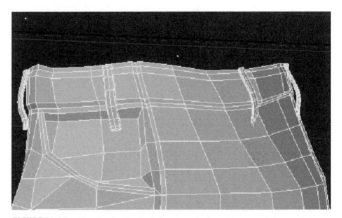

FIGURE 13.25   Duplicate the belt loop and place it around the waist.

Utilizing the existing geometry, or by splitting in new faces, add wrinkles and creases. See Figure 13.26.

Now that the pants are finished, let's give Frank a top. We create a shirt in much the same way as the pants. First, set up splines using the human figure as a guide. See Figure 13.27.

Next, generate the surfaces from the splines. See Figure 13.28.

Add a collar and thickness in the same manner as for the pants and shirt.

One important thing to keep in mind, especially with clothing, is to make sure both halves of the model are not perfectly symmetrical. The

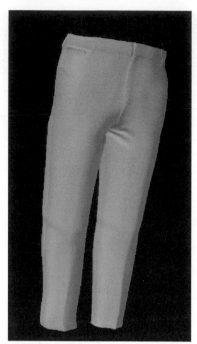

FIGURE 13.26 Add wrinkles and creases to the jeans.

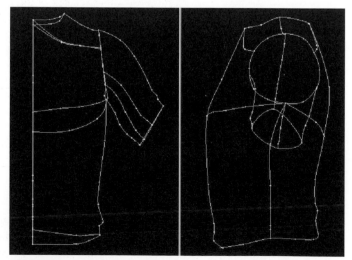

FIGURE 13.27 The splines for the shirt.

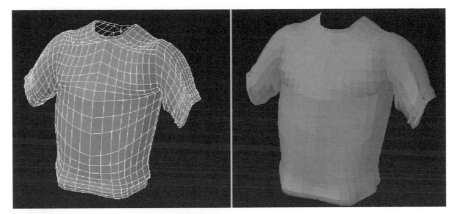

FIGURE 13.28   Generate the surfaces from the splines.

way cloth folds, bends, and constantly changes shape means that none of the wrinkles will match from side to side. See Figure 13.29.

FIGURE 13.29   Give the shirt thickness and asymmetry.

Finally, make sure the clothes fit your human. See Figure 13.30.

Once you have the basic clothes, you can deform them for animation and posing in the same way as you do a naked figure. Bones and displacements can alter the clothes just as they can skin. You can add special morph shapes on the clothes to create specific wrinkles and bulges as the figure bends and twists. (See Chapter 10.)

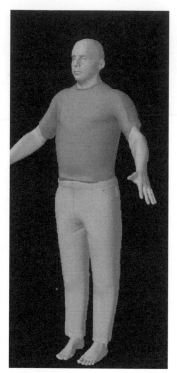

FIGURE 13.30   Fit the clothes on the person.

Some of the higher-end software, such as XSI, Maya, and LightWave, contain clothing simulators. These let you assign real-life characteristics to the clothing geometry (such as fabric type) and dynamics (such as collision detection, wind, and gravity) for added realism.

SUMMARY

Creating digital clothing presents its own challenges. Organic, yet not flesh, clothes are man-made items with a constantly changing surface. They reveal who we are in a time and place. Modeling tools such as splines and the surfaces they generate are a good starting point for creating the forms that cover our bodies.

WRAP UP

If you have made it through the book and built your own digital human—congratulations! You now have a model you can use over and over, improve, and alter. You can have him just hang out, looking cool, as in Figure 13.31.

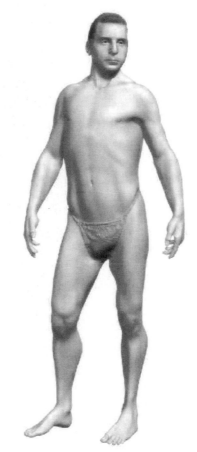

FIGURE 13.31   The digital human ready for action.

Or, you can present him with greater challenges, as in Figure 13.32. This brings us to the end of the book, but not the work. Studying the human form is a lifelong endeavor. Rest assured that every effort you put into it will be returned to you.

FIGURE 13.32 The digital human has his work cut out for him.

This book illustrated techniques for constructing a digital human. But without the knowledge and understanding of the figure, we are just blindly pushing polygons around.

ABOUT THE CD-ROM

The companion CD-ROM includes reference images of the live model so that you can construct the same figure as seen in the book, 3D models of the figure in various stages of completion, and all the illustrations from the book chapters in full color.

> **Figures:** All the figures from within the book in full color.
> **Models**: 3D models of the figure in various stages of completion
> **Reference**: Includes images of the live model to be used in your own construction of the figure

There are also full working versions of 3D modeling software Amapi v5.15 (Mac & PC) and 2D paint software Project Dogwaffle (PC only) to allow you to get started in modeling and texture painting right away. View the "read me" files in the programs folder for directions on how to install these programs.

SYSTEM REQUIREMENTS

Windows: 98, ME,2000,XP,NT or Mac OS 9 or OSX

3D modeling program with strong polygonal toolset such as *Lightwave 3D, Maya, SoftImage XSI, Cinema 4D, Amapi, Truespace*, and *3ds max*.

Image editing software that supports layers such as Abobe *Photoshop* or Procreate *Painter*.

INDEX